Narrativ

Therapis

Lives

by Michael White

DULWICH CENTRE PUBLICATIONS
ADELAIDE
SOUTH AUSTRALIA

published by

Dulwich Centre Publications

Hutt St PO Box 7192
Adelaide, South Australia 5000
phone (61-8) 8223 3966 fax (61-8) 8232 4441

printed & manufactured in Australia by:
 Graphic Print Group, Richmond, South Australia

cover artwork by: Susy Stiles, Torrensville, South Australia

100% recycled
paper

Contents

Contents (cont'd)

Introduction

I believe that most readers would be familiar with the extent to which experiences of demoralisation, fatigue and exhaustion are commonly expressed in the culture of psychotherapy. Here, I am referring to the experiences not of persons who consult therapists, but of therapists themselves. Many therapists speak openly about their sense of despair, and a considerable number 'drop out', suffering from what is often called burnout. Yet others all too frequently find themselves struggling with a painful sense of lack of direction in their work, often feeling that, despite their best efforts, they are only marking time, and just managing to keep their head above water while they do so. Although there are therapists who experience none of this, I doubt that many readers would be oblivious to the presence of these expressions of fatigue and despair in the professional networks of which they are a part.

In response to these experiences of demoralisation, fatigue, and exhaustion, it is not uncommon for therapists to find themselves reflecting on their choice of career in life, and to begin confronting questions about how and why they stepped into the counselling/therapy profession in the first place. At these times, early retirement or alternative career options are often considered. Many therapists are lost to the field on account of this.

Many different explanations are offered for this phenomenon. Some of these refer to the nature of the work itself - that it is demanding and at times quite overwhelming. Others problematise the self of individual workers: they are 'not cut out for it', they have 'unresolved issues', they are 'co-dependent', and so on. Yet other explanations refer to the institutional structures that provide a context for this work - to the fact that these structures are non-supportive and demoralising to staff - and to developments in service delivery that are being increasingly dictated by the economics of the 'free' market place, not by what might be in the best interests of persons according to criteria that are important to them.

This latter consideration is now beginning to receive significant attention. We all have good reason to be concerned about these institutional structures and many of the market-driven decisions about service delivery. In response to this, workers are just now beginning to find more ways of sharing these concerns with others - that is, with other service providers and with persons who are seeking services - in their efforts to open more options for collaborative action in addressing them.

Although these matters that relate to work-place structures and decision-making about service delivery are highly significant in considerations of the life and the work of the therapist, these are not the subject of this book - at least not in any direct sense. Instead, here I will explore yet another hypothesis about therapists' experiences of despair, fatigue and burnout. This is one that proposes that these experiences are also very significantly the outcome of (a) how therapeutic practices are generally conceived of, (b) the relational practices that structure the interaction between therapists and the persons who consult them, and (c) the practices of the self of the therapist that structure the therapist's management of their own identity.

In this book I present some alternative conceptions of the therapeutic endeavour, and draw out some of the relational practices of therapy, and practices of the self of the therapist, that are associated with these conceptions. These alternative conceptions are those that are informed by what are commonly referred to as 'narrative ideas', and by poststructuralist thought. The relational practices of therapy and practices of the self of the therapist that are associated with these alternative conceptions will be offered as partial antidotes to therapist despair, fatigue and burn-out, and as sources of sustenance and inspiration to therapists in their lives and their work.

Although many of the ideas and practices that are drawn out through this book appear in pieces that I have previously published - for example, the first section of this book includes a review of the sort of 're-membering' practices which prominently figure as 'experience of experience' questions in 'Saying hullo again: The reincorporation of the lost relationship in the resolution of grief' (White 1987) - and although I have given some space in some of my published pieces to a consideration of the implications of these ideas and practices for the life of the therapist, this is the first time that the life of the therapist has been exclusively the focus of my writing.

In workshop contexts over the past several years I have presented all of the thoughts that are expressed in this book about addressing therapist despair, fatigue and burnout. According to the feedback from participants of these workshops, this is a topic that is deserving of a significant, if not urgent, priority in a writing project. This feedback, and the encouragement that has been expressed in this, has contributed significantly to the impetus to write this book.

The publishing of this book was significantly delayed by a bicycle accident in February of this year. The injuries that I suffered in this accident have taken some time to heal. Although the main part of this text had been mostly written at that time, until very recently I just hadn't been able to attend to the preparation of the final draft. I was in physical pain for a considerable time and, try as I might, wasn't able to concentrate on this task. Through this difficult time, my experience of this writing project changed. What was started in enthusiasm and joy gradually came to cast a shadow on my life. And as my doubts that I would ever be able to complete this book mounted, I developed a 'writer's block' that further complicated my efforts to return to the task.

Cheryl White's timely actions in August of this year helped me to escape from this block, and from the gloom that was enveloping me in regard to this task She organised for a group of us, including David Denborough who is an editorial assistant with Dulwich Centre Publications, to book a cabin at Hanson Bay, a very beautiful location on Kangaroo Island, for two or three days. I found that sitting in this cabin and looking out over this bay and its winter seas, while going over my manuscript with David, re-invigorated me in this writing project. When I returned to Adelaide I was able to proceed with the task of preparing the final draft of this book.

Had it not been for Cheryl's action, this book would still not be. But her contribution to this project is much more than this. Right now I am thinking particularly of her wisdom and her consciousness of, and persistent questioning of, the power relations of local culture in all that she does, and the part that this has played in the shaping of my work. I will here also thank David Denborough, not just for helping me to get started again, but for the spirit with which he did this - I was warmed and lifted up by this.

As I reflected further on the history of the ideas and practices represented in this book, I found myself reminiscing a little, and then reliving some of the experiences that have been powerfully reinforcing of these ideas and practices - experiences that have also significantly contributed to the shape of my work and my life more generally. Some of this reminiscing took me to my conversations with the many therapists who have attended intensive training workshops at Dulwich Centre, and who have, in the course of these workshops, made themselves available to be interviewed about their lives as therapists. In their readiness to experience narrative practices from the inside, and to engage in personal explorations of their work and their lives in this context, they have contributed significantly to the shaping of this book. It is my hope that, in what is written here, I have been able to successfully capture something of the spirit of these conversations. It is also my hope that the participants of these workshops will find the many regions of this book that have been powerfully touched by the ripples of their expressions of life and of work.

To all of the folks who were so enthusiastic about contributing to this project by opening their lives to readers in the way that they have, I want to say how wonderful it has been for me to experience being in such great company, and to further expand my sense of community. So thank you Sophia, James, Louise, Pat Schumm, Ian Hanslow, Greg Stanton, Sally, Paul, Maria Fiorito, Michelle Murphy and Kathy, Aileen Cheshire, Brigitte, Mem, Sue, and Veronika. I would also like to thank David Epston, Amanda Kamsler, Jill Freedman, and Gene Combs, for their comments on an earlier draft of this book, Melissa Raven for her copy-editing efforts, Linda Higgins for transcribing the interviews that are published herein, and Jane Hales for preparing this book for printing.

A note on the use of language

For some years I have been exploring the tradition of poststructuralist thought and practice, and it is in this tradition that I have sought to locate what has come to be known as narrative therapy. The pursuit of poststructuralist understandings of human action has taken me to studies of critical philosophy, to literary theory, to cultural anthropology, and to postmodern ethics. These studies are far removed from the orthodox psychologies and counselling/ therapy theories which are informed by the structuralist discourses. Poststructuralist studies engage us in thinking outside of what is routinely thought in the culture of counselling/psychotherapy. They engage us in terms of description that are not the taken-for-granted terms when it comes to matters of life and to human action - terms of description that are unfamiliar.

In that it is these explorations of poststructuralist thought and practice that are the subject of this book, here I engage with terms of description that are not the familiar ones that are taken up when the subject is life and human action. I am aware that this may raise some difficulties for the reader. And quite probably some questions as well: 'Why doesn't he just say this in plain English?' 'Why does he have to use jargon which obscures what he is saying?' 'Instead of talking about lives that are "thinly described", why doesn't he just say that the person lacks self-esteem?' 'Instead of talking about work that is "more richly describing of a person's knowledges and skills of living", why doesn't he just say that this work leads to self-fulfilment?'

My response to these questions? Firstly, words like self-esteem and self-fulfilment are not considered jargon because they represent taken-for-granted notions about life and human action in contemporary western culture. Notions like these have become our culture's 'facts' about human nature. But they are nonetheless products of the structuralist discourses. Secondly, there is no equivalence between terms like self-esteem and self-fulfilment on the one hand, and terms like 'thin description' and 'knowledges and skills of living' on the other. It is not just that these terms lack equivalence, but that they speak to notions that are associated with distinct and different practices of life, and, for that matter, distinct and different practices of therapy. For example, the relationship with one's life and the proposal for action that is shaped by the conclusion 'poor self-esteem' is quite distinct from the relationship with one's life and the proposal for action that is shaped by the conclusion 'thin description'. Taken-for-granted terms like self-esteem and self-fulfilment are in fact inconsistent with those informed by poststructuralist thought, and they also contradict what it is that I am describing in this text. I believe that this will be made quite evident in this book.

Thirdly, poststructuralist thought provides a direct challenge to many of the 'facts' of this culture that are expressed in the taken-for-granted ways of describing life and human action. Poststructuralist thought provides options for the deconstruction of these 'facts'. This is a deconstruction that is identifying of the ways of thinking and living that these 'facts' are emblems for, and of the sort of individualities that these ways of thinking and living are reproducing of and that are venerated in contemporary culture.

On any account, it is not possible for me to express the ideas and practices of therapy that I wish to through conventional ways of speaking and writing. In this book, I have chosen particular descriptions only after careful thought. I accord these descriptions precise meanings that the regular and taken-for-granted terms of the culture of counselling/psychotherapy cannot convey. Although some readers may consider some of these terms to be jargon, I would ask that they avoid re-translating these into the more familiar words and phrases of the conventional discourses of counselling/psychotherapy, for to do so will change their meaning. I believe that it was Richard Rorty who once said that 'a fact is a dead metaphor'. Perhaps, following Rorty (1991), it would be helpful for readers to regard many of the terms of description that are used in this book as metaphors that stand apart from the 'facts' of life, and that are thus 'a source of the new'.

In this book I frequently use the terms 'therapy' and 'therapeutic conversation'[1] as a description of what it is that occurs in contexts in which persons are seeking consultation about their concerns/problems, and in which other persons called 'therapists' respond. However, I remain dissatisfied with these terms as a description of the ways of being in work and in life that are the subject of this book.

A note on thought

In this book I haven't been content to just provide an account of my translations of poststructuralist thought. Rather, I have gone to some lengths to render transparent much of the thought that I take to be a guide in this work. I do this not only to provide the reader with a firmer sense of where I am coming from, but so that they might have a better opportunity to derive their own translations of the thought that I have concerned myself with, and to place these translations alongside mine in our ongoing explorations of narrative practices.

I do realise that this commitment to transparency has added a level of complexity to the discussion in some sections of this text. However, it is my hope that readers will find persevering with this complexity to be rewarding.

Note

1. I have borrowed the term 'therapeutic conversation' from the work of Harlene Anderson and Harry Goolishian (1988).

PART I

Re-membering
and
Definitional Ceremony

Introduction

In this section of this book, I refer to the shift in what counts in terms of legitimate knowledge in regard to matters of practice when persons are inducted into the culture of psychotherapy. In this induction, the more local or folk knowledges that have been generated in a person's history are marginalised, often disqualified, and displaced by the formal and expert knowledges of the professional disciplines. I also refer to the shift in what counts in regard to the significant memberships of a person's life. In this process the associations of the monoculture of psychotherapy are substituted for the diverse, historical and local associations of persons' lives.

Thirdly, I refer to the shift that takes place in terms of what it is that is deemed appropriate in regard to forums of acknowledgement; a shift in what is considered appropriate as an arena for the knowing performance of knowledge. And fourthly, I refer to the shift that takes place in what constitutes appropriate practices of witness that are to be expressed in these forums of acknowledgement. In these shifts, the more informal arenas and practices of witness are displaced by formal and specialised arenas and practices.

I propose that, for the therapist, the outcome of all these shifts is that their work and their lives become thinly described. This contributes significantly to experiences of burden, fatigue, and exhaustion, and to circumstances that establish a vulnerability to despair and to burn-out.

I then introduce 're-membering' practices. These are practices that assist therapists to reclaim and privilege the significant historical and local associations of their lives, and to explore possibilities in the incorporation of yet other persons into their lives and their work. I propose that this re-membering of life contributes to therapists experiencing themselves as knowledged and skilled in their work, and in their lives more generally.

Discussion then turns to an exploration of the notion of 'definitional ceremony'. This notion is one that introduces options for the structuring of alternative forums of acknowledgement, and alternative practices of witness. Participation in these forums is powerfully authenticating of therapists' knowledges and skills, and contributes to their work and their lives being 'thickly' or 'richly' described. I propose that participation in these definitional ceremonies is sustaining and inspiring of therapists.

As I started the task of committing to paper these ideas about re-membering practices and definitional ceremonies, I began to reminisce. This took me to stories of my personal history. I have decided to include one of these stories here. I do this for the sake of transparency, and for other reasons that will become clear as this book unfolds.

The mouse stories[1]

I am the father of Penny, who is nineteen years old. When Penny was young, just a very little girl, she came bursting in the front door of our home after visiting my younger sister, her Aunt Julie. 'You never told me about the Mouse stories', she exclaimed, with hands on hips, as if I had withheld from her one of the more important keys to life on this earth; information of critical importance to the entire course of her present life, and perhaps to her next one as well. 'Mouse stories. Mouse stories. Oh, *those* stories!' I exclaimed, recalling the stories I had told Julie, who is four years younger than me, when she was a young girl. Although I'd never made a conscious decision to withhold this episode of my history from Penny, I had never been all that impressed with my story-telling abilities, and hadn't thought that this would be something that I would ever pick up again in my life. But now that Julie had let the cat out of the bag, so to speak, I could see that I had some explaining to do.

I don't know how or when exactly it all started, but when Julie was a young girl I told her stories about a little girl mouse who was very competent, clever, skilled in problem-solving, strong and fair-minded, fun-loving, and quite adventurous. She was respected for her sense of community and, at the same time, for her independence of thought. I should add that this little girl mouse was also somewhat wilful, and, at times, according to whim, a rascal. Although I don't recall how or when I stepped into this story-telling, I do recall some of the reasons why I continued the practice through some period of my sister's childhood. First and foremost, I recall that Julie pestered me for these stories. She was in fact very good at this and, because I loved her so, this pestering was difficult, if not impossible, to resist. Second, Julie was a really 'gutsy' little kid in a world that in every way was highly disqualifying of such qualities in females. Even all the cartoon heroes were male, and I recall thinking that this was so unfair. Third, although at times I and my brother referred to Julie as 'leach', I did enjoy the world more when she was hanging out with us - the bright eyes, the playfulness, the determination, the honesty.

With Penny's discovery of this episode of history, I found myself in a crisis of confidence. Was I up to it? Could I recreate the adventures of the little girl mouse? Could I again put together the plots and the characters of the story-telling of my distant past? I was quickly rescued from this crisis. Penny made it clear that, as her father, I was obliged to share these stories with her, and she was just great at insistence. Cheryl, my partner, and Penny's mother, encouraged me with: 'Yes, you can do it. Of course you can. You know you can'.

Before I knew it, I was recreating the different series of the Mouse Stories: 'The Girl Detective Mouse', 'The Mouse in the House with Ten Cats', 'Alley Mouse' and 'The Hills Mouse'. The leading characters in each of these series are girl mice who express the very same personal qualities and commitments of the girl mice of a generation before. Penny's responses to my initial efforts were entirely reinforcing. These became her regular bed-time stories (although they didn't work at all well in getting her off to sleep), and before long I found that I was also looking forward to the next instalments.

Soon Penny made a decision to record these on audiotape. In this way, she built up a collection which she treasured. What happened to this collection? Lots of things, many of them untoward. For example, once a pot of glue was up-ended on some of these audiotapes, only to be discovered at a later time. To Penny, this was a tragedy, and she was inconsolable. Would she ever recover? Eventually yes. Other tapes have been lost in the passage of time, and to the disorder of a busy and adventurous life. But some still survive today.

As I was preparing this piece, in looking back over this period of my relationship with Penny, I found myself revisiting the different ways that these stories have been important to me. For example, they provided a powerful medium of connection with Penny when I was absent and she was young. When I started to travel to distant places with teaching, I would record Mouse Stories that were set in the cities that I was to visit. Penny would listen to these during my absence, and in this way I reckoned that she could keep track of my life, and have at least some experience of being with me. And knowing this, I reckoned that I might have at least some experience of being with her. As well, on these travels I carried with me a tape-recorder so that I might record yet further stories. I knew that Penny would be eagerly awaiting these upon my return. But more than this - much more - recording these stories on these travels assisted me to get through the persistent and seemingly incurable wrenching feeling in my heart that I felt at being so far away, apart from Penny, at times apart from Cheryl, and apart from others whom I also love. Recording these stories in my hotel room at night was the only antidote that I could find. Nothing else would work.

I recently happened across a few of the Mouse tapes that had withstood the ravages of time. I am going to include here a brief transcript of one of these tapes. My purpose in doing so is to provide you with some sense of the co-production of these stories. The narrating of any story is powerfully shaped by the listener's response. This cannot be emphasised enough when the listener is also the subject of the story, which in this case is Penny. This transcript is taken from the standard introduction to the stories of the Detective Mouse series. Although Detective Mouse is not without foibles (for example, at times she is a touch pedantic), she is a rather extraordinary mouse who has even managed to solve many of the mysteries that proved too difficult for Sherlock Holmes to unravel.

In the Detective Mouse series, each episode begins in the middle of the night in the forest where Detective Mouse is fast asleep in her wonderfully cosy tree-house. For some perverse reason, Detective Mouse is never summoned at a reasonable hour, but always in the dead of night. Now Detective Mouse is rather a heavy sleeper, so she never hears the knocking on the door. So, whoever is summoning Detective Mouse at this inconvenient time must knock firmly, then more firmly, then even more firmly still, until they are pounding heavily on the door. Eventually the door gives way. Wrenched from its hinges, it crashes to the ground heavily, raising a cloud of dust and splinters. This usually serves the purpose of alerting Detective Mouse to the fact that her presence is required. Needless to say, such a rude awakening hardly does wonders for Detective Mouse's mood at the beginning of each episode. In fact, at this stage in the story she is invariably grumpy. In the following transcript, Penny's contribution appears in italics:

Tap, tap, tap. [gentle knocking]

Girl Detective Mouse, fast asleep, doesn't even twitch.

Rap, rap, rap. [firmer knocking]

Still Girl Detective Mouse doesn't move.

Thud, thud, thud. [yet firmer still]

Girl Detective Mouse shifts in her sleep, and wrinkles her nose briefly. Then again she is still.

Penny giggles.

Thump, thump, thump. [getting radical]

Penny belly-laughs.

Girl Detective Mouse pulls a pillow over her head. Otherwise, she remains comatose.

Bang, bang, bang. [over-the-top radical]

Craaaaaaaaaaaaaaaaaaash!

The door is wrenched from its hinges and smashes onto the ground. Girl Detective Mouse opens one eye - just a slit - and peers into the gloom, through the cloud of dust and past the pile of wood-chips that was once a door.

Oh, no! Not again! Why does this always have to happen in the middle of the night? Aaaaaagghh! [exclaims Penny, taking over the story-line in her four-year-old voice]

Why can't everyone come at a more sensible hour? [continues Penny]

Slowly and crossly, Girl Detective Mouse swings herself out of her soft, warm, bed and drags herself to the doorway. Standing just outside she sees a little boy, all alone.

Ohhhh! [Penny exclaims lovingly]

'Who are you? What are you doing here? And why did you break my door down?' fires off Girl Detective Mouse, extremely annoyed.

This time a longer belly-laugh from Penny.

'I didn't mean to break down your door. I'm only a little boy. I knocked on your door because I needed your help. But when you didn't come, I just knocked a bit harder, that's all.'

Girl Detective Mouse, softening some, responds: 'What do you mean, "that's all"? Breaking down someone's door, that's a lot! And it was oak too! New two weeks ago! Now tell me, how can I be of service to you?'

I know! I know! [exclaims Penny. And so we are off, joining the famous Girl Detective Mouse in another extraordinary adventure.]

Now to the question of my purposes in including here this episode of my personal history. I don't believe that there is anything unusual about this account of story-telling. And it certainly isn't at all unusual for people who are involved in the care-taking of young children to engage in story-telling. I'm sure that many readers could relate interesting accounts of their own story-telling history. So why did I choose to do this? My chief purpose in telling this story about story-telling is to introduce explorations of the sort of 're-membering' practices that are taken up in some detail in chapter one - re-membering practices that I believe to be a potential source of generativity for therapists, and that can provide a source of ongoing sustenance to us in our work. This re-membering is not simply recollection, but a practice that actually contributes to the identification and acknowledgement of those persons who have contributed significantly to the generation of our stories of identity and to our knowledges and skills of living.

Over the years I have been consulted by many parents, and other adults who have care-taking roles with children, over various concerns that they have about the children who are in their care. I have always greatly enjoyed meeting with these care-takers and children, and engaging with them in the exploration of different possibilities for action in the service of addressing their concerns. Although I don't mean to imply that I have at all times found this work to be seamless, or without glitches, I have consistently experienced joy in joining with these children's ways of knowing, and in the exploration of the practices of therapy that support and take up these ways of knowing. This has provided wonderfully imaginative options for action in addressing the concerns that are at the centre of the consultations.

In reflecting on this, I found myself thinking about the sense of familiarity that I have with this joy, with these special ways of knowing, and about the development of these therapeutic practices. How am I to explain this? What is it that informs my connection with these ways of knowing? What is it that shapes these therapeutic practices? Maybe some theory of child development? Not likely. Certain texts on working with children? Helpful perhaps. But to me this is not a satisfactory answer. Rather, I believe that any thorough-going response to these questions would have me engaging in reflections on my relationships with Julie, with Penny, and with a number of other young children whom I've known. I believe that it is in the context of these connections, of these memberships of my life, that I have become knowledged in this work with children. Julie, Penny, and these other young children have joined with me in the co-authorship of these knowledges and therapeutic practices.

Early in 1996 I found some Mouse tapes that were assumed lost. It was wonderful to re-visit some of these stories of a decade and a half ago. They gave me pause to reflect on the history of this story-telling, and took me into conversations with Penny and with Julie about what I understood to be their contributions to the spirit of my work with children. As an outcome of these conversations, I have been aware of their voices having an even stronger presence in this work. And Cheryl's voice is there as well, for she had so appreciated these stories that she had never heard, was confident that I could re-create them, and in so many ways reinforced the telling of them. About this I feel joyous, and I experience a greater consciousness of what it is that sustains me in this work.

The actual writing of this story about story-telling has been a further exercise in the re-membering of my work - it has provided me with further opportunity to acknowledge a few of the memberships of my life that have provided contexts for the generation of some of the knowledges and practices of my work with children. In making this acknowledgement, I am not denying my contribution to the generation of these knowledges and practices. And I am not stepping into a one-down position (any more than I would be prepared to step into a one-up position), or giving something away. Rather, for me not to engage in this sort of re-membering would render my work with children 'thinly' described[2], and so much would be forsaken. This would close down options for me to revisit the knowledges and skills that were co-generated in these significant memberships of my life. This would shut down opportunities for me to take steps that contribute to my work being more 'richly' or 'thickly' described. And it would close the door for me on new possibilities in the work itself.

Later in this book I will reflect further on this story. I also plan to explore in more detail the metaphors of 'thin' and 'thick' description. Next, however, I will provide a more formal introduction to re-membering practices and the relevance of these practices to the work and life of the therapist.

Note

1. This story also appeared in the book *The Personal is the Professional* (White & Hales 1997). I have reproduced it here in the belief that it contributes well to introducing what I want to say in this book about re-membering conversations. The thought that later reflections on this story could assist in clarifying important distinctions around some of the conceptions and practices of narrative therapy provided yet further impetus to include it here.

2. For an account of the juxtaposition of thin and thick description in the poststructuralist tradition of thought, see Geertz (1973), 'Thick description: Toward an interpretive theory of culture'.

1

The Culture of the Professional Disciplines

The regulation of knowledge and of the membership of one's life

When a person enters the culture of the professional disciplines they are confronted with a shift in what counts as knowledge. The culture of the professional disciplines is a culture that produces particular, highly specialised, and formal knowledges that constitute systems for the analysis of persons' expressions of life, which are constructed in terms of behaviours. It is claimed that these systems of analysis provide, for professional workers, privileged access to the objective truth of these expressions. In this culture, those ways of knowing the world that relate to the more popular and more local discourses of 'lay' communities are marginalised - often categorised as quaint, folk and naive - and frequently disqualified. These other ways of knowing, those that have been generated in the immediate contexts and intimate communities of a person's daily life, mostly don't count in terms of what might be taken for legitimate knowledge in the culture of the professional disciplines.

There is another shift in what counts when a person enters the culture of the professional disciplines. This is a shift in what counts in regard to which persons, and which institutions, might constitute a person's significant relationship and affiliative network - those relationships and affiliations that are deemed to be significant and that are to be privileged in regard to matters relating to the practices of work, and in regard to the knowledges of life that are relevant to this work. In taking up Barbara Myerhoff's (1982) metaphor, in imagining lives to be 'membered', in this discussion I will refer to the persons who, and the institutions that, feature as the significant relationships and affiliations of a person's life as constituting the 'membership' of that person's life. In these terms, the shift that is required of persons entering the culture of psychotherapy is a shift in what counts as the significant membership of their lives.

In the culture of the professional disciplines, when it comes to matters of professional conduct, there is an overriding expectation that the membership of a person's life will be constituted of others who have succeeded in meeting the eligibility requirements of the formal organs of these disciplines - that is, universities, professional associations, clubs, committees, boards, and so on. These eligibility requirements establish powerful restrictions on who might participate in these organs, and impose an exclusive membership criterion for 'professionals' in their working lives. In this formalisation of the membership of a person's life, the 'common' memberships of life - the 'ordinary', everyday and historical associations - are dishonoured. These are not considered relevant to the performance of knowledge.

There are many structures and processes at work in the culture of the professional disciplines that powerfully reinforce this exclusivity. Many of these structures and processes are quite explicit - for example, the ever-present and highly visible emphasis on top-down accountability - and others are more insidious. For example, upon entering the culture of psychotherapy, in various contexts and as part of training and supervision, it is not at all uncommon for a person to be subject to systems of understanding that are pathologising of the significant relationships of their lives, and especially of their familial relationships (and, more often than not, of the relationship with their mother). This can be understood as part of an induction or initiation process, one in which the significant memberships that feature in the history of a person's life are downgraded and frequently disqualified. This paves the way for the substitution of the membership of a person's life - for the formalisation and professionalisation of this membership.

To summarise, I have proposed that entry into the culture of psychotherapy is associated with an induction in which the more local or folk knowledges that have been generated in a person's history are marginalised, often disqualified, and displaced by the formal and expert knowledges of the professional disciplines, and by a shift in what counts in regard to the significant memberships of a persons' life. In this process the associations of the monoculture of psychotherapy are substituted for the diverse, historical and local associations of persons' lives.

The regulation of forums of acknowledgement

To know that we know what we know, and to consciously embrace this knowledge as we live our lives, it is necessary for us to experience a degree of authenticity in our knowledge claims, whatever these claims might be. This sense of authenticity is not something that is achieved by referring to 'factual grounds' or 'objective data', but is instead something that is the outcome of processes of authentication. These processes of authentication require social arenas or forums in which persons might express or perform their knowledge claims before an audience that witnesses this performance, an audience that responds in ways that are acknowledging of such claims. It is through such processes of authentication that persons experience being at one with such knowledge claims.

In arenas of this sort, which can be formal and informal, the response of the audience is not passive, but is an active and knowing response. This response takes shape as a reflection on the person's expressions of knowledge, and is often in the form of commentary. These reflections are a re-telling of the knowledges that are evident in the person's expressions, and these re-tellings contribute significantly to the knowledges known. It is in this way that personal knowledges are co-constructed. And it is in this way that lives are membered by those who contribute to the co-construction of these personal knowledges.

In the networks that make up the social contexts of persons' lives, and in the flow of everyday life, there are many arenas in which a person might express or perform his/her knowledge claims before an audience. If a person's life can be considered a 'club', it is those persons who most regularly or most significantly participate in these arenas who make up the privileged membership of that person's life. But participation in these arenas achieves more than the authentication of a person's knowledgeableness. It is also through these arenas that people can achieve a 'full' or 'thick' description of these knowledges, and of their personal identities.

In the preceding section, I discussed the induction of persons into the culture of the professional disciplines, and referred to processes by which there is a shift in what counts as legitimate knowledge and what counts as the significant memberships of persons' lives in regard to the activities of the professions. But there is yet another shift. When persons enter the culture of the professional disciplines, what it is that constitutes appropriate forums of acknowledgement also changes, along with the criteria that specify to whom these forums are accessible, who might appropriately contribute to audiences for expressions of knowledge, and what it is that constitutes relevant practices or techniques of acknowledgement in these forums.

Exclusivity of professional knowledge and professional membership is accompanied by an exclusivity in regard to those contexts that are deemed appropriate for the knowing performance of knowledge. Forums of acknowledgement are governed by specific conventions and regulations that determine the structure of staff meetings, seminars, conferences, examinations, and so on. And, as well, there are regulations governing the practices of witness in these contexts - that is, the practices of acknowledgement and the practices of censure. These practices of acknowledgement include the techniques of the applause, of the evaluation, of the award, and of the polemic that is performed under the guise of feedback. In this shift, the more informal arenas and practices of witness are displaced by formal and specialised arenas and practices.

For the person stepping into the culture of the psychotherapy, the shift in what counts in terms of legitimate knowledge in regard to matters of practice when persons are inducted into the culture of psychotherapy, in what counts in regard to the significant memberships of a person's life, in what it is that is deemed appropriate as an arena for the knowing performance of knowledge, and in what it is that constitutes appropriate practices of witness, contributes very significantly to thin conclusion.

Thin conclusion and thick description

Clifford Geertz, a cultural anthropologist, juxtaposes 'thin description' and 'thick description' in his classic paper, 'Thick description: Toward an interpretive theory of culture' (1973). These terms he borrowed from Gilbert Ryle. Thin descriptions of a persons' actions are descriptions that exclude the interpretations of those who are engaging in these actions. Thin descriptions are also those descriptions that exclude the particular systems of understanding and practices of negotiation that make it possible for communities of persons to arrive at shared meanings in regard to these actions. Thin descriptions are typically those arrived at through the 'observations' of those considered to be outsiders who are studying the lives of other people and the communities in which these people live.

Conversely, thick descriptions of persons' actions are descriptions that are informed by the interpretations of those who are engaging in these actions, and that emphasise the particular systems of understanding and the practices of negotiation that make it possible for communities of persons to arrive at shared meanings in regard to these actions. A thick description of an action is one that is inscribed with the meanings of the community of persons to which this action is directly relevant.

To Geertz (1973), ethnography is thick description arrived at through the sort of interpretations *that take us into the heart of that which is the interpretation.* Ethnography is about events intelligibly described, and the interpreting involved in rendering events intelligibly described *consists in trying to rescue the said ... from its perishing occasions and fix it in perusable terms* (p.20). Thin description, on the other hand, is derived as an outcome of efforts to 'answer our deepest questions' of the world, of life, to extrapolate 'general visions' from 'local truths', to develop accounts of the 'universal properties of mind', and so on. Of these efforts in the construction of formal theories and systems of analysis of life, Geertz is sharply critical. He says of any description of action, that *any attempt to cast what it says in terms other than its own is regarded as a travesty,* as *ethnocentric* (p.24).

Others writers also take up these metaphors. For Renato Rosaldo (1992), thick description is that description that provides an account of events as *loosely tied bundles of informal practices.* This is an account that is derived through the sense made of these events by those who are directly engaged in these practices, and by the understandings of those whose lives are directly influenced by them. Thin conclusion (or what Rosaldo at times refers to as monographic description) is that description that constructs lives and communities *as well-formed systems regulated by control mechanisms* (p.94) that can be understood through the application of the sort of formal systems of analysis that are informed by the 'expert' knowledges of the professional disciplines.

Barbara Myerhoff (1982), also an anthropologist, embraces these metaphors too, and reflects on the actual practices that take place in communities of persons that contribute to the generation of thick or rich descriptions:

> *Private and collective lives, properly Re-membered, are interpretive. Full or 'thick description' is such an analysis. This involves finding linkages between the group's shared valued beliefs and symbols, and specific historical events. Particularities are subsumed and equated with grander themes, seen as exemplifying ultimate concerns.* (p.111)

So, to the question of how thick or rich description is generated, Myerhoff's partial response is that this is the outcome of the identification of the historical events of one's life with 'shared valued beliefs and symbols'. But Myerhoff also provides an account of the processes by which this is achieved. She proposes that it is through engaging with a community of persons in the telling and the re-telling of the preferred stories of one's history and of one's identity that lives are thickly described. It is in this context that the stories of persons' lives become linked to shared values, beliefs, purposes, desires, commitments, and so on. It is in the context of the telling and re-telling of the stories of one's life that meta-texts, and texts that are meta to these meta-texts, are generated.

The outcome of this is the production of lives that are multiply contextualised. It is the multiple contextualisation of life that contributes to the generation of narrative resources, and thus to lives that might be well read - to quote Geertz: *Texts require multiple contextualisation in order to be well read* (1983, p.176-7). These narrative resources contribute significantly to the range of possible meanings that persons might give to their experiences of the world, and to the range of options for action in the world. And, in that this range of options for action would not be available to persons whose lives are poorly read, these narrative resources are constitutive of life - they contribute to the shaping of life; they make life up.

Thin conclusion and the life of the therapist

Many readers will have some familiarity with a critique of expert knowledge systems on the basis that these structure power relations that are subjugating of the persons who consult therapists. But what about the life of the therapist? What is the effect on the therapist's life of this formalisation of knowledges, of the professionalisation of the membership of their lives, and of the regulation of forums of acknowledgement?

I believe the consequences to be profoundly significant. In the formalisation of knowledge, persons become differently knowledged. A class of knowledge that is modest in its claims (local, particular and 'experience near'[1]) gives way to a class of knowledge that is immodest in its claims (global, universal and 'experience distant'). Rich descriptions of life that are multi-storied give way to flat or 'monographic' descriptions, descriptions that are generative of 'thin conclusions'. And, despite the promises of these global 'truth' claims, the specificity and authority of expert knowledges, which are distributed from the top down, make it difficult for persons whose working lives are located in the various sites of the culture of psychotherapy to ever experience the attainment of an adequate grasp of knowledge. No matter how much they know, it is never enough. Requisite knowledge is always beyond the horizon. In this culture of psychotherapy, therapists find it ever so difficult to escape the sense that they have failed to know what needs to be known. The outcome is that the lives and the work of therapists become 'thinly described', and this very significantly narrows available options for action in life generally, and in 'work' more specifically.

As lives become professionally membered in the monoculture of psychotherapy, and in the dishonouring of the memberships through which local and folk knowledges have been co-generated through personal history, much is forsaken. The outcome for many is a dis-memberment that contributes to a loss of history, and a loss of a particular sense of the self. It is also a dis-memberment that deprives persons of the opportunity to join locally with others in connecting the specific experiences of their lives (including their work) to the shared values and beliefs that are privileged in different communities of persons, and to experience so doing in relation to the significant themes and meanings of life. So often, a professionally membered life turns out to be a 'dis-memberment' that contributes significantly to thin descriptions of personal identity and of life generally.

And what of the formalisation of forums of acknowledgement? The governing of forums of acknowledgement through the conventions and regulations of the culture of psychotherapy closes options for informal, common and spontaneous expressions of knowledge. This reduction in available forums for the expression or performance of knowledge restricts options for persons to experience the authentication of knowledge claims, and for these knowledges to be more richly described. The formalisation of practices of witness renders a broad range of common and everyday practices of witness, or practices of acknowledgement, irrelevant. And the general limits on the locations from which persons might legitimately express these knowledges denies them access to contexts that might contribute to a sense of being knowledged.

As well, in the culture of the professional disciplines there is little equality of access to these forums of acknowledgement. Persons who have relatively junior status in the culture of the professional disciplines are less likely to find themselves the subjects of acknowledgement than are those persons who have senior status[2]. And the formalisation of practices of acknowledgement renders a broad range of common and everyday versions of these practices irrelevant.

The thin conclusions about one's work that are the outcome of this shift in what counts as legitimate knowledge, in what counts as the significant membership of a person's life, and in what is deemed appropriate as forums for the knowing expression of knowledge, contribute very significantly to therapists' vulnerability to despair, fatigue and burnout. In the chapters that follow, I will review some practices that provide at least a partial antidote to these experiences. But first a proviso.

Limits of critique

I have reviewed here some of the shifts in what counts when persons are inducted into the culture of the professional disciplines - in what counts as legitimate knowledge, in what counts as the significant memberships of person's lives, and in what structures are deemed appropriate as forums of acknowledgement. I have also reviewed some of the effects of these shifts on the lives of persons who step into the culture of psychotherapy. This review constitutes a critique of expert knowledge systems, and I believe that it is important for me to be clear about the limits of this critique. This clarity might be best achieved by stating here what it is that I am not proposing in this review.

I do not intend this review to be in any way read as a general disqualification of the knowledges of the professional disciplines. Instead it is a critique of a class of knowledge; that is the formal and systematised knowledges that establish global truth claims about the nature of life - of social organisation, of human development, of the workings of the psyche or of the family, and so on. And it is a critique of how these formal and systematised knowledges are taken up in and inform particular operations of power in the culture of psychotherapy.

I do not believe all that appears in professional texts to be reproducing of these expert knowledges and these practices of power. Many texts include ideas and practices that stand outside of these systematising theories, and many others have embedded contradictions to these systematising theories. As well, there are many examples of texts that give expression to ideas and practices that are directly challenging of much of this - although these texts are often somewhat marginalised. The ideas found in these texts that I refer to here are not those that are taken up into the familiar operations of power of expert knowledge systems, and they are not those that are rendered exclusive theories - they are not those ideas that are associated with practices of power that marginalise and disqualify the local knowledges of personal history.

I also do not intend this critique of the formal knowledge systems to be in any way read as a veneration of the local knowledges that are generated in the significant memberships of personal history. I am not generating a proposal that these knowledges be substituted for the expert knowledges and assigned some elevated status - that these other more 'local' knowledges be granted the sort of veracity that would assign to them global truth claims or universal validity. Rather, I have critiqued the global and systematising nature of the formal and specialised knowledges, and the practices of power that are associated with them, in relation to the extent to which they contribute to a dismemberment of persons' lives through the disqualification of the local knowledges of personal history, and the extent to which they inform monographic accounts of life.

In critiquing the expert knowledges of the culture of psychotherapy, I am not suggesting that these knowledges are expressions of a false consciousness or that the local knowledges of personal history are expressions of some true consciousness. Nor am I suggesting that the expert knowledges are fabrications that provide a disguise for operations of power, or that the local knowledges are the 'authentic' knowledges that stand in opposition to operations of power. Rather, following Foucault (1980), I understand that all knowledges are socially constructed and constitutive or potentially constitutive of life, and that power and knowledge are inseparable - all knowledges are associated with and inform practices of power[3].

Further, in engaging in this critique of the expert knowledges of professional culture, I am not proposing an idealising of local culture - I am not engaging in some romantic veneration of familial, wider kinship and friendship networks, or any of the other intimate associations and institutional affiliations of personal history that provide the context for the generation of the multiple, often contradictory, and frequently contestatory local knowledges. Rather, I have critiqued the extent to which the culture of the professional disciplines and the expert knowledge discourses marginalise and disqualify local culture, and introduce a professional monoculture. And I have critiqued the extent to which this establishes an exclusivity in regard to what are deemed to be the credible memberships of persons' lives[4]. The effects of this on persons whose lives are located in the culture of the professional disciplines is perhaps best described by Barbara Myerhoff: *Without Re-membering we lose our histories and our selves. Time is erosion, then, rather than accumulation.* (1982, p.111)

Notes

1. I have borrowed this term from Clifford Geertz (1973).

2. I wish to say little here of the practices of censure that are also expressed in uniquely convened forums in the culture of the professional disciplines, except that, in number, these tend to eclipse those forums in which a person might be subject to acknowledgement - except, of course, for those who inhabit the more senior positions in the institutions of the culture of psychotherapy.

3. Although all operations of power are associated with and contribute to the production of knowledge, there is not an identity between the practices of power that are associated with the various knowledges.

4. In regard to this point, I am not proposing that the memberships that are available to persons in the culture of the professional disciplines are necessarily, of themselves, dis-membering of persons' lives. It is the exclusivity of these memberships that achieves this.

2

Re-membering

In the foregoing critique of the expert knowledge practices of the culture of the professional disciplines, I took up Barbara Myerhoff's notion of membered lives, and reviewed some of the conventions of this culture that can be dismembering of persons' lives. The image of membered lives brings into play the metaphor of a 'club' - a club of life is evoked. This metaphor opens up options for the exploration of how a person's club of life is membered - of how this club of life is constituted through its membership, and of how the membership of this club is arranged in terms of rank or status. As well, this metaphor suggests unique possibilities for action in the form of re-membering practices, which inform a 'special type of recollection'. I will here quote Myerhoff (1982) on this subject:

> To signify this special type of recollection, the term 'Re-membering' may be used, calling attention to the reaggregation of members, the figures who belong to one's life story, one's own prior selves, as well as significant others who are part of the story. Re-membering, then, is a purposive, significant unification, quite different from the passive, continuous fragmentary flickerings of images and feelings that

accompany other activities in the normal flow of consciousness. (p.111)

This notion of re-membering, and the club metaphor, suggests possibilities for persons to engage in a revision of the membership of their club of life. This is an engagement that provides persons with the opportunity to have a greater say about the status of particular memberships of their club of life. Through re-membering practices, persons can suspend or elevate, revoke or privilege, and downgrade or upgrade specific memberships of their lives. Various classes of honorary membership can be established and bestowed, including life memberships. It is in this way, through re-membering practices, that persons can have more to say about whose voices are to be recognised on matters of their identity, and about who might be authorised to speak on such matters. And, apart from contributing to persons having a greater say about the status of the existing memberships of their club of life, re-membering practices also contribute to options in regard to the selection of new memberships from persons and groups of persons who might be available and willing to join - from persons and groups of persons who might be invited to take out preferred memberships in one's club of life.

This notion of re-membering also suggests possibilities and provides opportunities for persons to more directly acknowledge the important and valued contributions that others have made to their lives. When these opportunities are taken up into re-membering practices, these other persons generally experience this as significantly honouring of them. As well, in engaging in these acknowledgements of the contributions of others, one experiences one's own life being more richly described. Such acts of acknowledgement can also have persons re-activating dormant memberships through re-engaging with some of the figures of their history. In these acts, a person experiences the stories of their lives linked to the stories of the lives of others around particular themes and shared values and commitments. And, more than this, these practices of re-membering generally make it more possible for people to experience, in their day-to-day lives, the fuller presence of these figures, even when they are not available to be there in a material sense (for example, in the case of persons who have died or from whom a separation has occurred). The sense of being joined in this way, and of experiencing one's life more richly described, contributes to new possibilities for action in the world. It also renders persons less vulnerable to experiences of being alone in the face of adversity - it provides an antidote to a sense of isolation.

Through these re-membering practices, in the revision of the membership of a person's club of life, those memberships that are honoured or elevated in status can be considered to be those that have provided the context for the generation of the person's preferred knowledges of life and skills of living. These are frequently the historical associations that have been significant in the derivation of the person's preferred account of their identity. In reviewing these associations, those knowledges and skills, and those accounts of identity, can be identified and explored in their particularities - the significant discoveries, realisations, conclusions, learnings, problem-solving practices, and so on, become more thickly described. This contributes very significantly to a person's sense of being knowledged, to the shaping of new proposals for action in their lives, and to specific expressions of these proposals.

Before proceeding to review the relevance of re-membering practices to the work and to the lives of therapists, a diversion is warranted - one that provides an account of re-membering practices as they might be expressed in narrative work with persons who consult therapists. This diversion will take the form of a brief review of the history of re-membering practices in my work, and three stories of narrative practice, the first of which is principally a transcript. These stories are unique in the sense that the narratives of persons' lives always are; in the sense that every therapeutic journey evolves in ways that could not have been predicted ahead of the journey itself, and in the sense that each journey brings with it options for entering new territories of thought and practice. However, these three stories of narrative practice are not unique in regard to the general effects of re-membering practices - these practices invariably make a very significant contribution to lives being richly described, and to the development of a wide range of options for action in the social world.

Saying hullo again

About ten years ago I started to organise and to commit to paper some of the thoughts and practices that I had been exploring in working with people who were in 'trouble' with grief - persons who had been referred to me with diagnoses of 'delayed grief' and 'pathological mourning'. Twelve months later these thoughts were published as 'Saying hullo again: The reincorporation of the lost relationship in the resolution of grief' (White 1988). The thoughts expressed in this paper contradicted the idea that working with grief is about assisting persons to go through the stages of a well-known journey so that they might arrive at an acceptance of the loss, and so that they might then proceed with their lives without the lost loved one.

The 'saying hullo again' paper spoke to some conclusions that I had reached in my meetings with persons who were seeking consultation over 'delayed grief' and 'pathological mourning': (a) these persons were already profoundly bereft; (b) this was a powerful testimony to the significance of, and the love experienced in, the lost relationship; (c) the loss of the loved one had contributed to wide gaps in the person's sense of identity; and (d) further work oriented by the known and established grief maps was counter-productive in addressing these losses. Too much had already gone from the lives of these persons - an experience of the voices of, and the touch of, the lost loved ones was already an achievement that was too elusive to these persons.

In response to these conclusions, I began to explore 'saying hullo again' conversations - conversations that were reincorporating of the person's relationship with the lost loved one, conversations that contributed to making available to persons, in their day-to-day lives, experiences of the touch and the voices of the lost loved ones[1]. Persons' responses to these conversations were dramatic - they broke from the desperation, from the despair, and from the sense of emptiness that had become the central experience of their lives, and reclaimed a familiar and comforting sense of identity. The 'saying hullo again' conversations that I discussed in this paper were in part oriented by what at the time I called 'experience of experience' questions, and which I now more regularly refer to as 're-membering questions'.

In providing here some account of the history of re-membering practices in my work, I thought it appropriate to briefly revisit these practices as they are expressed in the context of addressing profound grief in relation the death of a loved one.

Sophia[2] and Bill

I first met Sophia fifteen years ago. At that time she was struggling with a pervasive depression and with an anorexia nervosa that was constantly threatening to deprive her of her life. This struggle wasn't new. Over many years this depression and anorexia nervosa had driven her into actions against her own life, and had precipitated admissions to hospital. Sophia was tiring of the struggle.

At first, Sophia was decidedly unenthusiastic about meeting with me and about pursuing yet another course of therapy. She had no confidence that this could lead to a good outcome, but had decided to go along with it for the sake of her partner, Bill. He had refused to be discouraged in his efforts to join with Sophia in search of a solution to the depression and the anorexia nervosa, and had remained steadfast in his belief that she would find a better life. Bill was a force for life.

Over the course of our meetings, Sophia identified, and gradually broke her life from, the voice of self-hate and the voice of anorexia nervosa. As she did so she began to explore and step into other accounts of her identity. Bill's contribution at this time was invaluable. He was ever ready to support Sophia in the meaning-making conversations that we were engaging in, and in the exploration of the proposals for action in her life that were informed by these conversations. And at no point in this work did he assume that he could have a voice for Sophia. As Sophia began to embrace life, Bill initiated a critical reflection on his ways of being in his relationship with her, and, as an outcome of this, took many steps to ensure that Sophia would be unhindered in this embrace. This was Sophia's chance, and for this Bill would move a mountain if this was necessary. Bill's presence in these conversations also warmed and sustained me.

For Sophia, her embrace of life was not a reclaiming of it. She believed that life had never been in her grasp. As part of what Sophia referred to as 'being born' as a person, she developed an interest in making small stuffed creatures. This she found to be life-giving, and it was through this project that she developed new connections with the outside world. As Sophia's life went forward, we had many causes to celebrate together. Through the next years I would hear from Sophia from time to time, sometimes a letter, sometimes a call

- and in this way I was an audience to the many developments in her life, including her enrolment in a women's studies program. Bill's voice was always there in these developments too - always believing, always acknowledging.

I knew that Bill had decided to take early retirement in 1996. He and Sophia were looking forward to spending more time together, and had planned many adventures for this phase of their lives. Then suddenly, in early 1996, Bill died of heart failure. I was called by Sophia's general practitioner. She was in hospital, recovering from a major overdose - now off the critical list, but depressed and furious with him and the hospital staff for having saved her life. She had intended to kill herself, and was now assuring everybody that the only outcome of the medical intervention would be a brief reprieve. Sophia was determined to be successful in the next attempt on her life, and was asserting that the medical intervention had extended her life by a matter of weeks, not months or years. It was her desire to be six feet under the ground, lying alongside Bill. This was the only place that she wanted to be. During the telephone conversation, the general practitioner informed me that Sophia said that she would speak to me, but that she would be entirely intolerant of anyone's efforts to talk her out of her resolve to join Bill. Knowing Sophia and Bill as I did, I appreciated that this resolve was a testimony to the powerful love that they had for each other, and to the wonderful contribution that they had made to each other's life.

I visited the hospital, and sat with Sophia. She was indeed angry, and just so miserable. She talked flatly of her desolation and of the greyness that had enveloped her life, of the gift of being that had now been withdrawn, of the impossibility of proceeding in life without Bill, of the lost hopes that they'd had for his retirement, of her desire to be lying alongside him, and of her conviction that nothing could stop the inevitable - the medical intervention had saved her on this occasion, but it had only put off what was inevitable. Sophia also made it clear that she would not spend time with anyone who had an agenda of talking her out of her resolve to join Bill. I gave her my undertaking not to do this, but asked if it would be okay with her if we had some conversations about options that would enable her to again be with Bill, to experience his presence, but that did not require her to be six feet under the ground. This was acceptable to Sophia, and so began a series of conversations that were oriented by the 'saying hullo again' metaphor.

The following transcript is of an interview that took place nine weeks after Bill's death, and constituted one of the turning-points in our work. In this interview, Sophia had been talking of the advice that she had been receiving from many quarters - to grieve, to let go of Bill, to accept the loss, and to get on with her life. Sophia just knew that this 'common knowledge' was not right for her. We explored how it was that Sophia had been able to respect this conclusion, and discovered that she had achieved this by keeping faith with and relying upon her 'uncommon knowledge'.

Transcript[3]

It's a knowledge that seems like an uncommon knowledge in a way? Do you mean it's not a knowledge that everybody can relate to?

It just seems like everyone else, apart from a few close friends, think that it's time just to move forward and put everything else behind me.

Put this behind you and move forward - is what most other people seem to think this is all about?

[Sophia nods]

What are you thinking about right now?

I'm thinking about what Bill would think.

Yes. Can you tell me about what he would think?

Well, my Mum and some other people reckon that he would be really angry with me for not just getting on with life. But I don't think he would be at all. I think he would understand. I don't think he would be angry at all. [tearful]

What's it like for you when other people set themselves up as an authority on his voice? What is that like for you when other people say these things - that this is what Bill would have said, that he would have been angry with you for not doing ...?

It makes me feel sick inside.

It makes you feel sick inside ...

My sister's husband told me the day of the funeral just to: 'Get out there and be strong. Bill would have wanted you to be strong for him'. But I said, 'No, he would want me to be myself'.

This was your brother-in-law? Who said that Bill would just want you to be strong and go out there? And you said, 'No he wouldn't, he would want me to be myself'? What do you call that when other people somehow believe that they have the right to step into Bill's shoes? What's a good name for that?

I reckon that it's exceptionally egotistical on the behalf of that person doing it.

'Exceptionally egotistical' - that's a pretty kind description. It's a fairly kind description of something which seems, quite frankly, outrageous. But your sense is that Bill would say, 'No Sophia's doing the right thing for herself'? If he was here, is that what he would be saying?

[Sophia nods]

Do you have a sense of what else he would be saying if he was here? If I could just ask him right now, 'Bill, what is the most important thing about what Sophia has been saying?' what do you think he would be saying about that?

I think he would want me to do whatever it is I need to do for as long as I need to do it.

So, he would be saying, 'Sophia will do what she needs to do and that's right'. How would he respond to your resistance to all of these other people who pretend that they can speak with Bill's voice, or pretend that they know what is right for you? What would he say about your resistance to that? Would he be supportive of it, or would he ...

He would be very supportive.

How would he be supportive of it? What would he say?

He would tell me to listen to my own voice.

He would say listen to your own voice.

Yes.

What else would he say that would be supportive of your resistance? I'll just tell the group [turning to the reflecting team which is behind the one-way screen] that Bill wasn't a man of many words, was he? But what he had to say was very profound, wasn't it? When he spoke about things, he had a way of saying things that was very strong, quite economical ... but strong. Would you say that's true?

Yes.

So, what would be one of his economical and strong statements of support, for your resistance, that we might hear from Bill?

He would say that only I know what is right for me.

That's what he would say: 'Only Sophia knows what's right for her'.

[Sophia nods]

Is there anything else that occurs to you that he might say? Apart from: 'Listen to your own voice'. 'Only Sophia knows what's right for her'?

He always told me just to be me.

Just to be you? Okay ... I would like to ask a few more questions, but first I would like to know how this conversation is going for you. In the conversation that we are having here now, are we talking about the right things to be talking about?

Yes.

Why is that?

Because I have been beginning to doubt whether or not what I'm doing is right.

Because you've been beginning to doubt whether what you are doing is right. What's our conversation doing to that doubt?

It's reinforcing the belief to listen to myself, not to everyone else I know.

It's reinforcing your belief in listening to yourself, not to others?

I've spent too many years doing what other people thought I should be doing. It took me a long time to figure out what to do for myself. What felt right for me.

Can I write that down? Is that okay? You said, 'It took me a long time to figure out what to do for myself'. Is that what you said?

[Sophia nods]

Then you said something else.

I've spent such a long time doing everything that everyone else thought I should be doing.

What's it been like for you here to actually bring Bill into the room in the way that you have, just by sharing with me what his reactions would have been to our conversation? Is that something that has been a positive or negative experience for you? Or neither? To bring Bill's voice here.

I felt like he was here already anyway.

You felt he was here already?

When I was sitting downstairs.

When you were sitting downstairs, you felt he was here?

It just made me think about when we used to come here.

Is that a recent development for you, to actually experience him being with you in that way?

No. The other times when I've been here too, it's been the same.

It's when you come here that you've experienced that? You actually have a sense of his physical presence? What's that like to find him present physically like that when you come here?

It gives me moral support.

Gives you moral support? And you have that sense that he is right here with us now in a sense ... like ...

Yes. Where he always used to sit, next to me.

Sitting right next to you. Always on your left side?

On my right side.

On your right side ... sorry, I meant right side but I'm looking at you from here, on *my* left from where I'm sitting. On your right side. Has that happened anywhere else, Sophia, or is it just coming here that you experience his presence like this?

It's only here.

It's just here?

I think it's because Bill played such an important part here in helping me find me.

Yes, he did play a pretty powerful part didn't he? I'm just writing some things down, just in case I manage to get some of these down in a letter.

It's okay.

If you had this experience more, not just here at Dulwich Centre, but in other places too, would that be a positive or a negative thing? I was just thinking about what you know about your own healing.

It would be a positive thing.

'... it would be a positive thing'. [writing]

One of the things I find most scary is that he is not there to help me along the way any more.

But if he was there for you like he is here now, that would be a positive thing?

Yes.

How would that be helpful to you in terms of helping you along the way? If you could experience him in your life like you experience him here, in this room?

It's like whenever Bill was there for me even though he wasn't at the same place I was at ... not necessarily physically present ... but he was always there in my mind. There was a real safety in that.

Safety. So, he didn't have to be with you. He could be out and about. He didn't have to be there physically, but there was a place there that he occupied that contributed to safety for you?

It's a bit like having a guardian angel, I think.

A guardian angel! Do you think that this supports your understanding about what's healing for you - to have Bill in your life more, not to turn your back and get on with life?

I think it does, because otherwise I wouldn't feel his presence so easily.

You have actually ... brought forth Bill's presence for me more strongly just by what you've told me about feeling he was with you here and in the waiting room ... [tearful] And I can just see him. Didn't he used to slap his knee? Do you remember that? Wasn't that a common gesture - slapping his knee? What were some of his other common gestures? I remember that one so clearly. He would often just slap his knee ...

He would cross and uncross his legs.

That's right. Cross and uncross his legs, I remember that one too. And he would often be slightly outside of the situation, looking in on it, wouldn't he? He would be thinking all the time.

Lots of times I would be talking to him and I would think he wasn't quite listening, and I would say, 'Do you want me to continue saying what I'm talking about, or don't you really want to know?' He would say, 'I was listening all along'. I'd say, 'Well, what did I say?' So, then he would tell me. It was like he was always listening but thinking at the same time.

That brings back memories for me about talking to Bill here and thinking that he'd tuned out ...

But he didn't.

No. And I'd say, 'Bill, I don't know if you've been listening', and he would say, 'Well, I have been'. And I'd say, 'Well what did Sophia just say?' and he could give it back word for word.

[Sophia nods]

What's your guess about how I'm feeling?

I think you'd be feeling a sense of loss as well. At the same time, it's not like it's a total loss. [tearful]

You've hit the nail right on the head. I can speak about how it might not be a total loss, but you've helped me *experience* that it's not. Do you know what I mean? It's one thing to say it, but it's another thing to really experience it. What are you thinking about now?

Some of the time it just seems like it is a total loss for me.

Some of the time it does. Do you know ... you've evoked his presence here very powerfully. I'm experiencing it as well, and I'm just wondering whether you know how you do that. Do you know? Because I know you said that it is partly coming here, but you go to other places that Bill was with you at. Do you know how you did that? You said that the first time that you came back here, a couple of months ago, you experienced his presence in the waiting-room. Do you know how you did that? Was it something you thought about before coming here, or was it something that just happened when you ... ?

It just happened when I went in and sat down.

Do you know what sort of state of mind that you were in, that you got yourself into, that made that possible? Do you have any sense of that?

I just thought of Bill and when I thought of him it was like he was sitting there with me.

So, you thought about that in a way that didn't just evoke loss - it also evoked his presence as well?

I was just thinking about Bill, about his 'being', not just thinking about him as not being here physically any more.

So, you weren't thinking of that ... you were thinking of his being. That's what you were thinking about? If this could work for you in other places, if you could think of his being in the way that you did when you sat down in the waiting-room, would that be positive or negative or ... ?

I think it would be positive.

I can tell you that it's been positive for me. Even though it's been very emotional, it's been a positive experience for you to introduce his being here in the way that you have. I'm just wondering if we could figure out how you could take this sense of him being with you away from here and into other places, about how you might do that. Because it's not by chance it's happened here. I understand why you might do it here first, because of the part that Bill played in you having a life, having a voice. I'm just wondering what might make it possible for you to do this in other places. Do you have any thoughts about that? You said that you came here and you weren't thinking about ... what did you say you weren't thinking about?

I wasn't thinking about Bill in relation to loss necessarily. I was just thinking about him.

So, you were just thinking about his being ... his being.

I wasn't particularly thinking about him being dead.

I'd like to think of some questions that I could ask that would help me get more in touch with that skill of actually evoking Bill's presence in the way that you have - just to understand more about how you did that. I can understand that you came here and that you sat in the waiting-room and you just started thinking about his being, not his loss, and that's a part of it. Are you sensing his presence still with you right now?

He's here all the time in this room.

He's here all the time in this room. Okay. So, what he knew about you is present too. The really important understandings he had about you as a person, they're here as well?

[Sophia nods]

You've actually shared some of those understandings already, some of the understandings that he had of you. Some of the knowledges that he had about your life and about what works for you.

That's one of the scary things, because I don't know if I can do that.

You don't know if you can do it?

By myself, without having him ...

Present. Yeah.

His support and encouragement and just ... trying to understand. Not necessarily always understanding, but just accepting.

Accepting. And you were re-experiencing his acceptance here? His acceptance of you? His understanding of you? Accepting what he didn't understand, is that right?

[Sophia nods]

How does that affect you to experience that acceptance? Like right here. What is this doing to you to be experiencing this here?

It's like total affirmation of ... just me.

Total affirmation of you?

Whatever was happening for me, whatever I was trying to struggle with, Bill just affirming that it was me and I could struggle with it. It wouldn't make me a bad person. Just me. Who I am today.

So that Bill could be with you in other places as well. And, there are some skills that you use in making him present, even for me - would it be okay if we talk about these skills? Are you interested in that?

[Sophia nods]

Why would you be interested in that?

It might help me in other places. And when I get into really black spaces it might be helpful to try and draw on that.

Yeah. That makes a lot of sense. Bill died about two months ago, is that correct?

Nine weeks today.

Nine weeks today, is it?

It's nine weeks since the last time that I saw him alive. He actually died on Wednesday morning.

Wednesday morning nine weeks ago. His acceptance of you didn't die and his understandings of you as a person have stayed with you because you've actually reintroduced them here today in this room.

Rupert

For a time our conversation took up further explorations of the knowledges and the skills that Sophia was expressing in bringing forth Bill's presence, and then she and I became an audience to the responses of the members of the reflecting team/outsider-witness group[4]. Their rich re-tellings of the stories of Sophia and Bill's life were powerfully acknowledging of their relationship, and of the contributions that each had made to the other's life. These re-tellings also included accounts of how our conversation had powerfully touched the lives of some of the team members, and had presented them with options in the re-membering of lost loved ones in their own lives.

After the re-tellings of the reflecting team/outsider-witness group, and following Sophia's response to these re-tellings, I wondered aloud if she could identify anything in the room that she might take away with her and that could be a symbol of Bill's presence. I was thinking of Rupert. Rupert is one of my stuffed team-members. He was gifted to me by Sophia over fifteen years ago, at a time when she was making her first tentative steps into life - Sophia is Rupert's creator. He is an extraordinary bear who had been making wonderful contributions to the lives of others for more than a decade and a half by teaming up with them in support of their desire to break free of the problems in their lives.

In response to my wondering, Sophia cast her eye around the room, and concluded 'There is nothing here that could do this'. I asked if she would look again. In response, she asked, 'Is Rupert here?' He was. He had just returned to Dulwich Centre after being away with a family of a young child. On his return trip, he had suffered a misadventure. He had been riding in the family's car with his head out the window - something he loves to do - when he overbalanced and toppled out, to be run over by a bus. Fortunately Rupert is made of hardy stuff, and we soon managed to squeeze him back into shape, although we'd had to make an appointment at the Bear Clinic to have his ear repaired. He was still waiting on this appointment.

Sophia now had Rupert sitting on her lap. She was holding him affectionately.

Transcript (continued)

You were saying?

He [Bill] *was really rapt. I might take him and fix the ear* [referring to Rupert's injury].

You'll take him and fix the ear? You know that Rupert ...

We used to call him Stupid Rupert. [laughs]

'Stupid Rupert'! Did I tell you about what Rupert's done for a lot of the children that come along here? Are you aware of this? Do you know why he is so well worn?

Because he's been loved. [now smiling]

He's been loved. He's goes home with some of the children who come here, and helps them out with their problems. And it is really interesting ... You were talking about Bill's acceptance, do you know what children experience with Rupert? Acceptance. No matter what they do, Rupert knows they're trying and he honours it.

I don't think he's stupid at all.

No, he's not is he. I think he's a comrade of Bill's. I think they're sort of comrades or something like that.

This is a kind of different teddy to the one I made and I always used to think that Rupert was a stupid-looking bear. That's why I called him Rupert the Stupid. [laughter]

He's turned out to be very smart. He doesn't tell me a whole lot about his wisdom - he keeps it to himself. He's a person of a few words, but these are pretty powerful words.

Like Bill!

Yes.

[Sophia is now tenderly stroking Rupert] *One of the things I've really missed is touching Bill.*

Do you think that taking Rupert away with you will play a part in contributing to you bringing Bill's presence forward in other places? ...

Postscript

Over the next couple of weeks Sophia had something of a breakthrough - she began to experience Bill's presence in her garden, particularly when she was tending his favourite shrubs. I wondered how it was that she had achieving this. Sophia's response: 'Anyone can do it. It is just natural. It is just a matter of clearing away the blocks and getting in touch with your strengths'. I asked Sophia how she would name these strengths, and wondered what else was at play here: 'Others can also name similar strengths. Yet, despite identifying these strengths in this way, experiencing the presence of the voices of their lost loved ones remains an elusive achievement. Could I ask some questions about what it is that you are bringing to these strengths?' Sophia was interested, and so a conversation was begun that was identifying of some of the skills and knowledges that she was expressing in bringing forth Bill's presence.

It was in this conversation that Sophia for the first time became conscious of the fact that she had kept a place in her life for her father's voice since his death, when she was a young girl, twenty-eight years ago. As she spoke of this realisation, and of her father's life, she related stories of his sisters, her aunts, who had remained in Holland and whom she had never met, but whose images had been sustaining of her in the many difficult times in her life. 'How is it that you knew them so well when you had never met them? How do you understand this?' I asked. Sophia spoke of her father's stories of life in Holland, and of the central part that his sisters played in these stories. We talked for a while about what it was about her father's story-telling that had so powerfully evoked the images of her aunts. Sophia then concluded that her father must have had the knowledges and the skills that made it possible for him to experience the ongoing presence of the voices of his sisters when so far away from them and from his birthplace in Holland, and that this must have been very sustaining of him in his life in Australia. Sophia also concluded that her father had passed these knowledges and skills on to her, and that it was through these that she had been able keep a place for his and for her aunts' voices in her life, despite all that she had been through. Further, in this conversation, Sophia stepped more fully into the realisation that she had been putting these knowledges and skills to work in my room and in her garden in her desire to have Bill rejoin her life.

In reflecting on our conversation, I asked Sophia: 'If you have put these knowledges and skills to work in keeping a place in your life for your father for twenty-eight years, do you think they might do the same for you in maintaining your connection with Bill? And if so, at what age will you be before you need to worry about whether or not there is some risk that you could leave Bill behind?' Sophia believed these knowledges and skills would continue to be available to her, and figured that she need not worry about the risk of leaving Bill behind until she was seventy-two years of age. This was a startling realisation, and with this she felt significant relief. What Sophia had feared most was that her life might go forward and that Bill might be left behind.

As our conversation turned to Rupert's contribution, I became aware of the fact that Sophia was already passing these skills onto her grand-daughter, Latoya. Latoya had become very attached to Rupert, and whenever these two were together, she would speak to Sophia of her 'Poppy'. Over the next few months the experience of Bill's presence became increasingly available to Sophia. He was re-membered into her life.

James[5]

James and Elaine Johnson, along with their three children, were referred following the concerns of teachers from the local primary school that these children attended. It was the behaviour of the two older children that was the source of these concerns. Some interactions that had been witnessed between the parents and the children, and particularly between Mr Johnson and the elder son, John, had reinforced these concerns. In the opinion of these teachers, what they had witnessed constituted emotional abuse. For the sake of the children's well-being, this was something that they believed to require immediate attention. After a series of conversations and negotiations, an agreement was reached with the parents to attend an appointment with me, 'just to see how it goes'.

I understood from the very limited information that I had about this situation prior to the appointment that James had been relatively reluctant to take this step. This understanding was immediately reinforced at first contact. When I introduced myself in the waiting-room, Elaine seemed happy to meet me, the children appeared not to notice my presence, and James gave me a decidedly cool reception. As we walked upstairs to my room, I pondered on how everyone's assumptions about this meeting might be addressed in a way that might make it possible for James to be present to our conversation.

When we entered the room, James and Elaine took a seat, and the three children began to busy themselves with my collection of stuffed toys. I attempted to engage James and Elaine in a conversation about our different understandings of what the meeting was to be about, but quickly lost James. The children were engaged in some argument over the stuffed toys, and James had begun shouting orders at them. In this he was particularly demeaning of John, calling him a lot of bad names. I then lost Elaine as well. She had joined James in shouting at the children. Two of the children were now crying. This turn of events weighed on me heavily.

In response to this, I found myself confronting one of those dilemmas that are so familiar to most therapists. The shouting and demeaning of the children were quite painful to witness, and I was very concerned about their real effects on these children's stories of identity. What was happening here conflicted with my chosen value position, one that has me opposing abusive parenting practices. I knew that I couldn't just 'shelve' these values. I also knew that I had to find a way of expressing these in a way that was non-imposing and that would open space for the exploration of new possibilities regarding parenting practices, rather than close this space down.

For me to have expressed this value position through the assertion of some 'authority' - to simply inform James and Elaine that their parenting was abusive, and to engage in some efforts to teach them 'better' ways of parenting - would not only have had the effect of closing this space, but would also have been reproducing of patterns of disqualification that are so totalising of persons' lives. It is likely that the outcome of such an approach would have been a confirmation of James' suspicions about the referral, and a strengthened resolution on his behalf to have nothing to do with this therapy. This authoritative approach is often taken by persons who do not have the special responsibilities that therapists have - that is, ethical responsibilities for the real effects of their expressions of such value positions.

In my efforts to embrace the responsibility that I have for shaping the expression of the values that have me opposing abusive practices, I soon found some spaces in which to begin asking James and Elaine some questions about their experiences of parenting. I wanted to know whether or not there had been times in this demanding task when they had found themselves somewhat stressed, maybe even at their wits' end. Before they responded to this question, I said that although in my entire career I hadn't found parents who could respond to questions of this sort in the negative, I was open to the possibility of James and Elaine being the first to do so. They glanced in each other's direction. Elaine then responded to the question in the affirmative, and soon after James followed suit. 'At these times', I asked, 'have either of you ever found yourself saying or doing anything in your relationship with your children that went against your better judgement? Or that compromised your wisdom? Or that in some way contradicted how you want things to be in your relationship with your children?' Again, before they responded to this question, I informed Elaine and James that I hadn't yet managed to find parents who could answer this question in the negative, but that I was open to the possibility of them being the first to do so. After a brief pause, Elaine responded to this question in the affirmative. Soon after, James followed suit.

These responses presented me with the opportunity to interview Elaine and James about this better judgement - about this parenting wisdom that they get separated from when things are not going well, when things are getting tough in their relationship with their children. I encouraged them to express their ideas about this better judgement, and wanted to know what this looked like when it was effective in shaping their interaction with their children. Elaine led the way in responding to these questions, but she was supported by James in this. On an occasion or two, I managed to consult John about this account of his parents' better judgement: 'When things get stressed between you and your parents, would it be better if they handled this by staying true to this better judgement that they are now talking about, or would it work better for them to lose this?' Following some clarification of this question, John's response was instantaneous and unequivocal. As children invariably do on these occasions, he voted for the better judgement. Although better judgement became more significantly described as the interview progressed, I knew that for James it remained a relatively thin trace, and that, because of this, it might not be strongly constituting of his further interactions with his children.

Towards the end of our meeting, I began to ask James and Elaine about the history of this better judgement. How had they reached their conclusions about what was parenting wisdom? Had their experiences of parenting and of being parented played a part in clarifying for them what was better judgement in their interactions with children? If so, what were these experiences? If not, what experiences had they taken their clues from on this? What else had contributed to the sort of realisations that had assisted them to distinguish how they wanted things to be for them in their relationships with their children from how they didn't want things to be? Both Elaine and James were interested in a return visit, so we made a time for this, and I wrote a list of these and other similar questions for them to take away and reflect on between meetings.

Elaine and James turned up to this second meeting without the children. They had decided that this was best as they wanted an uncluttered space in which to talk about the questions that I had left them with at the end of the first meeting. Elaine opened the conversation with an account of the history of her connection to better judgement. This was an account far more richly described than the one that she had given in the first meeting, and it included some 'discoveries' that she had made during the interval between the meetings, and her thoughts about the implications of these in her relationship with the children. James sat quietly listening to this account unfolding. Then it was his turn. He said that he didn't have much to tell. Both parents had been abusive of him. He couldn't recall good experiences of being parented. He had learned some things from Elaine over the years, but was not able to respond to the questions about why it was that he had related to the better judgement that she had expressed in her relationship with the children. He also said something quite disarming - that it was more likely that he would lose it with his children than Elaine, and that he had more difficulty sticking with better judgement than she did.

Despite the fact that James was now taking a position against those practices of parenting that stood outside the realms of better judgement, I was concerned that having 'nothing much to tell' would restrict him in the exploration of better-judgement options in his relationship with his children - that this alternative account of parenting might remain a thin trace, one not significantly constitutive of his actions as a father to these children. In response to this concern, I said that it was my understanding that conceptions of better judgement in parenting practices don't come out of the blue, and asked if it would be okay for me to join with him in further explorations of the questions about the history of this. James said that he was open to the idea of me joining him in this, and so began a series of exploratory conversations that took up the rest of this session, and that were further extended on in the next, which James chose to attend alone.

There were two very significant outcomes in these exploratory conversations of the history of better judgement in parenting practice in James's life. One was an explicit recognition and an acknowledgement of Elaine's contribution to options for his expression of this better judgement. The other outcome was that James recalled a episode of his personal history that he had never before spoken of, and that had been nearly lost to memory. He informed me that when he was a child he would leave home as early as he possibly could on school-day mornings because his household was not a good place for him to be at those times. On the way to school he would walk by Frank's (a school friend's) place, and then retrace his steps to wait outside the front gate until he estimated that the members of this household were up and dressed and having breakfast. At this time, if he hadn't been discovered standing there, James would go and knock on the front door. He would always be shown in by Frank's parents, Mr and Mrs Georgio, and invited to join the family at the breakfast table. Mr Georgio would always give him watermelon. And this was a treat.

I asked James why it was that he was telling me this story. What was it about this experience that was important to him? He said that perhaps it provided some answer to my questions about the history of this better judgement in parenting practice - perhaps this was his introduction to other possibilities in parenting. I wanted to know from James what ways of parenting were expressed by Mrs and Mr Georgio at these times, and why it was that James so related to these expressions. James was lost for words. He had no names for these expressions. So, I asked him to tell me more stories about Mr and Mrs Georgio's interactions with him and with their own children. I acted as the scribe. I then went over my notes with James, and together we speculated about names for what was being expressed by these parents. 'Understanding', 'respect', 'tolerance', 'kindness', and 'giving' were just some of the names that James settled on. 'It is good to get more of a sense of what you stand for, James', I remarked. 'Well, it is good for me to get a better sense of what I stand for too', came back the response.

After talking with James about his thoughts on why it was important to get more of a sense of what he stood for in regard to the practices of parenting, I wondered if it would be helpful to him to achieve an even better familiarity with this. He thought yes. In discussing the options for this, I said that I had an idea that might seem a little far-fetched, but wanted to suggest this anyway: 'What about the idea of getting in touch with Frank and his parents so that we might have the opportunity to more directly learn about these parenting practices that struck such a chord for you?' James was initially open-mouthed at the idea, but began to warm to it as we approached the end of our meeting. He departed saying that he would try to contact Frank and his parents, but that he wasn't at all sure he would be able to locate their whereabouts as he hadn't 'seen Frank for eons'.

James called me three days later. He had located Frank. Mr Georgio had died of heart failure six years ago, but James did have Mrs Georgio's telephone number. He was asking me to write this down. 'Why?' I asked. 'So you can contact her.' 'Why me?' 'Don't know if I feel up to this myself', replied James. 'Do you really want me to go ahead with this?' 'Yes.' 'You're sure?' 'Yes.' 'Okay. So what do you want me to tell her?' 'Tell her everything. The lot. Mary's her first name.' Not satisfied with this, I went over with Frank what I thought might be helpful for Mrs Georgio to know. He okayed this, and I made the call that afternoon. I was relieved when Mary Georgio said that she not only remembered James, but that she had often found herself wondering what had become of him. She had vivid memories of his visits to her home early on those school mornings.

Mary reminisced a little, and then she told me what James had never known. Mary had figured that James was being subject to abuse at home, and had talked to the school and to some neighbours about what action to take on this realisation. This was more than two decades ago, well before the conspiracy of silence over abuse was broken, and the little advice Mary received from these consultations encouraged her to do nothing: 'There's not enough to go on. If you act on this, James will just cop more bother. He won't be able to keep his friendship with Frank. And he won't be allowed to visit your home ever again'. Mary and her husband, Bob, were anguished. What could they do? The only course that seemed available to them was to provide James with whatever nurturing they could in the limited opportunities that were available to them. Mary remembered the watermelon, and told me that it was not by chance that Bob developed the habit of serving James with generous helpings of this and other treats.

And there was more that James didn't know. The fact that James was frequently discovered at the front gate in the early mornings was not by chance either. Mary and Bob had made it their business to be aware of his presence, and would discover him by 'accident' as they went to fetch the paper or turn on the garden hose. They had told James that he could come right in and knock on the door instead of waiting outside, but he never took this invitation up. So, Bob and Mary just went right on discovering him. I informed Mary of James' parenting project, of how she and Bob had figured in our discussions of this, and asked if she would be prepared to join this by coming to a meeting in my office. Her response: 'I would be delighted'.

I immediately called James. As I was waiting for him to answer, I pondered the question: 'Should I catch him up on the conversation that I'd had with Mary over the telephone, or should I arrange a time to meet with him?' This was a question that I couldn't resolve, so I shared it with James. He said he couldn't wait. As I recounted my conversation with Mary, he became very emotional. When I got to the parts that he hadn't known, about Mary and Bob's consciousness of what he had been going through, about their anguish, about what they had resolved to do about this, about the watermelon, and about being discovered in the mornings, James started to sob. Then, not able to speak he hung up. I was crying too. Over the next thirty-five minutes, James called back four times. He then went off to talk to Elaine about it all. I later apologised for having shared this news over the telephone, instead of arranging to meet with him. James said no, that doing it as we had had given him a chance to process the information in the way that worked better for him.

The meeting with Mary went ahead. In her presence, I had the opportunity to ask some questions of James about the project that he had embarked upon - to understand more about what he stood for in his parenting practices, and to stay closer to these understandings in his relationship with his children. I also asked him to review how it was that, in explorations of the history of this better judgement, a line was traced back to the contribution of Mary and Bob Georgio. Mary was so visibly touched by what James had to say.

When James stopped speaking, I asked Mary if she would speak of her experience of this telling. It was 'wonderful for her to hear', and she'd felt so relieved to know that what she and Bob had done in response to James's plight, and in response to their anguish, 'had been for something'. She wished that Bob could have joined us in this meeting, as it would have meant a lot to him too.

Mary also said that although she understood that everything hadn't turned out how James might have hoped it would in his relationship with his children, nonetheless it was an extraordinary thing that James had taken up, into his life, some of these other understandings about what it meant to parent children, despite all that he had gone through as a child. It was clear that James was warmed by this. I asked Mary if we could ask her some questions about what it was that she and Bob had stood for in their parenting, about the know-how that the two of them had expressed as parents, and about the history of this in their lives. In response to this latter question, Mary spoke of various figures in their personal histories, and powerfully invoked the image of her maternal grandmother, Maria, who had such a strong voice on matters of fairness and respect. This conversation, which was extended over a few meetings, contributed very significantly to James's better judgement being more richly described, and to it being more deeply rooted in history. He talked later of the connection that he felt with Maria, and the gratitude that he felt over Mary's willingness to share this connection with him.

I encouraged James to formulate this better judgement, which he was now ever so much more familiar with, into a series of proposals for how he might respond to his children when things were going off track. James, Mary and I then met with Elaine and the children to catch them up on developments, and to consult them about these proposals for action. The feedback that James received was very reinforcing, and provided clarity around which of the proposals would be most likely to have a desirable outcome for Elaine and the children. I wondered aloud how James might stay in touch with these proposals under stressful circumstances. Various suggestions were offered. Mary said that it would be fine for James to call her at these times. This was the option that James took up.

At follow-up I learned that things had been working out much better all round in the Johnson family. It wasn't that there hadn't been some difficult moments, but James and Elaine had stood together through these, not allowing themselves to become separated from respectful parenting practices. James had spent some time informing the children's teachers of developments in his project, and they had been supportive of him in this. These teachers also reported that the children appeared less stressed, and were becoming more confident in classroom and school-yard contexts. The Johnson family had become part of the Georgio family's extended kin network - James and Frank's reclaimed friendship was looking more and more like a brotherhood.

Although my work with James was shaped by various narrative practices, what seemed to make the most significant contribution were the re-membering practices. It was through these that Elaine's, Mary's, Bob's, and Maria's memberships of his life were elevated and honoured. It was through these re-membering practices that James's alternative knowledges and skills of parenting were more richly described.

Louise[6]

Louise sought consultation in the hope of dealing with some of the 'remnants' of the abuses that she had been subject to by her father and by a neighbour (a man who had lived two houses away from her family home) during her childhood and adolescence. Over more than a decade she had taken many steps to reclaim her life from the effects of these abuses. The two therapists that she had consulted during this period had been very helpful to her in this project, and life was now going quite well for her. There were, however, still occasions upon which Louise found herself entertaining negative thoughts about her identity, and upon which these thoughts recruited her into self-accusation. Although she had developed ways of shaking off these negative thoughts, and of freeing herself from these self-accusations, and although she knew that these negative thoughts and self-accusations would not prevent her from having a good life, Louise was hoping that further steps could be taken that would eradicate these experiences from her life.

In consulting Louise about her experience of these thoughts and self-accusations, she said that at times it was almost as if she could still hear, in them, the voices of her father and the neighbour. Apart from the way that these voices were linked to the negative thoughts and self-accusations, Louise said that the presence of these made it difficult for her to be open to the positive things that others had to say about her identity. I asked Louise to check my understanding of her concerns: 'Is it that your father and this neighbour claimed a privileged say in matters that relate to your identity, and that, because of the steps that you have taken to reclaim your life from the abuses, you are now only vulnerable to these claims at those times when you find yourself in stressful circumstances?' 'Yes, this is a good understanding', came the response. 'And is it that you would like to take steps that would dispossess your father and this neighbour of any say whatsoever at these times?' Louise again responded in the affirmative.

At this point in our conversation, I was thinking of the life-as-a-club metaphor, and wondering about the appropriateness of a re-membering ritual. So, I asked Louise if, in thinking about her life as a membered club, it would fit for me to speak of her father and the neighbour as having claimed an elevated membership status in her life. 'This makes sense', said Louise. 'In this case, perhaps a re-membering ritual might be helpful.' I then began an explanation.

'Have you ever been a member of any club that had a constitution or charter?' I asked. 'I was a member of a tennis club when I was nineteen', replied Louise. 'Do you know whether this club's constitution had clauses for the suspension or revocation of membership?' Louise didn't know the answer to this question. However, she did know that there were procedures for the honouring of certain memberships. She knew this because she had acted as secretary for a brief time during which a life-membership was awarded to one of the club members. 'Would it be possible for you to obtain a copy of the constitution of this club?' Louise said that she could try, but didn't know if the club still existed. If it didn't, she wasn't at all sure that she would be able to trace the whereabouts of ex-committee members.

'Why do you want these documents?' Louise asked. I explained that these documents might provide a basis for the structuring of a re-membering ritual, in which the memberships of her father and the neighbour could be down-graded or revoked, and in which some of the other memberships of her life could be upgraded and honoured. 'Perhaps, through such a ritual, you might find yourself having a lot more to say about which of the members of your life are granted some authority on matters of your identity.' I then explained the proposal for a re-membering ritual, and Louise said that she was enthusiastic to give it a try.

Louise's attempts to obtain a copy of the constitution of her old tennis club came to naught. She had returned to her old neighbourhood to find that the tennis club had been disbanded and the courts torn up. She did manage to locate two ex-committee members, but they were unable to assist in her search for a copy of the club's constitution. She had talked to a work-mate of this quest, of her frustrations in it, and of the proposed re-membering ritual. This work-mate informed Louise that she belonged to a service club, and offered to fetch her a copy of the constitution of this club. Louise accepted, and produced this at our next meeting. She had already highlighted the sections relevant to the suspension, to the revocation, and to the honouring of memberships.

We read together the relevant clauses and began the task of translating them into documents that would become part of a ritual that would provide Louise with an opportunity for the revision of the status of the membership of her life. Louise had made a decision to expel the neighbour from her club of life, but not her father. Rather, it was her intention to very significantly downgrade his membership so that his voice on matters of her identity would cease to have a hearing.

Louise's translations of the relevant clauses were quite formal:

You are hereby given notice of the following charges (see below) in regard to actions that are in contravention of the regulations governing membership of Louise's club of life. These charges will be heard by the ethics committee on September 7th, 1996. You are advised that you have the option of making submissions regarding these charges. The deadline for any such submissions is September 1st, 1996. These submissions must be tendered in triplicate, and via registered mail.
Without prejudice,
Louise, Chief Executive Officer.

Louise had also reached decisions about which memberships of her life were to be upgraded: that of a friend, Pat, her Aunt Helen, one of the counsellors, Jane, who had been so helpful in assisting her to reclaim her life from the effects of the abuse, and a psychiatric nurse, Pauline, who had stood with her through some particularly difficult times.

The very writing of the notices to her father and the neighbour had a powerfully invigorating effect on Louise. She deliberated as to whether or not to mail these notices, along with the lists of charges. Ultimately, she chose not to do so. We then moved on to the preparation of the notices that were to go to Pat, Helen, Jane, and Pauline. These notices advised these women that, on account of their contributions to challenging the voices of abuse in Louise's life, they were to be granted honorary life membership of her club of life. Before mailing these notices, Louise would call these women to provide some background, and would ask them if they would be willing to join, as members of her 'ethics committee', in a ritual ceremony in which the charges against her father and her neighbour would be read. She was also to ask these women if it would be acceptable to them if the contributions they had made to an antidote to the voices of abuse in her life were honoured in this ceremony, and if they would join her in a celebration afterward.

Louise received a positive response from all of the women, and three weeks later we assembled for the re-membering ritual. In the first part of this ritual, Louise, with the assistance of some questions from me, spoke to the purposes of the ceremony, and of her determination to dismantle the authority of her father and neighbour in all matters that related to her life.

Pat, Helen, Jane and Pauline were then asked to engage in a re-telling of what they had heard. I assisted in this re-telling by introducing some questions. 'What has touched you most?' 'What images of Louise were evoked for you as you witnessed her action in addressing the injustices she had been subject to?' And so on. Next, Louise was invited to reflect on the re-tellings of the outsider-witness group. 'What was most capturing of your attention?' 'Did this re-telling contribute to further realisations about your identity?' 'Do you have any predictions about how these realisations might affect your life?' And so on.

Louise then read aloud the charges, and asked that the ethics committee join her in reaching a decision on these. It was confirmed that Louise's father and the neighbour had breached many of the membership regulations of Louise's club of life. A unanimous decision was taken to expel the neighbour from Louise's club of life, and to downgrade her father's membership to an associate and provisional status.

Following this, Louise spoke of the significant contributions that those present had made in assisting her to reclaim her life from the effects of the abuses that she had been subject to. This included an acknowledgement of the extent to which the voices of Pat, Helen, Jane, and Pauline had so challenged the authority of the voices of abuse in her life. These women were then invited to again engage in a re-telling of what they had heard. In this re-telling, they responded to some questions: 'How have you been able to join with Louise in this way?' 'What is it that has you acting against these injustices?' 'What is it like for you to know that Louise has included you in her life in this way?' 'What did it mean that the voices of abuse haven't been able to silence your voices?'

In these responses, Pat, Helen, Jane and Pauline shared some of the stories of their own lives that had linked them to Louise's, and that spoke to shared values, concerns and themes. For example, Jane spoke of her parents' contribution to her own consciousness of injustice, and of the part that this had played in her joining Louise in her project of reclaiming her life from the effects of the abuses she had been subject to. Louise spoke to what it meant to her to be connected to the lives of these women in this way, and offered to them life memberships of her club of life. These life memberships were readily accepted. We then moved on to the celebratory part of this ritual.

This ritual had a powerful effect on Louise's experience of the voices of abuse. From this time on, under circumstances of stress, these voices were never more than a whisper - and at these times they were quickly dispelled by the voices of those who were life-members of her club of life. And there were other developments that were a direct outcome of the re-membering ritual. For example, Louise developed a connection with Jane's parents, and began to take steps to reclaim her relationship with her mother.

Notes

1. At times it has been assumed that this work that is oriented to the 'saying hullo again' metaphor is also informed by a notion of a spirituality that is immanent or ascendant, and that is associated with forces that are other-worldly, or of another plane or dimension. These notions are not ones that have shaped the development of this work, and this is not what I have intended to propose. Rather, work that is oriented by the 'saying hullo again' metaphor assists persons in the development of skills in the resurrection and expression of significant experiences of their relationships. These are experiences that these persons have lived through - that are part of their stock of lived-experience.

2. Sophia, c/- Dulwich Centre, Hutt St PO Box 7192, Adelaide 5000, South Australia.

3. There was a reflecting team/outsider-witness group present for the interview that this transcript was drawn from. Because Sophia spoke very quietly, I reflected back most

of what she said so that the members of this reflecting team might hear our conversation. For those readers who are unfamiliar with the concept 'reflecting team', this is discussed in this book in the section on 'definitional ceremony'.

4. A discussion of the notion of the reflecting team as an outsider-witness group, and of outsider-witness practices, can be found in this book in the section entitled 'Definitional Ceremony'.

5. By 'James's' choice, all names are pseudonyms.

6. By 'Louise's' choice, all names are pseudonyms.

3

Re-membering and Professional Lives

In this chapter I will review the relevance of re-membering practices to the work and the lives of therapists. Lest there be some residual misunderstanding about what is proposed in this work that is identifying of, elevating of, and more richly describing of some of the alternative knowledges and practices of persons' lives, I will here comment further on what it is that I am not asserting in this proposal.

Local wisdoms

In challenging the systematising knowledges of professional culture, and in introducing re-membering practices in the identification, thick description, and performance of the local and historically situated knowledges and practices of persons' lives, I am not engaging in some veneration of local wisdoms. I am not ranking the specific knowledges and practices of local wisdom above other knowledges and practices of life - these are not knowledges and practices of life that can be accorded priority through recourse to some criterion of correctness. I am not here constructing these local wisdoms as the superior knowledges and practices of life. And these local wisdoms are not being assigned an objective reality status - they are not being taken as speaking in some way to the 'real' truth of the world, or to a condition of 'true' consciousness as opposed to a condition of 'false' consciousness.

The knowledges and the skills of the local wisdoms that were more richly described in the work with James in chapter two did not represent the 'truth' of his identity, or his 'authentic' ways of being as a father, or the 'essence' of his nature, any more or less than did those ways of thinking and being that constituted abusive practices in his relationship with his children. The development of proposals for other ways of thinking and being for James in his relationship with his children, and his expressions of these ways of thinking and being, did not reflect universal conditions of correct or healthy practices in the parenting of children. The local wisdoms at work here do not represent the discovery of some universal principle that might provide a reliable child-rearing guide to other caretakers of other children. Rather, the ways of being and thinking that constitute these local wisdoms are particular derivations of culturally known and constructed knowledges and practices of care-taking. The modes of life and of thought that inform these local wisdoms are generated through history and in the various institutions of culture.

Renegotiation of experience

In establishing conditions, through narrative practices, that make it possible for persons to deconstruct and take a position on many of the taken-for-granted ways of thinking and being that are shaping of their lives, I am not proposing an escape from culture. I am not proposing that this deconstruction establishes some option for persons to step into ways of thinking and being that are ahistorical and 'free' of what is constituted by culture; ways of being and thinking that are radically invented, that are adrift from the history of ideas and practices of our world. In regard to the living of lives, there is no vacuum to be found. Rather, I have proposed that the deconstruction of taken-for-granted ways of thinking and being presents persons with options for the negotiation and renegotiation of their experience of life in terms of alternative modes of thought and practices of life. I have further proposed that this deconstruction frees persons to more actively monitor the real effects of their ways of being and thinking, and that this has the potential to provide them with the opportunity to have more to say about which ways they might live, and which ways they might think.

Perhaps I could illustrate this point with an example. When I am working with men who are referred to me for perpetrating abuse, I often engage them in conversations that, amongst other priorities, contribute to the naming of the practices of abuse and to the identification of the attitudes that are reinforcing of and that are expressed in these men's justifications of these practices. In these conversations, the history of these practices and attitudes is explored, as are their real effects in the constitution of lives. It is through these, and other deconstructing conversations, that the ways of thinking and being that inform abuse cease to speak to these men about the truth of masculinity or of men's needs or of their identity in a more particular sense. It is through these conversations that these ways of thinking and being cease to speak to these men about what it means to be a man in relation to women, children and other men. As a result of this, it becomes possible for men to take a position that is challenging of these ways of being and thinking. But this position is not taken from a space that is outside of culture and history. In taking this position, these men are expressing values that are informed by other ways of being and thinking that have a cultural and historical location. In comprehending this, I understand how important it is for me to make it my business to engage with these men in other conversations that contribute to the rich description of the knowledges and skills of these other ways of thinking and of being in the world.

Professional lives

I am sure that readers will not find it difficult to appreciate the relevance of re-membering practices to their work with persons who consult them. But these considerations are also entirely relevant to the lives of therapists. Re-membering practices provide opportunities to turn back the effects of the processes of induction into the culture of psychotherapy described in chapter one, and to reclaim much of what is forsaken - to break from thin conclusion and to participate in the generation of rich description of therapist identities. In this way, re-membering practices become a source of sustenance to therapists' lives, and of inspiration in their work. Re-membering, so understood, becomes an antidote to the sort of dis-memberment that is so often accompanied by entry into the culture of the professional disciplines - and because of this, it is also an antidote to despair, to fatigue and to burnout. Re-membering practices can also be taken into forums of acknowledgement that are structured according to 'definitional ceremonies' (Myerhoff 1982, 1986). I have decided to devote a separate chapter in this book to this consideration.

In this chapter, I will illustrate some of the practices of the re-membering of the lives of therapists through recourse to transcripts of interviews. However, before doing so, I will briefly discuss some of the implications of this re-membering work; implications which challenge many taken-for-granted notions of the culture of psychotherapy, and which encourage therapists to deconstruct and to break from them.

Implications

(i) Attributional thought and the continuum

Re-membering practices are informed by considerations in the revision of the membership of persons' lives. These practices contribute to an identification of the preferred memberships of persons' lives, and to the privileging of these memberships. In response to the sort of thin conclusions that persons so often arrive at when questioning their personal performance in the different domains of their lives, re-membering conversations open possibilities for them to more richly describe the day-to-day knowledges of life and skills of living that have been co-generated in the significant memberships of their lives. This provides persons with new options for action in addressing their concerns.

In this way, re-membering practices make it possible for persons to break from the thin conclusions that are expressed in the sort of attributional thinking that encourages the location of problems in the various sites of their identity[1]. This location of problems in these sites of identity is a habit that is pervasive in the culture of psychotherapy, and in popular culture as well. The attributional thinking that informs this habit constructs personal deficits, and is associated with certain practices and instruments of personal judgement. These instruments include the classic continuums of human development[2] that are revered in the culture of psychotherapy - continuums of dependence and independence, of autonomy and enmeshment, of competence and incompetence, and so on.

Within in the context of re-membering practices, notions of dependence, enmeshment and incompetence are recast as thin conclusion. This is not trivial in regard to implications for practice. This recasting assists therapists to avoid participating in the routine and unquestioned reproduction of the dominant culture's venerated notions of individuality, and instead opens options for re-membering conversations in which persons find their lives being more powerfully joined with the lives of others. Elsewhere I have provided examples of the practical significance of breaking from this attributional thinking and from these continuums of human development, and of the recasting of notions of personal deficit as thin conclusion. I will draw on one of these examples here:

> ... *in this work, what people have determined to be dependency is reinterpreted. People step into alternative discourses about identity. Whatever 'dependency' was, it is no longer some psychological fact of the person's life that needs to be 'worked through', and the practices of self-accusation associated with this idea recedes. It becomes possible for people to approach those whom they have believed they were dependent upon, and to formally extend an invitation to them to join* [a] *nurturing team. As well, nurturing team membership can be increased by encouraging people to identify and to approach others whom they think might be willing to join. If, after these steps there is a shortfall in membership, therapists can put people in touch with others who are 'card carrying' nurturing team members who would be willing to play a part.* (White 1995a, p.105)

(ii) Economic and commercial descriptions of life

Re-membering practices provide persons with the opportunity to engage in the resurrection and the rich-description of the knowledges and skills of living that are co-generated in the significant relationships of their lives.

Inasmuch as it is these knowledges and skills that are constitutive of persons' lives, these re-membering practices distance us from the economic and commercial discourses on life, and from the employment of these discourses in explanations of the events and achievements of life. These economic and commercial discourses incite persons to review these events and achievements in order to make determinations about what personal credit might be claimed, and about the degree of indebtedness to be acknowledged; to determine to whom, and how much, credit and debt is due.

In that the events and achievements of re-membered lives are reflections of the knowledges and skills of living that are co-generated in persons' significant relationships, within the context of re-membering practices, the discourses of economics and commerce are not invoked; determinations of personal credit and debt are not accorded a priority. This consideration is not 'academic'. At the outset of this book, I shared an account of my story-telling history, and referred to the link between this and the familiarity that I have, in my work, in being with young children in joy and in their ways of knowing. In re-membering this work in the way that I did in this introduction - in acknowledging Julie's and Penny's contribution to this work - I was neither taking credit for it, nor giving this credit to others; I was no more interested in stepping into a one-down position than I was in stepping into a one-up position - all of which could only contribute to my work with children being more thinly described.

To enter into economic and commercial understandings of, and ways of speaking about and relating to, this work with young children, would close down options for this to be more richly described, and for yet new possibilities for being with children in this joy and in these ways of knowing. After discovering the Mouse tape last year, I engaged in conversations with Julie and Penny about what I understood to be the contribution of our shared story-telling histories to my work with young children. Subsequently I found Julie's and Penny's voices to be more present in this work, and that there were more options available to me in the creative engagement with young children. For me to enter these developments into economic and commercial discourses - to give and take credit for them, or to 'own' these developments - would contribute to a reduction in options for these creative engagements.

(iii) Contemporary identity categories

Re-membering practices provide the opportunity for persons to experience their lives more richly described through the identification and exploration of the history of their preferred knowledges and skills of living. In so doing, these practices take us past the modern preoccupation with the identity categories of the 'self' that are elevated and naturalised in contemporary discourses of identity - for example, those categories of personal 'qualities', like 'strengths', 'assets', and 'resources'.

This is not to suggest that to focus on these identity categories is unhelpful. And it is not to suggest that trafficking in these modern identity categories is something that can be entirely avoided - that we can totally break from a reproduction of the sense of personhood that is at the centre of contemporary western culture. Even as we engage with persons in the re-authoring conversations of narrative therapy, such identity categories are frequently filled out with identity descriptions that contradict the thin conclusions about personhood that are associated with the problem-saturated stories of person's lives - 'weaknesses' give way to 'strengths', 'deficits' give way to 'assets', and 'inadequacies' give way to 'resources'. No doubt this renegotiation of identity descriptions contributes significantly to the thick description of the alternative stories of a person's life, and this is constitutive of new options for action in the world.

However, in our narrative practices we do not have to be restricted to the reproduction of the dominant forms of individuality of western culture. And we do not have to be captive to the descriptions of these identity categories in a way that sets limits on our re-authoring conversations - limits that dead-end these conversations, limits on the exploration of different ways of thinking and being in the world. Instead, we can engage in the deconstruction of these identity categories by conceiving of the descriptions of these categories as representing specific ways of thinking and being in the world. So conceived of, we can ask new questions of these descriptions: 'What ways of being in the world are championed by these descriptions?' 'What is the history of these ways of being and thinking?' 'What other ways of being and thinking are rendered invisible in the privileging of these?' 'What are the real effects of these ways of being and thinking in the shaping of life?' 'Which cultural values are venerated in these descriptions?' and so on.

One outcome of this deconstruction is that contemporary identity categories become pockets of know-how. The various descriptions of personal strengths, assets, and resources become emblems for specific knowledges of life and skills of living. This deconstruction of these identity categories and the descriptions that fill them out provides further possibilities for thick description. For example, the alternative knowledges and skills that these notions of personal strengths, assets and resources are emblems for can be more richly described. This can be achieved in various ways, including through re-membering questions that are identifying of the relational contexts in which these knowledges of life and skills of living have been negotiated.

An example of the deconstruction of these contemporary categories of identity was presented in the postscript to the story of Sophia and Bill. In response to my curiosity about how it was that Sophia had experienced Bill's presence in the garden, Sophia initially responded: 'Anyone can do it. It is just natural. It is just a matter of clearing away the blocks and getting in touch with your strengths'. After inviting a naming of the 'strengths', I began to ask some questions that engaged Sophia in a deconstruction of these. In response to these questions, the knowledges and skills that this identity category of 'strengths' was an emblem for were richly described, and it was the identification of these knowledges and skills that Sophia subsequently judged to be a significant turning-point for her. To have been limited to the descriptions of the identity category that Sophia was initially invoking would have dead-ended our conversation.

In so challenging these taken-for-granted notions about identity in contemporary western culture, I am not here proposing to engage in a debate about whether or not things like strengths and resources actually exist. Nor am I expressing a negation of whatever it might be that notions of strengths and resources speak to, or making assertions about the relative merits of these notions. I am not denying that trafficking in these notions can have what are experienced as beneficial effects in persons' lives. And I am not proposing that all reference to such terms of description be abandoned. In fact, as I have stated, in many re-authoring conversations, through what I have described as landscape of identity or landscape of consciousness questions (White 1991,1995), persons are engaged in packing out these familiar contemporary identity categories with competing and preferred identity descriptions; identity descriptions which challenge the deficit-saturated versions that can be so disabling.

(iv) Self as a unitary and essential core of being

Re-membering practices reach past the identity categories of contemporary culture, and identify the 'self' of the person with the knowledges and skills of life that are co-generated in the context of the significant memberships of a person's life. Inasmuch as it is the identification of these knowledges and skills of living that contributes to a life more richly described and to new possibilities for action, these re-membering practices invite us to challenge modern notions of the self as a unitary and essential core of being that seeks expression through some singular voice that can, with 'genuine' authority, represent its own interests. Re-membering practices raise questions about the real effects on persons' lives of the ways of being and thinking that incite the great cultural pursuit of 'becoming more truly who we really are', and questions about which culturally dominant ways of being are constantly being recreated by this incitement. In this way, these practices encourage us to resist the unquestioned reproduction of this culture's venerated notions of individuality, notions that emphasise 'self-possession', 'self-containment', and 'self-actualisation'. And, rather than encouraging us to join the great cultural pursuit of 'becoming more truly who we really are', re-membering conversations raise options for us to be 'other than who we were'.

This challenge is not to dispute the fact that many persons have at times found ideas that are based on the notion of a unitary and core self to be helpful in challenging the circumstances of their lives. For example, the idea of speaking with one's 'own authentic voice' has on so many occasions been a powerfully effective strategy in challenging relations of domination, and in resisting the imposition of the voices of 'authority' on persons' lives. However, the challenge to notions of a unitary and core self brings forth a consciousness of and an examination of the wider discursive context of the contemporary 'culture of self'. This challenge encourages some exploration of the real effects of relating to one's life according to the practices associated with these discourses of the self, raises questions as to the necessity of understanding our lives in the ways that are informed by these discourses, and draws attention to the part that these discourses play in the generation of thin identity conclusions.

(v) Surface and depth

Re-membering practices provide the opportunity for persons to resist thin conclusions about their lives and to engage with others in the generation of rich descriptions of the stories of their identity. Inasmuch as it is these stories that persons live by, that shape their actions, these re-membering practices assist us to break from the habit of contrasting the metaphors of surface and depth. This contrasting of the metaphors of surface and depth is a habit that is informed by the tradition of structuralist thought - a habit that is endemic in the culture of psychotherapy.

In structuralist analysis, persons' expressions of living are constructed in terms of 'behaviours' that are considered to be surface manifestations of deeper elements or forces that inhabit the 'centre', elements or forces like drives, motives, wishes, and so on - or of disorders in these drives, motives, and wishes. That is, expressions of life are considered to be the surface manifestations of the psychopathologies. When it comes to social organisation (whether it be families, communities, states, or cultures), in structuralist analysis, expressions of living are again considered to be surface manifestations of deeper 'truths' - these expressions are read as symptoms that have a function or that serve a purpose for the organisation (usually conceived of as a 'system'). Structuralist analysis as applied to social organisation is often referred to as 'functionalism'.

In the tradition of structuralist thought, it is only through formal systems of analyses, which provide the 'necessary' rules of translation, that these surface manifestations can be reduced to the elements of which they are considered to be an expression. It is through these systems of analysis that the disorders, the psychopathologies, and the dysfunctions are constructed. This contrasting of surface and depth provides the foundations of the expert knowledge practices that establish a power relation in which therapists 'know' more about the lives of the persons consulting them than these persons know about their own lives. This is a power relation in which the professional knowledges and skills are privileged over the knowledges and skills of living of the persons who consult therapists, a power relation that is marginalising of the persons who consult therapists. In this power relation, persons' lives become the objects of professional knowledge.

In contrast, the re-membering practices defined in this book are associated with a poststructuralist tradition of thought. It is in this tradition that the metaphors of thin and thick are contrasted, not the metaphors of surface and depth. This contrasting of thin and thick frees us from the reproduction of expert knowledge practices that are objectifying of persons and that are disqualifying of their knowledges and skills of living. In joining with persons in ways that contribute to possibilities for them to break from thin conclusion and to engage in re-membering conversations that are generative of rich description, it is the knowledges and skills of living that have been derived in the history of these persons' lives that are privileged. And in that the therapeutic practices that are constitutive of the lives of persons who consult therapist is also constitutive of the lives of therapists, it is through this juxtaposition of thin and thick that we are able to break not just from the professional reduction of other persons' lives, but from the reduction of our own lives as well.

Re-membering conversations

I will here present illustrations of the re-membering of professional lives through transcripts of interviews with therapists who have visited Dulwich Centre to participate in week-long intensive training courses. In the context of the second level course, all participants have the opportunity to be interviewed about their lives and work. During these interviews, the other participants constitute the outsider-witness group who engage in re-tellings of the stories that are told in the interview. These interviews are routinely structured into four phases, and organised around the definitional ceremony metaphor. These phases are outlined in some detail in 'Reflecting team as definitional ceremony' (White 1995b) and I will not reiterate them here.

The transcripts reproduced here are accompanied by introductions, and by postscripts.

Pat[3]

Pat talked generally of her work, of her experiences of growing up in her family of origin, of emotional and sexual abuse that was perpetrated on her and other family members by her father, and of her concerns about her relationship with her mother which was troubled. Pat had a strong desire to resolve these concerns, and to restore this connection.

Early in this conversation I developed a sense of just how powerfully Pat stood for loving and respectful ways of being, and a general awareness of how the knowledges and skills of these ways of being were expressed in her day-to-day life - in her familial relationships, in her friendship networks, and in her work with the people who consulted her. I was curious about the history of these knowledges and skills, and about Pat's contribution to the crafting of them.

As the conversation evolved, I learned that, at the age of twenty-six, Pat did the extraordinary. Still isolated in her experience of sexual abuse, she managed to identify it for what it was, and to independently and directly confront her father. He demanded that she recant, and informed her that unless she did, she wouldn't see him again. Pat didn't succumb to this threat, but stood firm. She stood by her experience and her understanding of what she had been subject to. As a result, her father disappeared from her life. I found myself wondering how Pat had achieved this feat that had required of her so many things, including the ability to distinguish between nurture and exploitation, between love and abuse, despite the history of her father's persistent efforts to obscure such distinctions.

After confronting her father, Pat took the initiative in efforts to assist other family members to speak of what had not been spoken of, and to heal what might be healed. As to be expected, these efforts did not go without some complications. Although Pat's mother had supported her following her confrontation of her father, over a period of time Pat became increasingly conscious of the fact that there was something unspoken between her and her mother that was impinging on their relationship.

In response to this discomfort, Pat had, some years ago, taken the step of talking with her mother about the unspoken - a step that, under circumstances such as these, is invariably fraught. Pat spoke of the occasions upon which she had made efforts, as a young woman, to disclose to her mother the sexual abuse that she was being subject to. The conversation didn't go well. Her mother accepted that Pat might have tried to tell her about the abuse when she was a child, but said that she had not really known about this because she had interpreted Pat's disclosure to be the outcome of some misperceptions. Pat insisted that her mother had known, citing her paternal grandmother's explicit efforts to assist her to heal from the effects of the sexual abuse that she was being subject to, and her mother's presence during these efforts. Pat's mother made it clear that this didn't fit with her recollection of events, and it was not resolved - except that Pat thought that they had agreed to disagree.

Over the next years, Pat continued to feel unresolved about this, and knew that this was interfering in her relationship with her mother. More recently, Pat's sister related Pat's account of these events to her mother, who became distressed and called Pat to set things straight. Pat learned in this telephone conversation that her mother had assumed that Pat had accepted her version of events - that she was not present during the paternal grandmother's efforts to heal her. Pat managed to stand by her experience and her understanding of this experience, and didn't do what had so often been required of her in the past; that is, change her personal record of the significant events of her life. One outcome of this was that Pat's mother distanced herself, and only felt able to relate to Pat indirectly through her connection with the grandchildren. Both women were suffering greatly from this state of affairs.

I found myself reflecting on Pat's actions. In taking such a risk in speaking of the unspoken, what did this say to Pat about her hopes for her relationship with her mother? What was it about the history of Pat's experience of her mother that supported this hope? How had Pat continued to nurture these hopes through these times?

As the interview progressed, I had the opportunity to learn a little of what Pat understood to be her mother's experience of growing up. In response to my questions about this, Pat talked at some length of her maternal grandfather, a Swedish socialist, whom she had never personally met. But, nonetheless, Pat could speak clearly of what he stood for - justice, fairness and respect - and of what he opposed - exploitation and abuse. She had in her possession some precious stories about his life. How could it be that Pat could speak of this grandfather in this way, as if she had known him personally? How was it that Pat could have such a close-up experience of this grandfather whom she had never met? Who had provided her with such a vivid introduction to his life? Who gave her these precious stories? What was the significance, to Pat's life, of these stories and knowledges? I doubt that any reader of this piece would be at all surprised to know that it was Pat's mother who had placed Pat on such intimate terms with her grandfather's life and identity.

The following transcript is taken from the mid-way point in our conversation. This transcript provides some account of Pat's re-membering of her mother, and of her maternal grandfather, into her life and work.

Transcript

So, your mother somehow introduced her father to you, even though you never actually knew him?

Yeah.

And she introduced you to him substantially? You have a quite strong image of who he was and what he stood for?

Yeah. I can picture him. I've seen pictures. He's kind of a small man ... is, was. But very large in spirit and character. [Pat sighs]

What's that deep breath about?

It's just a powerful image. It gives me strength to think about it.

Do you think your mother might have known that it would give you strength? I was just wondering if that was ... ?

That's what I was thinking as I was telling you all of this.

Do you think her telling you was one of her responses to the abuse that you were going through?

Yeah. Even though she said she didn't know ... I mean she saw all kinds of abuse, she just didn't see the sexual.

Yes.

So, yes ... I don't think I realised it before, that it might have been intentional. But as I was telling you a few minutes earlier, I was starting to realise that ...

Yeah?

I thanked her for it, as if it was just something serendipitous. But I never really recognised it as ...

That there may have been some purposes?

Purposes to it? Yeah. I thought of it more as purposes to her.

How did that sustain you actually? Being introduced to your grandfather in this way by your mother?

I wished for him to be my father. And it was just important to know that there were other types of men in the world. And I connected him to my uncle, my mother's brother.

Who is ... ?

... My Uncle Ferd, Ferdinand. More than once I thanked him for being a different kind of man. Throughout my growing years, that relationship with him was very important to me. I just loved knowing he was a sweet man who could say, 'I love you'. He was the only man I knew who could say I love you, besides my brother ...

What would it mean to you if your mother's introduction of you to her father was her attempt to deal with something that she couldn't see?

It already means a lot to me, because it means I can go back and share that with my mother. I haven't known how to help her in her attempts to grab onto something that she did that was right. I've tried to give her some ideas, but nothing's meant that much. Actually, she might have told me that, but I just didn't hear it that way.

What does it mean to you to think that there was a purpose in this? That she was attempting to deal with something that she couldn't see?

I feel like she saved my life. [tearful]

Yeah?

I feel like ...

That she saved your life?

I think that I heard more of the stories [about the maternal grandfather] *than my brother and sister did. This means to me that she was giving me some piece of silk rope that I could hang onto to pull me up through those years - a really strong rope. I mean, I saw her attempts to get out of there, which sometimes she doesn't even remember. She just couldn't do it, she didn't have the resources ... she didn't have the resources. So I saw her as trying to help me get out by trying to help me be independent when I grew up, so that I could save myself at that point.*

Do you think that this image of your grandfather, and his way of being and the difference in his way of being, made it more or less possible for you to name what you named when you were twenty-six, and to see the abuse for what it was?

I think it made it very possible.

It made it possible for you to discern that?

Yeah. Because it gave me a sense that I was someone who had a right to be loved and treated with respect. [tearful] *I must write that one down.* [writing] *... I mean it sounds so simple, but I have to see it sometimes.*

What did you write down?

'I have the right to be loved and treated with respect.' ... [silence] *...* [sigh] *... I've been feeling more and more that's what brought me through the rest of my adult years. I think connecting this with that image* [of the maternal grandfather] *helps me hold onto it even more. Makes me even stronger. I can just connect it* [the fact of getting through it] *to that image. The pairing of the two makes it much stronger.*

So, in a situation where your mum didn't have many options for responding, this idea that she gave you something, something that she could give you, perhaps opened the door for you to develop that consciousness about your father's abusive ways of being? That's a pretty powerful thought?

Yeah. She called my grandfather a thinker - a great thinker - which allowed me to think that I could be a great thinker. If you're a great thinker, you can think for yourself, you don't have to take with you what he [her father] *tried to send me off with. I could think for myself.* [long sigh]

What's that sigh about?

Relief!

Relief?

I feel like I got some place just in this conversation. I feel like I just followed that rope right through to the present. And, that I have something really powerful within me, and a really wonderfully powerful connection with my mother. I just didn't know how to make her see it before.

I guess I was thinking about what had sustained you in this ongoing challenge to the effects of this abuse in your relationships. Not just in your relationship to yourself, but in relationships with other people in the family and in opening up the space for other members of your family to do what might be more healing for them. In the face of your sister's non-response to these letters, you kept on. [Pat had persisted in her efforts to reach out to her sister.] You won't allow it to stop you. Is that right?

I want her to know that I love her in spite of what's going on. I don't ever want her to think that I'm judging her. I just want her to know I'm there and for her to feel my strength. Sometimes I let the letters ... don't write all that often ... because it's hard for me. It's hard for me not to feel left out, but I admit that sometimes I can put that aside. What sustained me? My children. My three children ...

I am so glad that I got to where I am before I had them so that I could kind of pave the way for them, or lead the way for them. To stand for the values I want to stand for. I had to make changes in my life to do that, because it wasn't always that way. That's my attempt. So, that's my major sustenance. And the work that I do is incredibly sustaining, because it's a chance for me to give back what I've gotten. The response of the people I see seems to indicate that.

A chance for you to give back what?

A sense of being a person who is to be valued completely for everything that they are. And to be respected and to be loved.

To be respected?

To be respected, and who is always worth loving. And, who has knowledges all of her own that are to be acknowledged. All of these were hard for me back in my twenties. All of those were hard ones for me.

When I talked with you about what it meant to you that your mother had taken the steps that she could to introduce you to her father, and what that made possible for you, one of the things that you said was that 'It helped me to get to that place where I could say I'm to be respected, I'm worth love, and I do have knowledge'. She kept saying that your grandfather would say that you are a thinker too. And these are the things that you are passing along to the people who consult you. And I'm just wondering if that is also part of your mother's contribution to your work. Do you know what I mean?

Yeah. It's a very direct contribution.

I'm just wondering about how what your mother did is expressed in your work as well?

[silence]

What are you thinking about?

I'm thinking about my work, and seeing if I see evidence of that in my work. I know I'll look for it now. I remember at times thanking her for that. I know it was in the front of my dissertation. I thanked her there, but I wasn't sure why I was thanking her. I kind of had the general idea. I knew that it was important that she was there, but I wasn't sure why. Now I feel like I can more richly describe her contribution to me and to my work.

And I was also thinking that maybe those people who go away from you experience some of the things that you experienced in your relation to your grandfather?

Yeah.

That's what I was thinking about. I didn't want to impose that idea, but ...

Sometimes we [Pat and the persons who consult her] *get into exploring the influence of other people on their lives, and grandfathers and grandmothers often come up. So, now I'm going to see this while we're talking about those things. The other thing that my mother, just in her own being, has contributed to me, and that's where I think she doesn't ... I think she recognises it, but not as much as I would like her to. Just that she is someone who also struggled throughout life and worked so hard to make her life the way she wanted it to be and to contribute to the world the way she wants to. And I watched her do that. She went to college when I was going through high school, and she went to graduate school when I was in nursing school, which is where I first started out. That's how I know that I'm a model for my children. That's the thread which I give to my children. Because I saw my mother do that for me. So, now when I go and I see my clients, I'm going to feel the presence of a lot more people in the room!* [laughter] *I can even picture all three of those grandfathers. The two great-grandfathers and my grandfather sitting in these other chairs.*

Doing what? Listening to your conversation? How would they respond?

Good question. I think that they might even have different jobs. But my first sense is that they might be evaluating what's going on and helping me to keep tabs on 'Am I being ... ?'

Respectful of yourself? Loving of yourself ... ?

Well, I was thinking more: 'Am I being effective in what I want to do with them?' But maybe one of them could be doing what you just said, checking with me about whether I am respecting and loving myself, keeping space for myself.

How do you imagine they would be responding to his conversation? You said that you could imagine the three of these grandfathers ... ?

I could imagine one of them saying, 'Well good, I'm glad to see you're having this conversation finally. It took a long while getting there' [joyful] *and 'That's where you needed to go and we knew it all the time.' That's what I imagine them saying right now. If they were in this room right now.*

That would be a good thing for you to hear?

Yeah. It would be like they're really there with me.

What would they say about you including them in your life in this way? About inviting them to be with you in your work with people who are subject to lots of difficult things?

They would each say that they are pleased to be included and invited and that that's the kind of the thing they've always been good at. They've always been good thinkers about community and fair politics ... and loving people. They would say: 'That's what we're here for, so use us. That's what we're here for'.

Do you think they'd feel honoured?

Very honoured.

They'd feel honoured.

But I feel honoured by their presence as well. Just from the stories that I've heard about all my family, it seems that they would be very happy and vibrant and energetic about this new job. That I'd finally let them in ...

And they would experience a link between some of your ways of being in the world and what they stood for? You mentioned your grandfather's Swedish socialist values, and they would experience a link [between these values and Pat's values]?

Would they experience the link?

Yeah. Between what they stood for and what you stand for?

Yeah. Now I'm going to go back and ask my mother even more questions so that I can differentiate these three men and get an even clearer picture of what they might say. In fact, all of my family is very into talking about them, so I might ask a lot of different people questions.

How's this conversation going for you?

Incredibly well.

Is it? Why is that?

Well, what I wanted was a more rich description and what I got was gold. I feel like there are boxes of jewels everywhere. It comes in surprising ways. It's not new to me that these people are available to me, yet it's all so new. What I mean is that it really fits. It's not like I just pulled them out of someone else's ideas.

Postscript (authored by Pat Schumm)

Since my interview, I have gone into sessions with the people who consult me with much more confidence that I have something to offer them. When I sit with them I have the experience of sharing the room with my grandfathers, and the wonderful stories that I associate with them. I sense a richness to my own life that I can assist the persons who are consulting me to discover and to describe in theirs. So far, the results have been very positive. The room has been so full of important images, during our meetings, that I have had the fantasy that we were all sharing tea together.

When I returned home, I showed my mother the portion of the videotape of this interview regarding her stories of my grandfather, hoping to bring her as close to my discovery as possible. I wanted her to witness my public acknowledgement of her positive contribution to my life, an acknowledgement that was the outcome of these explorations of how it was that I knew my grandfather so well, without ever having met him personally. I had taken this for granted and, therefore, this hadn't provided me with an opportunity to effectively acknowledge this contribution to her. Prior to this, our relationship had suffered from thin description, as I had focused on how she had failed me. The pain and sadness I'd felt about my relationship with my mother had carried over into irrational worries about the future of my relationships with my own daughters. It had also carried over into my work with the persons who consult me about their relationships with their parents, negatively affecting my confidence that I could be helpful to these persons in addressing this issue.

I had found myself seeing my mother in a whole new way. Rather than seeing her as the typically 'weak and ineffectual' mother the literature describes, I began to see her as the strong, creative and 'actively trying to save me' mother I already knew but couldn't seem to reach, neither in my heart, nor in my interactions with her - because I don't think she was recognising it in herself. Once she saw the videotape of me reflecting on her expressions of personal agency, she was able to acknowledge this in herself, and we connected at a richer level. Her reaction to the videotape was that I had brought her a gift, one that she was more than willing to receive. As she expressed her joy to me over this, I wept. Everything had changed. She and I were now standing together in our story, rather than miles apart. We now shared a mutual path toward healing and integrity. We each voiced our sense of feeling wonderfully reconnected.

Serendipitously, I experienced another change from this interview. The effect of the team reflections on the stories of my life was one of a re-membering of me in my professional world. At the outset of the interview, when I was contemplating and articulating the problem I wanted to work on, that of a thinly described relationship with my mother, another problem kept coming to mind. I had been feeling somewhat invisible in relation to my colleagues. This was because, although I wished I could share with them more of my experience of being in my family of origin, I felt unable to do so. I knew other family therapists who often did this, but the more cut-off from my family I felt, the less this was a possibility for me. Because of the nature of the stories of my personal history, I didn't think that I should share this with 'work friends' in the way that I had been able to with the close friends of my life. I was concerned that I didn't know them well enough to be able to trust their responses. I worried that my story would elicit shock, horror, sympathy, etc., and only contribute further to a sense of being victimised and serving to alienate me from colleagues and from my own life. The reflecting team members who responded to this interview with a re-telling, some of them friends, but all of whom I also considered colleagues, focused on highlighting my own knowledges of life, on my personal powers, and on my love. I felt acknowledged as a human being. It was wonderful to be able to share my personal and professional self as one, rather than trying to keep them separate.

Ian[4]

Ian's work includes meeting with men who have perpetrated abuse. For him, working in this area is not a reflection of circumstance, but of choice. As a member of the dominant culture of men, Ian has a strong sense of a commitment to play some part in addressing the injustices visited on the lives of others by men of his culture. Before stepping into the responsibilities associated with this commitment, Ian had been conscious of the fact that his work choice would take him into an arena that would be challenging of him, and that at times this would be difficult. However, as he engaged with the men referred to his service, he found that he hadn't predicted some of the fear that he was experiencing in this work. While he understood that there existed lifetime experiences that would offer legitimate explanations for this fear, he was nonetheless concerned about the possibility that this could become an impediment to his work. So, he requested that this fear, and the implications of the fears that he experienced more generally in his life, be the subject of our consultation.

Men's culture encourages men to exempt themselves from taking any responsibility for what is perpetrated in its name. How was it that Ian had not exempted himself and avoided this responsibility? Ian did have some understanding of the difficult challenges that he would face in this work. What was it that sustained him in these challenges? Despite the fear that he spoke of, Ian had no regrets about this decision to work with men who abuse. What was the history of this commitment? In an attempt to understand the answer to these and other questions, I began talking with Ian about the events that led up to his decision to work with men who perpetrate abuse.

Ian's work as a therapist was the outcome of a mid-life change of career. He talked of some of the events that had influenced this career change, and of the training that he'd undertaken in preparation for this. In the field-work that was part of this training, he had found himself working under the umbrella of an agency that supported practices that were deeply rooted in the structuralist psychologies. These are those psychologies that encourage therapists to consider the complaints and concerns that persons bring to therapy to be the surface manifestations of deeper underlying psychological forces. These are those psychologies that establish therapists as experts in the translation of what these events of the 'surface' speak to in the lives of others. And since it is in this context that the pathologies, the disorders, and the dysfunctions are manufactured, these are also the psychologies that establish therapists as psychopathologists.

As part of his training in these structuralist psychologies, Ian was required to undergo personal therapy of the same ilk. Here he had a first-hand experience of practices that were profoundly disrespectful, and he quickly realised that he was not prepared to subject others to these practices - that there was no way that he could participate in the pathologising and the dishonouring of the lives of persons who sought consultation from him. So, he rejected the supervision and employment offered to him by this agency, and departed in search of a position that might resonate more with his personal ethics.

How was it that Ian had been able to resist this powerful incitement to engage in practices in the pathologising of other persons' lives? What was it that he recognised in these practices that made it possible for him to resist the reproduction of them in his work?

Transcript

So you couldn't do it because you recognised ... what was it you said? ... that there was no way that you could put people through that process? There were certain things that you actually recognised about this process? What were they?

I couldn't see myself as the sort of person who instigated more pain. I couldn't see myself as a person who was a tool of re-living trauma, and I couldn't stand the guilt that it was giving me to even think like it. I realised the burden and pressure that I was feeling as a therapist in trying to battle with 'I can't do this'. Expectations of a supervisor wanting me to do this. I am sure that they wondered if I was from another planet or something. I just thought, 'No way!' I thought, 'Listen to me'. I tried to get through to them, and I'd be just put down. They'd say, 'You have a problem'. I would say: 'I don't have a bloody problem. Don't you tell me that I have a problem. I'm listening to people with their problems and I am trying to help them, so don't give me any more ...'

So, a few things ... well, lots of things are catching my attention. One of them is that you said that in no way could you put people through this process. That it went against certain beliefs and values that you hold dear, about trauma and being a tool of trauma, and so on. And, also, somehow, this evaluation of you didn't work. You know ... the evaluation that it was your problem. Somehow that didn't really wash with you. You weren't so vulnerable to it ...

I resented it.

You resented it?

They had given me enough problems in putting me through this training and everything else. I knew how I was engaging with clients in this other way, and they weren't listening. So, I wouldn't have it. I was tenacious! [laughter] It was

difficult. I would leave the supervision feeling totally inadequate and feeling
very disempowered, not believing in myself as a person, or as a counsellor.
Every time I would walk off thinking: 'Why am I doing this work? It's a waste
of time. I'm killing myself in the process'. So, I think that's why when I met with
a different form of consultancy and supervision in Steve [a friend and
colleague], ... [one with a] *personal relationship coming into it, it was just so*
overwhelming - it was beautiful.

You said that you sort of broke from all of this. You started listening to
people's stories, and about what the events [of their lives] meant to them, and
found your own space to express respect. I would be interested to hear a little
about who has recognised this? Did anybody recognise this commitment that
you had to loving and caring ways when you were younger? Was anybody in
touch with the fact that you stood for something different? That what you stood
for contradicted all of that men's culture stuff [referred to by Ian early in the
conversation] going on around you? Do you think anybody had even a small
idea of this?

Yeah. There is an aunty who did.

An aunty?

Yeah. I was pulled ... in two ways. There were people who drew me into
negative stories about that. But, there was an aunty who was another mum to
me.

Can you tell me about her? Is that okay ... or ... ?

Yeah. She was a second mum to me. She was the aunty I would go to for school
holidays. She's the aunty who would go out of her way to see what I wanted.
She was the aunty who would just really care about you as a person, and would
want to know about you rather than put over what you've got to do to be
acceptable.

So, how old were you when you would go there for holidays? Were you quite
young?

I was quite young when I first started going. I would say I was five. I can re-
member going there once after having my tonsils removed and I wasn't very
well. She lived at Cronulla, near the beach. So I went off down there to
recuperate. 'Aunty Patty will feed you up, she'll get you well'.

Patty was her name?

Yes. She's a beaut[5] woman. She really looked after me in a different way, in a very respectful way.

Do you remember being surprised at that at the time? Surprised that you had someone asking you what you wanted to eat or ... ?

I think I can remember acknowledging the difference of it. It was nice. To a kid ... to a young person it was nice to have.

So, you're special to her in a way?

Special to her? Yes. I was like her adopted younger son. She has three children of her own and her three children were more like brothers and sisters than cousins. I was always invited to their weddings when other cousins weren't. So we were very close. We were like brother and sister. It was interesting, because Uncle could be a violent man. He was an alcoholic and my cousins would tell me stories of how they were thrown down the stairs and their eyebrows would be left on the wall. It was very interesting that those stories [about this aunt] came out of being cared for and connected in a loving way, in amongst that environment.

So, in some way she managed to share these loving, caring ways despite the violence that was around her?

Yes. It amazes me.

Would you say that would be tenacity?

Oh yeah! [laughter] *I'm not going to call it genetic* [refers to the fact that, earlier in the conversation, Ian had identified his own tenacity], *because it weakens the tenacity!* [laughter]

Why were you thinking about ... ?

I was thinking, 'Don't even get involved in calling it genetic!' Because, she would say things like, 'You know, it's in the Hanslow blood', and this sort of stuff. But I'm not going to call it that, because it takes away the strength of tenacity.

Yeah.

She is a very special person.

Is she still alive?

Yes. She is. I'll have to go visit her now - it's been a while - to catch up.

So, I understand a bit about what she expressed to you. Can you get a sense of what it was that she really appreciated, and connected with, in you? It sounds like you were a very special person to her.

I think she appreciated the person I was. And we could sit and talk. We would go down to the beach together and ride the dumpers [a term for surf]. *We had fun together. We'd laugh together. Tell jokes. We had a very warped sense of humour, a joint warped sense of humour. It was really an acknowledgement that I was okay ... that I didn't have to be anything different. I could just be myself, which was very different for me.*

Do you think that this played a part in you being able to embrace this other way of being? That you haven't been separated from despite the abuse and the bullying and a whole stack of other things? Do you think that this in some way explains why you've kept faith with this belief and ways? Do you think it played a part in supporting this, or not?

Yeah. Yeah. It has. Because, going to her place for holidays, which I would always really seek out and try and do every school holidays, whenever I could, was like going to a refuge. It was seeking that place where I could get away. Seeking the place I could get away from ... And I think that my mother knew that, because after a while she would say, 'Go and phone your Aunt Patty and see if you could go and stay'. So, I would go ring [call her] *and see if I could stay, and be very disappointed if I couldn't.* [laughter] *I'd get very close to heartbroken if I couldn't. Seeing her had the effect of getting away. That need to get away and experience that again. Interesting thought ...*

What was that, sorry ... ?

Interesting thought! Because I hadn't previously actually looked at the importance that Aunty Patty and that whole place ... that whole ritual of going, and needing to go on a regular basis. Like that injection of hope ...

Sorry? [meaning, 'What was that?']

Interesting ... injection of hope ... [laughter]

So, even then as a little kid, you knew you had a knowledge about yourself - you knew what you needed to do to sustain yourself. Can I just go back to Aunt Patty then? Do you know what you meant to her? Do you know what it was that you brought to her life? Like, you were a young man that was able to join with her in her humour, you could frolic around and have fun. Do you know what it was that you brought to her life?

I was special.

You were special?

I was special. I think I brought some fun into her life, actually, because it was her and me that would go off to the beach together and leave the rest at home or wherever. We would get out and do stuff. We would go to the pictures or whatever. We were the ones that would be together just doing the things that would be different. The alternative things. And um ... we got off on that! [laughter] *It was good. I gave her that joy and I also gave her my love and she gave it back. I remember when Uncle Jim died, her husband. I waited until a week after the funeral and sent her flowers then. It was some flowers to my other mum and that meant a lot to her. She rang afterwards and told me that she cried after that ... I wanted it* [the flowers] *not to be with* [the flowers of] *the others. I wanted them to be later and from the other son ...* [tearful] *... not just with the others. I wanted her to know that it was to my other mum. So, I gave her a little bit of love and caring in doing that ... I gave a lot of caring as well. It is very hard to know how much I did give her without knowing I'd been doing it. I think I put it into the category of just wanting to be nice.*

Do you think that you also gave her hope that things could be different? You know, that males could be different, because ... ?

It would be interesting to ask her that. It must have or otherwise ... that connection between us would not have remained ... her own fear of men would have come in to sever it and it never has. I could pick up the phone and ring her and say, 'How's it going, love?', and all this sort of stuff. It was real fun.

That's fantastic! [laughter]

And, I would kid her along and say: 'Have you been to the bowling club and met any interesting blokes?' 'What's the new boyfriend like?' [laughter] *'Anybody asked you to marry them again yet?' And all this sort of stuff.* [laughter] *I kid her about that. We usually had a good old laugh about that. I even got her heart going ... so I get her heart going.* [laughter]

What I was thinking about is that it's my guess from what you've told me that ... Aunt Patty had another image about how men could be, and that she experienced that in you and ...

Yeah. I think so.

And, that she made it her business to experience that and to, I guess, support it and acknowledge it. And, I'm just wondering whether she knows what you're doing to actually play your part in this world in changing men's culture?

She may not. She may not. I might need to bring her up to date on that.

And, the connection between what you are doing and her ... it does seem from our discussion a pretty powerful connection. And so, in a way, I guess she is implicated in that ... in a way ... she's implicated in what you're doing.

Yeah. Very much so.

Implicated in what you're doing. What would it be like to consciously ... I don't know if this is a good idea, or a bad idea ...

Chuck it out. [laughter]

... in terms of the fear that you've been up against and you've been challenging, what would it be like if you more consciously experienced Aunty Patty with you in those situations? If you more consciously experienced her standing with you? If that link was more powerfully acknowledged? Even if you were to introduce the people who were consulting you to Aunt Patty in some sense? I don't necessarily mean in a material sense, but I'm just wondering what difference this would make to your experience of the fear and so on ... ?

It's interesting that you say that, because I have found that recently, that I have actually done a version of that. Something like that. A version of that.

Have you? What have you done?

I've been in a situation with a client, fighting my fear, and I know that if the fear is not there, my work is real engaging and caring and respectful. And I have pictured Steve to one side, a little smile on his face, saying [laughter] *Great! ...*

Have you? Fantastic!

It has been good to have him there, and I smile within myself somewhere on the inside about that being there. But, it's interesting now with this coming through about Aunty Patty's importance - I can actually draw on another person to be there as well. And that whole image of being able to draw on different people at different times, I think will be very beneficial. Because, it breaks the isolation of some of the work at times as well. I think that's why I put Steve there in the first place, in this little visual thing. In being so isolated, in breaking with my own culture sometimes, I knew where he was and I knew where I am. And it's like we are in this together.

How did you achieve that? That's no easy thing to do.

Well ...

Postscript[6] (authored by Ian Hanslow)

This re-membering experience remains one that has far-reaching influences, through my life personally and my life as a therapist. Directly after the interview, I had a sense of peace I had not experienced in quite some time, but didn't have a clear understanding of what was happening with me. I had a sense of a space opening up to new possibilities that were exciting to me, and not feared.

The following week, I and another colleague met with Steve for our regular consultation, and, toward the end of our meeting, I asked if they would be witnesses to my reading of a declaration that I had written the night before. This declaration had evolved from questions I had been asking myself since the interview. It was a 'Declaration of Independence from the Effects of Fear'. Months later I found myself writing again, this time a poem which included the following verse:

> *One effect is a life renewed*
> *a life wanted, a life loved,*
> *a life with others surrounded by hope*
> *A life with others surrounded by love,*
> *care and heartfelt touch.*

My re-membering experience gave me a clearer and richer sense of the history that stands behind the ways I wish to live my life as a therapist and as a man. Prior to this, I did have a preferred story about how I wanted to be as a therapist and as a man, and although this was one that was getting stronger, it didn't seem to have a foundation. I had a purpose and could look at the future, yet I couldn't see a thread that gave my developing story of self a past - my future appeared to float. The re-membering experience gave me a foundation and told me that the loving and caring ways in my life were stronger than the fear, and that these loving and caring ways had existed in my life for years. The more I thought of the history of the events that reflected the strength of this loving, and how this had overshadowed fear in my life, the more I felt myself able to rise to take on new opportunities and challenges.

I had previously considered my caring, gentle and respectful characteristics in a negative light due to the many messages, throughout my life, that told me they didn't fit with the view of what was acceptable in a man. As I began to really honour and respect my 'caring masculine ways', this strengthened my image of how men can be in our culture, and strengthened my desire to support other men as they challenge dominant ways of being men. When I am faced with difficult situations in my work, I now prepare for these times by thinking about who will be there with me. I take with me a sense of these people standing with me. While I am physically alone, I know that the invisible 'team of concern' is with me.

The images of those I love and care for remain more clearly with me now through the times when I'm working with people, and this assists me to speak of and to challenge the fears. I also find that these people are with me when I reflect on my life, supporting me in my preferred notions of being a man, and as I attempt to challenge our dominant male culture.

My team of concerned people has in recent times extended to include those that I have not even met yet that have viewed a part of my story. Michael has shown parts of my interview on video at some workshops and seminars. In response, people have written notes of encouragement to me, telling me that one of the ways in which they now sustain themselves in their work is by taking the image of me with them into their work - and their images are in my work, sustaining me. I received a telephone call only a few weeks ago from a worker whom I didn't know. Her words were: 'Thank you for adding to my learning experience and enriching it'. I have been close to tears and in wonderment at these responses that show how a special connection between a boy/man and his aunty can reach out and mean something to other people.

My Aunt Patty's love and acceptance of me as a boy and as a man sustains me to this day. Our conversations still include laugher, and this lifts me. Remembering what my aunt meant to me, and still does, and the way that her life influenced me, has assisted me in recognising expressions of love and hope in others' lives. I also find that when I meet with people and listen to stories that can so easily overwhelm, I now more readily notice those times in their lives when someone has been an Aunty Patty to them.

Writing about Aunt Patty's contribution in this way evokes the presence of others: my connection with Steve Armstrong, with whom I meet for consultation, and with whom I share a rich and caring friendship, has nourished my work, as has my connection with Rae Flatters, a loving friend who has stood with me as I challenged fears in my life, and whose response to my Declaration of Independence from the Effects of Fears was so affirming. And always there are the voices of my partner, Narelle, expressed in her love and unfailing support, and of my children, Ben, Nathaniel, and Marissa, who keep me in touch with what is so wonderful about life.

Greg[7]

Greg talked of the questions that he had in relation to the events of the contexts of his workplace and his studies, and of the dilemmas thrown up for him by these questions. He talked of some of the experiences of life that had provided him with the foundations upon which to think such questions; of his relationship with poetry and music, of his participation in the student protest movement, of his experiences of his family of origin, and of his friendships. These experiences, and others, were expressed in his conception of the persons who consulted him as 'co-conspirators'; in his respect of their knowledges and skills, and in his appreciation of their acts of resistance to all manner of impositions, including those that are at times perpetrated in the name of therapy. It was evident that the challenging of 'fixed ideas' was a recurrent theme in Greg's personal history.

As the conversation drifted into re-membering, Greg talked of a good friend, Kevin, who had died of AIDS in 1993. Kevin was a vibrant person, very much alive to the world around him. Greg had understood and deeply respected what Kevin had stood for, and had related strongly to his wisdom. After his death, Greg had kept an honoured place for Kevin in his life, and so was able to continue to experience his presence in life's journeys. I wondered aloud how it was that Greg was able to so carry others forward in his life. This was a skill that turned out to be a familiar one to Greg, and without further prompting he re-membered several other very important characters into his life and work.

Transcript

I guess I've always had something of a sense of being able to take people along with me. People is probably too narrow a description really. It's got to be wider than that, because when I think of what's come forward with me in different parts of my life, it has included animals too. Terry, my first Cocker Spaniel when I was growing up, Sam-Fang, a particularly distinguished Hamster. The cats, all of them, from Cinderella to Rude-Boy ...

How many cats are there?

There are ten.

Ten cats!

Yeah.

Do you have ten cats?

No. They have me.

They have you. Where are they now while you're away?

They're in my apartment being cared for by my stepmother. She lives within, I guess, a mile or so, and she will hop on the bus and come down and spend an hour or so with them every day. In fact, I was able to call back and get the report on who was doing what, and who was missing Dad the most. All of that.

Is that right?

Yeah.

So, your stepmother joins you in this? She really has a strong appreciation for your appreciation of these characters?

Yeah. And, it's funny too, because I think that my appreciation for my cats has been a part of her connecting with parts of herself that she also values. In bringing up memories of cats that she had when she was a little girl, which is probably closer to back around the turn of the last century than either of us would like to admit. All the way back to there and her bringing forth some of those stories on occasions.

What is the age of your stepmother?

She works on what we jokingly refer to as the Jack Benny theory. She has been thirty-nine for ever. Let's see ... in fact, her last birthday was when we hit the real conflictual point, because I said that there was something too paradoxical about her having been thirty-nine for the last forty years. So, I don't know how to work that out. My best guess is that she would be probably be five or six years younger than my dad. And my dad, were he still alive, would be ninety-three today. So, she's in her middle eighties I would think.

And she's visiting every day and ... ?

Yeah. Oh, she is a really remarkable lady in a lot of ways. She gets out, hops on the bus and goes to New York City and goes shopping in Maceys. When there's a sale on, forget it, she's elbowing people out of the way: 'Let me have that blouse!' [laughter]

Does she know all your cats individually?

Yes. The names of each of them? Yes. Their characteristics ... When I called, she was catching me up on Pumpkin's actions particularly. She had just been over to visit that day. She had opened the outside door and he was already in the vestibule. He looked up, saw it was her and said, 'Oh, it's only you', and turned around and went back in through the inside door and into the house. He was expecting it to be me by now. And it wasn't, so he wasn't all that interested. Or Descartes. Descartes got her name actually because of how vocal she is. We made the assumption that her philosophy was, 'I meow, so therefore I am'. [laughter] *So, she got the name Descartes through that. And 'Dayky's' been talking a lot, I've been told. I guess one of the questions that comes forth from Dayky is: 'Where's Dad? I miss him.' It will be good to get back to them.*

I mentioned that there was a man that lived not far from here that had many cats?

Yes.

I'm sorry that you didn't get to meet him.

I think that would have been really a special opportunity for me.

And how come ten cats? Like, how is this? You've collected them from different places or ... ?

Yes. Over a long number of years. Rude Boy actually was the son of Snowy. Snowy was a cat that when I was working in a warehouse ... she was found on the roof of the warehouse in the middle of a snow-storm in January of 1980. And, another of the guys who worked in the warehouse was going to adopt her and take her home with him. That lasted one night. His existing cat was having nothing of sharing a house with another feline. So, she came back to the warehouse the next day and she didn't have any place to go. Then she did because I volunteered. I figured that I'd work that out with my housemates later, but this cat has a home. And Snowy showed her gratitude by gifting us with five kittens eventually, and Rude Boy and Charcoal were part of that litter. Controversy was rescued from a group of young teenagers or pre-teens who were really engaging in some abusive behaviour towards him. He was probably about four months old or so. A young, very trusting kitten. And they were picking him up and they were waiting for the traffic light to change so that there would be cars coming. And they would throw him out to the middle of the street when cars started coming. And he was getting missed by the cars and coming straight back to these young boys and they would pick him up and repeat the process. When I discovered that, I took him away from them and I brought him home. Dayky and her sister Halloween and their brother Scruffy, who has since gone on to another household, were part of a litter of four that was left on my back doorstep when they were a day old and I had to bottle-feed them along the way. Each of them has their own different points of entry and their own stories, but they are all quite special to me.

So, you've been very active in parenting them, even with bottle-feeding and ... ?

Yes. They've been a really important part of my life.

What will it be like when you go back home into your apartment? What do you imagine will happen when they see you?

When I return home from a trip ... ?

Will they forgive you?

Most of the time. What I like to do is, I like to get my luggage inside the door first and then I kind of walk in and just lay down in the middle of the living-room floor. And everybody comes and starts crawling all over the place. [laughter] That's usually the first part of my return home. The second part is when we get to the important stuff - getting out the can-opener and ... [laughter]

And, this has this been very sustaining of you? You take this back into your work with people? Is that right? You said, there are people - like you mentioned Kevin - but you also mentioned these other folks in your life that you take ... So, how does this get taken back into your life and your work and where you stand in your ethics class and where you stand in relation to imposing practices?

I think about my friend Stephen up in Rochester, or Maitland, or any other people in my life, and the certain attributes and attitudes that they have that kind of help to bring some of that forth for me. But the cats, when I specifically think about them, I think about curiosity, and I think about stubbornness. And those are I think two things that have been assets for me, that have been useful in my work in a lot of ways. Especially the stubbornness. The willingness to stand for something and not be swept away in some flood of some other ideas floating past. So, in some ways, I guess reminding myself that this is a very cat-like tendency has been helpful.

Yes. Helps you to embrace that more and to respect this more in yourself?

Yes.

How is this conversation going for you? Are we talking about what is important for you to be talking about?

Yes. It has touched on things that are important for me, because it has helped me to kind of begin to connect some things of those different threads that I wasn't quite sure how exactly wove together. I think I'm beginning to see the loom in some ways.

Yes. I guess I'm getting to understand a more about the history of your connections in this work. What about your - I don't know what you would call it - your caring for that kitten that was on the roof and the ability to read the behaviour of creatures? And the significance that you attach to things that normally get missed? I don't know whether you would call it a reverent sort of attitude to a lot of the special things you mentioned. The sorts of things that you can find in big cities that are so often lost in the rush of life and in the preoccupations that people have with what they're doing. I don't know how you'd describe that. Whether you would you say it's like more of a reverence for some of these dramas of life that are happening, that you take into your life. Obviously they make your life a rich place. Is this something that is unique to you and your family, or are you linked to anybody else you know in this? What would you call it? Do you think that my description of it is one that you can relate to, or is it said quite differently by you?

That description [reverence] fits actually ... It gets me thinking about other things that I know of my life that fit very well with that description. Even in that job-setting that I've been in it for the last four-and-a-half years, one of the things that made it very easy to be relaxed and to present myself in the interview that led to me getting that job was passing by on the bus and looking out of the window and seeing a whole flock of Canada Geese on this rolling front lawn of this townhouse housing development. Basically, these geese were in the process of eating the lawn! And just looking at that and really saying: 'Wow that's great! That's just the neatest thing'. And, over the course of the next several years, every time on the bus passing that point finding myself anticipating: 'Are they going to be there today or not? Or have they flown off for the day and gone on a tour of the neighbourhood?' But looking for the geese, attending to things like that? Yeah.

And does this mean it's not such a hard thing for you to orient yourself to the little sparkling events of persons' lives that get missed in so many ways? That don't get responded to by organisations like the one that you work in? Do you think this feeds into your work?

I think it comes from the same kind of place because I think it's a meeting of curiosity with the ability to value those small events somehow. To notice them, but to notice them in a way that takes them in somehow. Not just have them float past.

Do you have an idea that's something that is just more with your life than in the lives of people whom you've grown up with or with whom you've known, or ... ? I was just thinking a little about your stepmother, who knows all the names of your cats, and her attention to detail.

Yes. It fits very well with my stepmother at least. Yes. It also, actually - it fits with my friend Stephen, now I think about it.

Stephen?

Yeah. Stephen was the bass player in my band for a number of years ...

Postscript (authored by Greg Stanton)

Over the past few months, I've thought about the interview this transcript is drawn from, and about the still-emerging sense of tying together or interweaving threads of my experience of various and diverse life situations. I've noticed quite a bit more the enduring value of, and nurturance that I take from, the connections that have informed my life, and have become more aware of the ways in which these connections shape my work - which I have come to view as a conspiracy of life.

Far too often, the persons with whom I consult have struggled hard to resist the imposition of practices that seek to define 'normalcy' in terms quite foreign to those persons' experience, only to feel swept aside by the sheer weight of this imposition. Standing as a co-conspirator against the injustice of externally inflicted and often unfitting definitions of self and relationship (for example, the dominant conceptions of addictive 'disease' and co-dependency) is a role I continue to value, and one that connects with my own story of standing against inequitable practices of many sorts. I often find myself puzzling with others about who else stands with them in their own projects of resistance, and in turn, becoming more curious about who stands with me ... and I'm sometimes surprised by the current versions of answers. It's not so easy to identify these figures today. I remember well the days of the anti-war movement (Vietnam), when thousands of people formed a visible or overt presence in standing with each other. Nowadays, fitting the puzzle together about who stands with whom seems more like a surreptitious and subversive project.

I've asked a current client, whom I'll call Sean for the purposes of this writing (respecting his preference to remain anonymous), to allow me to pass along the story of our recent conversations as a way of illustrating what this co-conspirator relationship is about for me, and he has graciously consented.

Sean and I began our work together after he had completed a four-month inpatient psychiatric hospitalisation. The 'diagnostic impression' included with his discharge paperwork described a 'schizo-affective disorder' (thought to be quite serious, and partially characterised by social withdrawal and a scepticism or cynicism about human relationships) and 'polysubstance abuse'.

As our conversation unfolded, Sean mentioned his connection with the lizards he had cared for over the past two years, who were now residents of his parents' home while he shared quarters in a supervised group home with three other psychiatrically labelled men. As my curiosity about his relationship with each of these small green beings unfolded, I was able to pass along stories of my experiences with my friend Dino's iguanas (Ralph, Alice and Harold), and Chinese water-dragons (Hops Sing, Brandon and Bruce), and we found ourselves in a rapidly evolving discussion centring on the valuing and honouring of the smaller ones we had each known. Sean then chose to tell me a story about cats ...

Sean was very young at the time, no more than eight or nine years of age. His family had adopted a sizeable brood of stray cats from their neighbourhood, who found shelter from wind and storms beneath their back porch. There these cats also found dry food and water, as well as leftover table scraps, in a tidy series of bowls, and enough love to stay - to be petted and to, in return, give forth enormous purrs of gratitude, all within the embrace of his sizeable working-class family. As Sean's family did not have enough money to have these cats spayed or neutered, the population grew over the years, until thirty of the smaller ones inhabited the yard.

Then Sean's neighbour purchased a vehicle, one of the first of its kind (El Camino), and of which he was very proud; rather than parking it in his garage, he always left it in the driveway, the better to show off his prized possession. As time wore on, he became increasingly vocal in his complaints about the cats occasionally walking on his car, leaving small paw dirt-prints in the shiny black finish ... but he still refused to park it in his garage.

One late spring day, Sean came running home from school, the cheerful news of an unusually good report card clutched in his hand ... only to find all thirty of his smaller friends writhing in various stages of convulsive dying in the yard, poisoned by generous portions of enticing food laced more generously still with strychnine. I felt my own tears well up as he recounted the story, and then my anger over the senseless injustices human arrogance can promote, fuelled by the grand discourses of consumerism and capitalism. And I became so much more aware of my intention to join Sean in developing his new project of life.

Sean had gotten into his first tangle with the psychiatric 'care' system soon after the poisoning of his small friends. His stance toward his neighbour became increasingly hostile, and there were ensuing incidents of property damage. This provoked an engagement with the psychiatric services, and a diagnosis of 'oppositional defiance disorder'. To my way of thinking, this was an odd way to describe an angry, frustrated, and frightened child in search for some form of justice. For twenty or so more years, his unheard story was continually discounted by professionals seeking to 'help' him through their diagnostic systems and treatments.

Nowadays, others have joined me in standing with Sean, including his parents who once abetted his recruitment into a discourse of 'illness', but who now gently hold small green creatures waiting for the day when Sean will return to them, group members with their own stories of love of fins, fur, feathers, and scales, and of the breath that is drawn through each creature in the vibrant expression of life, and others at the animal rescue shelter where

Sean has taken to volunteering his time. In contradistinction to the asocial stance associated with the encumbering psychiatric label once applied, Sean's sense of who stands with him continues to grow.

If there is a poetry of subversion, a musical, evocative enchantment of the small acts of resistance, I have begun to see a part of the richness possible in new patterns of this sort emerging in others' lives, and in my own. The stubborn curiosity that my housemates always remind me of isn't a map so much as a compass, guiding a search that sometimes leads to useful questions, or to a powerful sense of acknowledgement ... and these often seem like stepping-stones toward a more fruitful path.

Pumpkin is meowing loudly right now, insisting on my attention in a way that serves to remind me how much he values our being in each other's life, while Chatsworth sleeps peacefully at my feet, in a posture of secure tranquillity that, since I sat down to write, has been interrupted only by a yawn and a series of loud purrs. Being able to notice these small things, and to find the warmth imbedded in them, informs my day-to-day work and life in ways that suit me well; standing up for the small ones, for those who have no voice to form their own words, and in turn feeling valued for taking that stance, helps me in my project of standing with others in their own projects.

I have given a great deal of thought to how I would like to conclude this postscript, and the story that has come to mind most insistently concerns Charcoal, a large grey tabby whose presence in my life was a rare gift. As Snowy's daughter, she was one of the earliest small fluffy persons to enter my life and, sixteen years later, she was still a source of rare joy and boundless energy. When I returned home from a conference in March of 1996, she was among the first to greet me at the door, and to join our ritual of re-inclusion on the living room floor. And that evening, she insisted that she be allowed the privilege, as each member of my community is occasionally allowed, of sleeping in the bedroom with me - a request that was quickly granted. She slept beside my pillow snoring periodically, and when we awoke at the time I needed to be off to work, she moved to a queenly position atop a pile of laundry, happily immersing herself in the smells she associated with her deepest human connection. I petted her lovingly, told her what a good girl she was, and headed off to work. She was still in the same spot when I returned, and it was then that I learned that her insistence of the previous evening had been a gracious request for a chance to say goodbye.

If I allow myself to remember her insistence on connecting to those she most valued, her desire to bring forth a few more moments of alliance in this project of life, I'll likely remain powerfully aware of the value of standing with others as these strands continue to weave ... and of the enduring ways in which each of these moments, each of these memories, and each of the dreams shaped by these, has influenced my own growth. And perhaps, this conspiracy of life will continue to grow.

Notes

1. The sites of personal identity that I refer to here are constructions of contemporary culture.

2. These classic continuums of human development can be considered instruments of 'normalising judgement', and of social control. Thus, the insertion of a person's life into such a continuum is an act of power. See Foucault (1979).

3. Pat Schumm, PO Box 424, Leverett, MA 01054, USA.

4. Ian Hanslow: (a) The Gunedoo Centre, The Upper Blue Mountains Child Protection Service Incorporated, Katoomba, NSW, Australia; (b) Macquarie Cottage Counselling Services Incorporated, Springwood, NSW, Australia. Address for correspondence: PO Box 475, Springwood NSW 2777, Australia.

5. Significant term of praise in Australia.

6. This is an edited version of Ian's postscript. The full version can be obtained by writing directly to him.

7. Greg Stanton, 845 Bergen Ave, Suite 192, Jersey City NJ 07306-4517, USA.

4

Definitional Ceremony

When cultures are fragmented and in serious disarray, proper audiences may be hard to find. Natural occasions may not be offered and then they must be artificially invented. I have called such performances 'Definitional Ceremonies', understanding them to be collective self-definitions specifically intended to proclaim an interpretation to an audience not otherwise available. (Myerhoff 1982, p.105)

I have discussed the role of forums of acknowledgement in the knowing performance of knowledge and in the authentication of persons' knowledge claims. In that these forums are contexts for tellings and re-tellings, they are also contexts that potentially contribute to the generation of thick descriptions of persons' lives. However, in the culture of psychotherapy, the processes that are dis-membering of persons' lives, the shift in what is deemed appropriate as forums for the performance of knowledge, and the regulation and exclusivity of these forums can have a such a significantly fragmenting effect on a person's community that 'natural audiences' may be hard to find.

When this is the case, the option of establishing alternative and 'artificial' social arenas for appearance can be taken up. Arenas can be established for the specific purposes of providing an audience for the performance of particular knowledge claims. These will be arenas in which the audience is conscious of the responsibility that they have to contribute to the lives of others being more richly described. Under these circumstances, this audience contributes significantly to the acknowledgement and to the authentication of the person's knowledge claims. These specially convened 'artificial' arenas provide contexts for what Barbara Myerhoff (1982, 1986) calls 'definitional ceremonies'.

Myerhoff's use of the term 'artificial' is not synonymous with dishonest or ingenuine, and the idea of convening an artificial definitional ceremony is not a proposal for something that is a poor copy of something else. Artificial arenas are not 'second-best'. As previously stated, these arenas can be powerfully authenticating of persons' knowledge claims, and contribute significantly to the rich description of the stories of their lives. And, in many circumstances, the 'artificiality' of these definitional ceremonies can provide for a bonus in that special attention can be given to certain particularities or special considerations of the performances, and, as well, to the very practices of acknowledgement engaged in by the outsider-witness group.

The definitional ceremonies that I am referring to here usually take place in structured forums which provide a space for persons to engage in expressions of the stories of their lives - these might be stories about their personal projects, about their work, about their identity, and so on - and for the expression of the knowledges of life and skills of living that are associated with these stories. These expressions constitute a performance that is witnessed by an audience, one that is specially convened for this purpose. Following the performance, the outsider-witness group is invited to respond with a re-telling of the stories told and of the knowledges and skills expressed. At this time (the second stage), the persons who are at the centre of the ceremony participate as an audience to these re-tellings. The re-tellings of the outsider-witness group have the effect of *rescuing the said from the saying of it* (Geertz 1973), the told from the telling of it.

In these re-tellings, many of the significant expressions of life that would otherwise pass like a blip across a person's screen of consciousness, and disappear off the edge into a vacuum, are pulled down into the story-lines of their life. But, more than this, the re-tellings of the outsider-witness group encapsulate the first telling, but exceed the boundaries of it. In this way, these re-tellings contribute significantly to the generation of rich descriptions of the stories told and of the knowledges and skills expressed.

Then, in the third stage of these definitional ceremonies, the persons whose lives are at its centre have the opportunity to reflect on what they have heard in the re-tellings of the outsider-witness group. This is an extended reflection, one that is begun in the presence of the outsider-witness group, and then taken back by persons into the intimate networks of their own lives. This second re-telling - a re-telling of the re-telling - invariably encapsulates the first re-telling in significant ways; this second re-telling also exceeds the boundaries of the first re-telling, contributing yet further to the stories, to the knowledges, and to the skills of persons' lives being thickly described.

Before engaging in explorations of the ways that the definitional ceremony metaphor can be taken up in the structuring of therapeutic contexts, I would like to emphasise the performative aspects of these tellings and re-tellings. In Myerhoff's account of the definitional ceremony, it is not 'life as text' that is being proposed, but 'life as the performance' of text. This emphasis on life as the performance of text is one that shapes the expression of the practices of telling and re-telling that are discussed in the next section on reflecting team as definitional ceremony. For the purposes of underscoring this emphasis, I will here quote Edward Bruner (1986) on this subject:

> *A ritual must be enacted, a myth recited, a narrative told, a novel read, a drama performed, for these enactments, recitals, tellings, readings, and performances are what make the text transformative and enable us to reexperience our culture's heritage. Expressions are constitutive and shaping, not as abstract texts but in the activity that actualizes the text. It is in this sense that texts must be performed to be experienced, and what is constitutive is in the production.* (p.7)

Reflecting team[1] as definitional ceremony

In reviewing here the practices that structure forums for tellings and re-tellings of the sort that contribute to multiple contextualisation and to thick or rich descriptions of persons' lives, I have decided to revisit the outsider-witness practices that are informed by the notion of definitional ceremony. In

'Reflecting team as definitional ceremony' (White 1995b), reflecting-team members are conceived of as outsider-witnesses to the significant expressions of the therapeutic conversation. The re-tellings of this outsider-witness group are oriented by the practices of narrative therapy generally, and by the maps of re-authoring conversations and by the idea of transparency more specifically. This is a transparency that is achieved through the deconstruction of team-member responses to the therapeutic conversation. As part of this deconstruction, team members situate their responses in the context of their own lived-experience.

In the first stage of these definitional ceremonies, the members of the outsider-witness group (herein referred to as the group) listen intently to the therapeutic conversation. At this time they orient their listening to the purposes of the persons seeking consultation, maintain a consciousness of what it is that catches their attention as the significant expressions of these persons' lives, and reflect privately on how these significances might provide a point of entry to re-authoring conversations. There is always so much that is expressed in these conversations that might be rendered significant: the effort that persons are putting towards having more of a say about the course of their lives, their persistence in keeping faith with intentions for a life differently lived despite all that might be discouraging of this, information about events that contradict the dominant plots of persons' lives and that might speak to the subplots of their lives, outcomes that are judged by persons to be the preferred events of their lives, and more.

During this first stage, apart from reflecting privately on these significances and on how they might be taken up in re-authoring conversations, group members also reflect on those aspects of their own lived experience that link them to whatever it is that is capturing of their attention. These reflections often trigger images of their own lives, and a consciousness of how these images are linked to the expressions of the persons who are at the centre of these consultations.

In the second stage of this definitional ceremony, that I have described as the 'second interview', group members have the opportunity to engage in re-authoring responses to those expressions which they believe might be significant, and to deconstruct or to embody these responses by situating them in the contexts of their own purposes, their imagination, and their lived experience. This occurs within the context of an interviewing process, with group members joining each other in these explorations through relevant questions. At this time, group members often find themselves responding to these questions by talking about some of the particularities of their own histories, particularities that have been made relevant by what it was that the therapeutic conversation evoked for them.

Outsider-witness practices of this sort are not achieved without challenging some taken-for-granted ideas about what it is that constitutes an appropriate response to the expressions of the therapeutic conversation. In 'Reflecting team As definitional ceremony' (White 1995b), I discussed the tendency of persons in the outsider-witness group to construe their responses as a form of positive reinforcement. I also discussed some of hazards of the practices of acknowledgement that are informed by this conception - that is, the hazards of 'pointing out positives', and of other versions of the 'applause'. However, the reading of acknowledgement as 'applause' is hard to resist. This reading has wide currency in the contemporary world, and can be difficult to break from. The applause, in its various forms, now has an exulted position in regard to most matters that relate to achievement in life, and is not easily dislodged; persons are increasingly encouraged to 'hang out' for the applause, and to participate in the practices of acknowledgement that are shaped by this conception. I believe that a familiarity with alternative and diverse practices of acknowledgement is being lost to the near global success of the applause.

The applause

This critique does not constitute a disqualification of applause as acknowledgement. No doubt there is a place for the applause, and for it to be valued in its different forms. To be congratulated can be validating and gratifying, and can have effects on persons' lives that are judged to be positive. And general applause for significant achievement in the social domain can bring with it a powerful sense of recognition for one's efforts. But the practices of acknowledgement that constitute the applause do not represent those practices of acknowledgement that I have proposed for the outsider-witness group in the sort of definitional ceremonies that I have described here. The practices of the applause do not engage the members of the outsider-witness group in the sort of re-tellings that contribute to the rich descriptions of life that are the outcome of these ceremonies.

What of the hazards that are associated with various forms of the applause - particularly those that are associated with the practice of pointing out positives? The practice of pointing out positives can be experienced as patronising and condescending by those persons who are subject to it. Or the persons who are subject to these practices can read these as a reflection of the fact that any significant understanding of the experiences of their lives is beyond the grasp of the members of the outsider-witness group. Thus, pointing out positives can be quite alienating of the outsider-witness group. At other times, persons interpret this practice as a reflection of the privilege of members of the outsider-witness group - privilege in terms of class, race, gender, sexual preference, and so on. Also, being subject to pointing out positives can have the effect of setting up a context in which the spectre of failure looms ever larger - failure to meet the expectations that are constructed by outsider-witness group members. The sense of this potential to fail the therapist and the outsider-witness group can be very disabling of persons who are often already struggling with failure accounts of their identity.

But even when the practice of pointing out positives is not experienced in these ways, this practice is nonetheless evaluative: it invariably requires acts of judgement of the events of persons' lives against criteria that are informed by socially constructed norms. This practice signifies an assumption that those of the outsider-witness group have the knowledges, and thus the wisdom, by which to make these judgements. So, although different forms of applause can be experienced as positive, and although the receipt of applause strikes such a powerful chord in a culture that exults it so, questions can be asked about these practices as acts of power that contribute to the regulation of persons' lives. Apart from these concerns, the practices of the applause represent more of a telling than a re-telling, and run the risk of contributing to thin conclusion rather than to rich description.

Conflating the practices of acknowledgement of narrative therapy with the applause is not the only misreading of this proposal for the responses of the outsider-witness group. The emphasis on the deconstruction of outsider-witness group responses is often read as a proposal for engaging in a class of personal sharing that is generally referred to as 'self-disclosure'. But self-disclosure refers to a broad range of practices, many of which contradict the class of sharing that is proposed for outsider-witness group members - a decentred sharing that continues to prioritise the experiences, the concerns, and the agendas of the persons who are seeking consultation. This decentred sharing is a purposeful and directed sharing that contributes significantly to the generation of rich descriptions of the lives of the persons who are at the centre of these ceremonies. In order to address this misreading of this class of sharing as non-specified personal disclosure, in the next section I will draw out the practices of acknowledgement that I have proposed for members of the outsider-witness group in the structuring of definitional ceremonies.

Decentred sharing

I plan here to provide clarification of the class of sharing that shapes the outsider-witness responses that are of a decentred tradition. In invoking a principle of transparency, I have elsewhere referred to these responses as 'situated' or 'embodied' responses that are deconstructing of the contributions of outsider-witness group members:

There is always an unequal distribution of power in the therapeutic context, regardless of the steps that are taken by therapists to render the context of therapy more egalitarian. And as previously discussed, the potential for this unequal distribution of power to be disqualifying and objectifying of people is greater in team contexts. In view of this, it is important that steps be taken to counter possible toxic effects of this power imbalance, to reduce the potential for harm. One contribution to such steps is for the reflecting team members to assist each other to deconstruct their responses. This can be achieved if team members invite each other to embody their comments with, or to situate their speech acts in, the history of their personal experience, interests, intentions, imagination, and so on. If reflecting team members take responsibility to deconstruct their comments and questions in this way, this does provide at least some safeguard against the sort of impositions of 'truth' that are the outcome of disembodied speech acts. (White 1995a, pp.187-188)

Before proceeding to further describe outsider-witness responses that are of the tradition of decentred sharing, I believe that it would be helpful for me to clarify what it is that I am not proposing by invoking this tradition.

Catharsis

The class of sharing that I propose here does not fit at all well with theories of catharsis that inherently value 'pouring-it-all-out' responses. Although such responses are invariably well-meant, I am sure that readers will be able to recall examples of heartfelt sharing responses that have been experienced by others as profoundly displacing, disqualifying, disrespectful, and discouraging. At times such responses take the shape of moral stories and homilies - advice and judgements are smuggled in under the guise of sharing. Accounts of how life might otherwise be lived are delivered, against which others are invited to compare and evaluate their own performance, invariably concluding that they fall somewhat short of the mark. These conclusions contribute significantly to thin descriptions that others have about their lives.

Self-disclosure

The class of sharing that I propose here is not sufficiently specified by the word 'self-disclosure'. The notion of self-disclosure itself is associated with a whole range of unexamined cultural assumptions about healthy and authentic ways of being in the world. Many of these assumptions constitute life according to the ways of thinking and practices of living that are most culturally valued. As well, the general and unquestioned value attributed to self-disclosure tends to centre the experiences and expressions of the outsider-witness group members, rather than the experiences and expressions of the persons whose lives are at the centre of definitional ceremonies.

This unquestioned value attributed to self-disclosure obscures the responsibility that outsider-witness group members have for the shape of their expressions, and for the real effects of these expressions on the lives of the persons who are seeking consultation. Thus, there are practices of self-disclosure that contradict the ethics of the decentred responses that I am wanting to clarify here - those ethics that place a priority on the centring of the agenda and the lived-experience of the persons who are seeking consultation, and on the accountability of the therapist and of the outsider-witness group for the real-effects of their re-tellings in the shaping of these persons' lives.

In order for the responses of outsider-witnesses in definitional ceremonies to contribute to the rich descriptions of persons' lives, it is important that the agenda and the concerns of the persons seeking consultation be honoured, and that these persons' expressions of life be at the centre of the consultation. This being the case, it is the responsibility of the outsider-witness group to ensure that, in the embodiment or deconstruction of their responses, their sharing is of a decentred form. In later chapters of this book, I explore in some detail the various decentred practices of narrative therapy. Here I will limit the discussion to decentred sharing within the contexts of outsider-witness group responses.

Outsider-witness practices

How can outsider-witness group members ensure that their responses are decentred in form? In the first place, this is not the responsibility of any one member of the group, but of the group itself. When a group member is engaged in a recounting and a re-living of some of their experiences of life, a recounting and a re-living that has been evoked by the expressions of the person who is at the centre of the consultation, it is not reasonable to expect this member to see to it that this recounting is decentred in form. Rather, it is the responsibility of the other group members to respond to this recounting and re-living in a way that re-centres the agenda, the concerns, and the lived experience of the person seeking consultation.

An example: in response to my conversation with Sally, who was a sole-parent mother of a six-year-old son, Nicholas, whom she had some concerns about, an outsider-witness group member, Max, talked about how he had, as a child, experienced difficulties quite similar to those faced by this son. Max went on to describe his mother's response to these difficulties in a way that was revering of her. It was obvious at this time that Max was engaged in a re-living of his experience of his relationship with his mother. In response to this, two members of the outsider-witness group took up the group's responsibility to ensure that such responses are decentred. In so doing, they began to ask Max a series of questions: 'What is it that has so powerfully evoked your mother's image? Did you see reflections of your mother in Sally's way of being with her son? What was it like for you to have Sally evoking your mother's image in this way? If you were to experience your mother's image in your own work with other women who are going through what Sally has been going through, how would this contribute to the shaping of the conversations you might have with them?' and so on.

Max's responses to these questions were very significant to Sally: he spoke of what it was that was expressed by Sally that was so evocative of his mother's image, of the fact that this had been a 'beautiful' experience for him, of the possibilities that this might open for him to experience his mother's presence more fully in his work, and of what this might contribute to this work - he predicted that he would, in some situations, be able to understand things that might otherwise be beyond his ability to understand. In this decentring of Max's responses, Sally experienced a powerful acknowledgement - the stories of her life were linked to the stories of another woman's life around shared values, purposes, and commitments, which were honoured.

Outsider-witness group members will find it easier to step into this tradition of decentred sharing if they seek to identify and to acknowledge the history of their experiences of the therapeutic conversation. This is an acknowledgement that speaks to the fact that whatever group members find themselves experiencing, during the therapeutic conversation, that they were not experiencing prior to the interview, is evoked by the expressions of the persons whose lives are at the centre of these conversations - by their words, their thoughts, their stories, their actions, their emotions, their gestures, and so on. If outsider-witness group members are able to stay in touch with this fact, they will be more able to appreciate and to speak to the history of their responses, and, in so doing, contribute to the recentring of the lives of the persons seeking consultation.

I believe that Bachelard's (1969) account of the 'image' is helpful to the development of these practices of decentred sharing. His interest was with the images of one's life that are evoked by states of reverie, and in how these images set off reverberations that reach into personal history. In response to these reverberations, certain experiences of the events of one's life light up through resonation. Through these resonances, specific experiences of historical events come into memory and form a story-line, one which represents the history of the image that is of the present. Taking this account of the history of the image into the definitional ceremony context that I have been describing here, the image that is of the present is one that has been evoked by the specific expressions of the person who is at the centre of the consultation, and by the therapeutic conversation itself. For outsider-witness group members, the reverberations that are set off by these therapeutic conversations frequently touch on many experiences long forgotten, and, as well, endow previously remembered experiences with a new significance.

Decentred sharing is facilitated by outsider-witness group members when they join with each other over explorations of the history of the experiences had in response to the therapeutic conversation. It becomes possible for group members to shape their responses in ways that are identifying of the images that set off the reverberations that these experiences of their history resonated with, and to do this in ways that honour what it was that evoked these images of their lives - that is, the expressions of the persons who are seeking consultation. This understanding that the history of the images had by outsider-witness group members is a reverse history, one that has its origins in the present, in what was evoked by the expressions of the persons seeking consultation provides group members with options for recentring the lives of the persons seeking consultation.

Outsider-witness group members can support each other in speaking to the experiences of the events of their lives that came into memory through these reverberations, of the images that set these reverberations off, and what it was that was expressed in the therapeutic conversation that was so evocative of these images. To honour the history of the image is to 'take it back' to the person at the centre. This engagement of outsider-witness group members is not neutral in regard to its effects on the shape of their own lives - it is constitutive. Through this engagement, group members become other than who they were at the outset of the therapeutic conversation. Therefore, for group members to honour the history of the images that are evoked by the expressions of the persons seeking therapy, is to acknowledge the extent to which these expressions contribute to their lives being more richly described.

In the purposive and decentred sharing described here, there is very little risk that persons who seek therapy will experience the responses of the members of outsider-witness group as homilies or moral stories. And there is virtually no risk that these responses will be experienced in any way as paternalistic or disqualifying. Rather, these persons will find that their agendas, concerns and lived-experience remains at the centre, that they are powerfully acknowledged in their expressions of life, and that, through the stories of their lives, they are linked to the lives of others around shared themes, shared values, and shared commitments.

In order to illustrate this decentred sharing, I will here include two transcripts of outsider-witness group responses to conversations with two therapists, Sally and Paul[2]. These conversations focussed on their lives and their work, and took place in week-long workshops at Dulwich Centre. The outsider-witness group for each of these interviews was composed of the other participants of these workshops. Paul and Sally, whose lives were at the centre of these conversations, and I, composed an audience to the re-tellings of the outsider-witness group. After these re-tellings, with the outsider-witness group again in the audience position, I asked Sally and Paul questions about what they had heard, ones that encouraged them to engage in a re-telling of the outsider-witness group's re-tellings that was more richly describing of these.

I have chosen these examples of outsider-witness group re-tellings because (a) they constituted such powerful experiences for Sally and Paul, because (b) it was their conclusion that these particular re-tellings played a very significant part in contributing to subsequent positive developments in their lives, developments that they hadn't expected, and, above all, because (c) Sally and Paul, and the outsider-witness group members, were keen to make this contribution to this book. Having said this, I do not believe that these examples of outsider-witness group re-tellings are exemplary - there are no exemplary examples. And further, I would add that outsider-witness group re-tellings that are oriented by the practices of narrative work, and that are of the decentred tradition that I have drawn out in the above discussion, are invariably shaping of persons' lives in ways that are judged to be beneficial, and often in ways that are unexpected.

The transcripts included here are edited versions. This editing was guided by Paul and Sally's responses to these re-tellings - the transcripts provide an account of those responses of outsider-witness group members that Sally and Paul considered most significant, and those that they appeared to relate most strongly to in their re-tellings of these re-tellings.

Sally

Upon interviewing Sally about the history of her presence in the workshop, she talked about her understanding of the extent to which an acknowledgement of the power relations of local culture is taken into narrative practice, and about how this fitted with her own consciousness of the significance of such power relations in her own work, and in her life more generally. Sally had put her consciousness of the power relations of local culture to work by gaining employment in contexts in which this could inform her joining with disadvantaged persons and groups of persons in challenging the wider community's practices of discrimination and marginalisation.

Sally's consciousness was significantly the outcome of growing up in a Greek family in a dominantly Anglo-Australian community - Sally was conceived in Greece and born in Australia. She was the eldest child in her family, and very much the 'go-between' for her family in its negotiations with the wider community - her father died soon after immigration and she was relied upon as the spokesperson for the family generally, and particularly for her mother who lived out her life in the company of Greek-speaking relatives, friends, and acquaintances.

The development of this consciousness was not without considerable cost to Sally. This 'go-between' position added several levels of complexity to her life, and she found herself consistently 'in the front seat' when it came to experiencing the wider community's practices of discrimination against minority cultures. As Sally spoke more of her experiences of growing up in this context, she talked about how 'she had gone off the rails' for a time in her adolescence. Amongst other things, her school performance deteriorated markedly, and she had 'got into lots of bother' with numerous authorities. She had concluded that she was a 'bad' person, and began to feel ashamed of herself.

In response to this, Sally's mother had asked a woman friend to do what she could to sort things out. This friend, Mrs Agostino, made a number of forays into the different domains of Sally's life, at times loudly advocating on Sally's behalf, at times severely admonishing her. Sally recalled vividly the embarrassment that she experienced in relation to these forays, and in regard to the 'Greekness' of them. However, as Sally had taken steps to reclaim many aspects of her Greek culture in recent years, she had begun to more highly esteem Mrs Agostino's interventions, and to regret the embarrassment - although she also regretted the fact that she had placed Mrs Agostino in such a position. Looking back, she wished that she had not caused so much trouble in her adolescence, particularly at school, and believed that the almost overwhelming insecurity she experienced from time to time was the outcome of this 'blot' on her history.

I asked Sally some questions about her school experience, wanting to know her thoughts about the extent to which this had contributed to her consciousness of injustice in regard to issues of culture. In response to this, Sally spoke of her outsider status, of the teasing that she had been subject to because of her 'Greek ways', of her school's expressions of ethnocentrism in all of the ways that ethnocentrism might be expressed. She also spoke of her awareness of the plight of some of her peers who were also from minority cultures. It was in this conversation that we both became aware of the fact that much of the bother that Sally had been in during her adolescence was informed by this consciousness, and of the extent to which this bother could be understood as a refusal to submit to what she was being subject to - as protest.

Transcript of outsider-witness group re-telling

Sue: *I was thinking a lot about what Sally said about her awareness of what some of her peers were going through at school ... other kids from other cultural backgrounds. And I was wondering how this awareness may have been expressed, and whether any of these other kid's lives would have been touched by this.*

Harold: *Do you mean actions that Sally took to defend, or to support ... or maybe to stand with other kids who were being put through the cultural wringer? And about what this would have meant to them?*

Sue: *Yeah. But not necessarily any of that ... not necessarily anything that Sally said outright, or actively did. But even the effects of the silent knowing that is expressed by people who are being subject to what these kids were subject to ... expressed, well, in unstated ways. Like with the meeting of eyes. You know, the 'I know what it is like. I've been there too. It is unfair and unjust. We both know what it is about. At least we are together in this awareness.*

And they don't know we know'.

Rob: *I was also thinking that Sally's consciousness must have been expressed in different ways ... And I think that you are onto something. That this would have been experienced by some of her peers ... and that it made a difference. Perhaps some sense of solidarity, or something like this. It would be great to meet with these people now, maybe to ... and to ask them for their memories of Sally.*

Harold: *And I was wondering how they would relate to the idea of 'bother' as a reflection of protest. How they would connect to this.*

Julie: *I had some thoughts about Sally's consciousness, and how she kept this up, maintained this ... Because there was a lot that would have been denying of it ... reducing it, or discouraging of it. Now, I'm only speculating, but I thought that some of this may have been supported by Sally's mother, who, after all, refused to give up, surrender what was so precious to her - her culture!*

Carol: *Yeah. I understand from Sally that her mother was really, really strong in this. Even vigorous in this. Could I come back and ask you about your initial reflection on what it could have meant to some of Sally's peers that she had this consciousness? Why was your attention drawn to this question? Could you say something about this?*

Julie: *Well ... hearing what Sally had to say about her experiences, about her history that is, had me thinking of some of my own experiences.*

Carol: *Would you be happy to talk about them here?*

Julie: *I'm from an Italian family, and also went to a school that was predominantly Anglo. Almost entirely Anglo. And sometimes it was really difficult. I was thinking about ... becoming more aware of ... the little unspoken sources of support that I managed to draw on, sometimes from surprising places. And when I was listening to Sally, I found myself wishing that I'd had a friend like her back then. It reawakened this longing. But in a way, and I don't know how, it also satisfied this. That's all.*

Carol: *That's a lot. What do you think it would have meant to you? To have a friend like Sally, I mean, when you were at school?*

Julie: *I know I would have felt less alone. I would have felt joined by someone strong. And I think I would have been much less self-conscious. I wouldn't have had to be so self-conscious, and this is something that has gotten in the way so much.*

David: *You were saying what is it like for you that Sally has reawakened that longing.*

Julie: *It's bitter-sweet. A sweet sadness, just acknowledging that to myself. And it has me thinking a lot about what some of my friends mean to me, and has me looking forward to telling them so. More than I have at least.*

David: *Could this be what it is like for the people that Sally works with ... for them to be with her in the way that she is?*

Sue: *And I was thinking about what Mrs Agostino might be saying if she was here ... What she would be saying about Sally's work, about her standing there and joining others with her consciousness in this way. And I was also thinking about how she might be feeling about the acknowledgement that Sally has given to her here ... about what it would be like for her to experience this acknowledgement in this place ... in this context.*

Rob: *I'm getting to understand what Sally was up against, and hopefully some appreciation of how she got through it all, and some appreciation of some of the skills and some of the connections that helped ... that contributed to this. And I have been thinking about ... lots about why it is so important for me to know this.*

Sue: *Well ... go on.*

Rob: *Well, I was on the other side of this. Although I wasn't the chief instigator, I certainly joined in discriminatory acts against some of my peers when I was at school. Nearly all of us kids did. These other kids were Italian, Greek, and from Yugoslavia. I played a part in giving them a hard time ... in pushing them out. This interview has given me cause to do a lot of thinking. I'm thinking about an apology that is due to some of these people.*

Sue: *Is that a proposal? Or what ... for real?*

Rob: *Yes. I've been sitting here thinking about the idea of contacting two of these people ... to say hullo and perhaps to ask them if they would be interested in having a conversation about the truth ... This would be a conversation triggered off by what has happened here. I mean by this conversation with Sally.*

Harold: *What do you think that could mean to them ... some acknowledgement from you about what you did, some acknowledgement about what you contributed to ... ?*

Rob: *I don't know. They might not be interested. But I could take some initiative. I could give it a try. I could ask them about it. And I would like to say to Sally that this is my commitment to do something.*

Nicole: *I was thinking about the hard time that my daughter has been going through with some of her peers, and I know it is partly to do with culture, although not all to do with this - my partner is Chinese Australian. I give her advice that never works ... She doesn't like this. Instead, following this - what I have heard from Sally - I'm going to ask her questions about what this does for her consciousness, who else this consciousness connects her to, and how it* [this consciousness] *is being put to work in what she is facing.*

Carol: *What effect do you think that could have?*

Nicole: *I don't know. But it is something I would like to try. And it gives me a sense of hope ... and a feeling that I'll be more appreciative of her trying, of her perseverance that is.*

Carol: *If your daughter could have been here, joining us, like as an audience to this conversation that we are having right now, how do you think she would have responded?*

Nicole: *I think ... and I don't know why I think this, but ... I think she would have cried. And I can imagine what it would have been like for them both, as young women, Sally and my daughter that is, to share their experiences with each other. I'm sure this would have been confirming. So, if it is okay with Sally, I would like to share this story with my daughter, and check it out with her (my daughter) - some of the understandings that have come from this conversation ...*

Paul

Paul chose a conversation about some of the stresses that he was experiencing in his workplace, and about some feelings of despair that he was finding increasingly difficult to shake off. He worked in an agency that provided services in the community to persons who were diagnosed with psychiatric illness - many of them considered to be chronically ill. As a worker engaged in 'front-line' service provision in this agency, Paul found the demands on him to be very high. It was his task not just to support the persons who were regarded as the 'consumers', but also the relatives and other carers of these persons, who were often quite exhausted. It was Paul's task to do this with few, if any, resources at his disposal, and in a service-delivery environment that didn't seem at all conscious of the well-being of its workers.

Further complicating of matters was the fact that there had been some recent developments in the workplace that had led Paul to conclude that the administrators of his service didn't understand what community mental health was all about. Despite his agency's stated commitment to working collaboratively and respectfully with consumers and carers in the identification and support of their goals, it was now expecting its workers to enter into contracts with consumers and carers that specified the number of contacts, the duration of these, and the goals to be achieved in this time. None of this took into account the realities of persons' lives, or their wishes about the provision of services. Paul believed this new 'top-down' policy about service provision to be market-driven, and to be against what he understood to be the spirit of community mental health. In this conversation, Paul also talked about the fact that he was experiencing increasing pressure to talk about consumers and carers in ways that were eroding of respectful practices, and that were marginalising of these persons' identities.

Paul hadn't been passive in response to these developments. With a couple of colleagues, he had taken initiatives to address these concerns with the administrators of his agency, and also to intervene at a policy level. He did feel that he was getting somewhere with these initiatives, and it wasn't this that he wished to focus on in our conversation. What concerned him most, and what he wanted to explore in our conversations, was that, despite his awareness of the context of the dilemmas he was facing in his work, he couldn't help but feel that he was failing the persons who were consulting him. It was this sense of failure that he believed was contributing most significantly to the despair that he had spoken of at the beginning of our conversation.

As we talked, I asked Paul some questions: 'Despair isn't something that persons experience without having had some hope that things would be different. Could we talk about some of the hopes that you have for the lives of others, those hopes that you have experienced being frustrated?' 'You said that many of your agency's recent policy decisions go against what you stand for. Would you talk about some of your values and beliefs that are contradicted by these decisions?' 'In regard to the sense of failure that you have spoken of, could you say something about your appreciation of the possibilities that are available to persons in their lives?'

In the conversation that was shaped by these questions, I also asked Paul to assist me to understand the history of these hopes, of these values, and of this understanding of the possibilities available to persons in their lives. In tracing the history of these hopes, values, beliefs, and this commitment to the exploration of the possibilities for persons' lives, among other things he spoke of his aunt's and uncle's contributions: of his aunt's habit of caring about the less fortunate and marginal people in her community, in ways emotional and practical; and of his uncle's frequent, and at times costly, acts of compassion that were directed at those who had fallen on hard times. It was this aunt and this uncle who had raised Paul.

Transcript of outsider-witness group re-telling

Debra: *It was good to get to know a little about the values and the beliefs that Paul takes on in his work ... and something about his personal commitment as well. Although these are not really recognised, not really acknowledged by the agency he works for, he hasn't allowed himself to get separated from them. It was clear that he hasn't even allowed the despair that he spoke of to take away these values and beliefs.*

Tom: *Yeah. From the way Paul spoke about his life and his work, these all seemed to be really just so precious to him. I was thinking about how he had managed to continue ... in the working environment that he described ... and to hang on to these values and beliefs?*

Lucy: *And his sense of commitment too.*

Amanda: *Do you have some thoughts about how he has managed this? Maybe ... about why he didn't get separated from these?*

Tom: *Yeah ... I think so.*

Amanda: *Do you want to share some of those thoughts?*

Tom: *Well ... er ...*

Amanda: *Do you want to pass on that question? It's okay ...*

Tom: *No, I don't want to do that ... It's just that ... that things didn't work out for me all that well in the family that I was born into, and for a while I went from pillar to post. Eventually I had an aunt who found a home for me with her best friend, and with her husband. I called them Aunt Beth and Uncle Jim, but they weren't really relatives at all. I was six years old when I went to live with them. They didn't really have anything much to speak of ... they were poor ... but they were a precious find. I wouldn't let go of them and they wouldn't let go of me. In the end, I was allowed to stay with them.*

Amanda: *So, there were things that Paul said that somehow made their images present for you?*

Tom: *I think it had to do with what Paul said about what his aunt and uncle stood for ... It sort of ... sort of helped me to understand more about what was precious to him. And it has had me thinking about things too ...*

Peter: *Do you want to say anything about them here?*

Tom: *They are a bit half-formed. But I know I am going to go away from here to have a conversation with Auntie Beth and with Uncle Jim ... a conversation that I wouldn't ... definitely wouldn't have had if it hadn't been for what Paul's been saying ... about what I know from them and about how this shows up in my work.*

Lucy: *There was something about the way that Paul refuses to put people in boxes. How he won't do it. He refuses to join in with abuses ... with abuses of power. But it is even much more than this ... I think. It is, it's more than being against something. It is something about how he can make connections with ... relate to the people who want his help. I don't know if I can put my finger on it ... perhaps it is a quality that he expresses ... I don't know ...*

Loretta: *Could the word be 'tenderness'? Or 'respectfulness'?*

Lucy: *Yes, that works! Both of these. And now I am trying to imagine what this must be like for the people he works with.*

Amanda: *It's my guess that some of them don't know how to handle this in the first place ... it is because these experiences can be so rare. But it is also my guess that it doesn't take long for these people to get in touch with this ... to get familiar with it, and to begin to seek it out more often.*

Peter: *What is your guess based on? What's its foundation? Like what ... ?*

Amanda: *This conversation has had me thinking of some of the folks who I work with ... most have gone through pretty terrible circumstances. At times I've had the idea that they are becoming dependent on me ... you know, that they want more than I can give. And I know that this is not a helpful way for me to be thinking about them ... or me either, for that matter. Listening to this conversation has given me some other ideas for dealing with what I had seen as 'demands'.*

Peter: *So, what are these thoughts?*

Amanda: *Well, to begin with at least ... to find some ways of talking to these folks about what it is they are looking for ... what they are seeking. And to acknowledge that this has to do with what they know about what is precious ... and a determination to hang onto this somehow. Somehow, I think that this acknowledgement is going to make a difference to all of us, and to how we are feeling about each other, me and the folks I work with.*

Debra: *That maybe this will somehow ... play a part in undermining the sense of burden? Is this what you are taking away from the conversation between Paul and Michael?*

Amanda: *Yeah. And something more than this as well. Another thought has occurred to me. That is to acknowledge how it is that these folks stand with us in what is precious to them ... and how talking about this could be very sustaining and supportive of what I value and believe, and of what this work is about to me ...*

Jill: *Could I go back to Paul's connection to his Aunt and Uncle? Because this seems such a great team ...*

Amanda: *Do you have questions about this?*

Jill: *Well, I do now.* [laughter] *You really are into this interviewing bit.* [more laughter] *I wonder if his aunt and uncle know about how Paul carries this torch. I was trying to imagine what they would say about who were the people who played a part in lighting ... who were the parties to the lighting of this torch ... because I guess there is more to the story. And I was also trying to imagine what they would say about what it means to them that Paul carries this torch in the way that he does.*

Debra: *Could I take up that thought?*

Jill: *Yeah. Go ahead.*

Debra: *I understand that Paul is in good company in the steps ... in the initiatives that he is taking to challenge the direction that things are taking in the agency he works in ... you know, the colleagues that he spoke about. I was wondering if these colleagues know what good company they are in.*

Jill: *What do you mean?*

Debra: *Well, I had this fantasy ... it's about the idea of Paul and these colleagues getting together with his aunt and uncle, and for them all to talk to each other ... to share some of these stories of their lives.*

Peter: *Wow! Would that ever make a formidable team!*

Notes

1. Tom Andersen introduced reflecting-team work to the world of family therapy with his 1987 publication, 'The reflecting team: Dialogue and meta-dialogue in clinical work'. It was his conception of this, and Karl Tomm's enthusiasm for it, that stimulated my own explorations of it.

2. According to the wishes of these two therapists, these are pseudonyms.

PART II

Politics
of
Practice

Introduction

Part one of this book focussed principally on the shift in what counts when a person enters the culture of the professional disciplines. This is a shift in terms of (a) the knowledges that are considered credible when it comes to matters of professional practice, (b) the institutional and personal memberships that are considered appropriate to a professional life, (c) the forums of acknowledgement that are deemed appropriate for the expression of these knowledges, and (d) the practices of witness that are judged to be suitable for these forums. It was proposed that this is a shift that serves to establish a professional monoculture, one that can be significantly dis-membering of therapists' lives. In that this contributes to thin descriptions of the work and the life of the therapist, it establishes a vulnerability to exhaustion, fatigue and burnout. Discussion then turned to practices that contribute to the work and the life of therapists being more richly described: to re-membering conversations and ceremonies of re-definition. These are practices that contribute to an antidote to experiences of burden, fatigue, and exhaustion.

In part two of this book I engage in further explorations of the professional discourses, with a focus on how they inform the conception of and the politics of the therapeutic relationship, and the ways in which these are not just shaping of the lives of the persons who consult therapists, but also of therapists' work and lives. Some discussion will be devoted to this latter consideration - to an exploration of the real effects of these professional discourses in the constitution of the life of the therapist. In this discussion, I propose that the conceptions and practices of the therapeutic relationship that are informed by the professional discourses also contribute significantly to therapists' experiences of burden, fatigue, and exhaustion.

I then explore alternative conceptions of the therapeutic endeavour that counter these negative real effects of the professional discourses, alternative conceptions that are experienced by therapists as personally renewing, and inspiring of them in their work.

This exploration takes me into a discussion of how these alternative conceptions shape therapeutic conversations, supervision and training.

5

Professional Discourses

Truth claims

The culture of psychotherapy is a culture of the professional discourses. These professional discourses are characterised by classes of knowledge that feature 'truth' claims about the human condition - claims that are ascribed an objective reality status and that are considered to be universal, speaking to 'facts' about the nature of life that can be discovered in all persons, regardless of culture, circumstance, place, era, and so on.

One of these classes of knowledge features truth claims about the 'self' - that, at the core of being human, there is a self that is the centre of identity, that is the foundation of personal knowledge and the source of human meaning. Another class of knowledge features truth claims about the nature of this self - about humanity, human development, identity formation, the workings of psyche, and so on. A third class of knowledge features truth claims about problem formation. These are the knowledges of psychopathology, of the disorders, and of the dysfunctions. A fourth class of knowledge features truth claims about the resolution of these problems.

Many of these knowledges of problem formation and resolution feature the repressive hypothesis in different guises - a hypothesis that proposes the existence of forces in the individual psyche that are said to frustrate the expression of human nature as it is determined by the knowledges about the self, and that deny this self the options for authentic states of being. These four classes of knowledge are operationalised in systems of understanding that, it is claimed, make it possible for therapists to engage with persons in order to decipher the truth about their existence and about their problems, and to assist them to break from the forces of repression, to discover who they really are and to live a life that is true to this discovery - that is, true to their real nature, their authentic needs, and so on.

In the culture of psychotherapy, these professional discourses shape the therapist's performance of 'truth' claims. This is a performance that is based on the assumption of the therapist as a knowing observer, one who has achieved, in regard to knowledge, an autonomous, detached, and disinterested status. The person who is seeking the consultation is regarded as the object of this knowledge, and is constituted, through this interaction, as the 'other'. In this way, these professional discourses are powerfully reinforcing of the subject/object dualism that is so pervasive in the structuring of relations in western culture.

The professional discourses that shape the interaction between therapists and the persons who consult them are also constituted of rules that govern the exercise of these different classes of knowledge. These are rules about what counts as legitimate knowledge, rules about how and where these knowledges are to be stored, rules about who is authorised to speak of these knowledges, rules about how these knowledges might be expressed, rules about the circumstances under which these knowledges might be expressed, rules about the positions and locations from which they might be expressed, and so on. Some of these rules have been the subject of part one of this book, and will not be further discussed here.

Technologies of power

These professional discourses are not only characterised by certain classes of knowledge and rules that shape the expression and performance of this knowledge, but they are also associated with certain 'technologies' which act as vehicles for the performance, the general privileging, and the ongoing production of these knowledges[1]. These are technologies through which not only the 'legitimate knowledges' are expressed but are also technologies of 'truth' seeking that ensure the ongoing production of these knowledges. These technologies include practices of the observation, measurement, and evaluation of 'behaviour', procedures for the location of problems at particular sites of identity, however these sites are constructed (for example, as 'psyches', as emotional 'centres', etc.), techniques for the categorising and classifying of persons' lives, and strategies that make it possible for therapists to operate on these sites - to intervene and to correct whatever it is that is assumed to be amiss.

These technologies are all informed by the modern preoccupation with the self-government of the self, and it is in this sense that they are technologies of power. These technologies incite persons to engage in self-surveillance, and effectively recruit them into the policing of their own lives in the reproduction of the 'truths' of human nature, and according to the norms of living that are championed by these 'truths'. There are many instruments of 'truth' seeking that are available to assist in this task. One such frequently employed instrument (that was discussed in chapter three of this book) is the continuum - of normality/abnormality, of autonomy/enmeshment, of independence/ dependence, of assertiveness/passivity, and so on. In the very act of entering one's life into these continuums, of locating one's place in the territories of these dimensions, persons are participating in acts that have to do with the calculated and precise management and administration of their own lives. These technologies and instruments of truth are not only centring of persons in the regulation of their own lives. They also incite persons to become agents in the 'optimisation' of their lives.

Upon reviewing the technologies of the professional discourses, we are confronted with the extent to which these constitute modern relations of power - a fact that should not be so surprising. In tracing the history of the modern professional discourses, Foucault (1984) has described the central role that these have played in the insertion, into popular culture, of new practices of power that have made possible, over the past few hundred years, spectacular advancements in the government of persons' lives. Whereas personal erasure symbolised sovereign power, the modern system of power that supplanted it:

... centred on the body as a machine: its disciplining, the optimisation of its capabilities, the extortion of its forces, the parallel increase of its usefulness and its docility, its integration into systems of efficient and economic controls, all of this was ensured by the procedures of power that characterised the disciplines: an anatomo politics of the human body. The old power of death that symbolised sovereign power was now carefully supplanted by the administration of bodies and the calculated management of life. (1984, pp.139-140)

Critique

There have been many critiques of the truth claims of these professional discourses, and of the relations of power that they reproduce. For example, I am sure that readers will have some familiarity with the many challenges that have been directed at the notion of a 'graspable objective reality', and with the numerous critiques of the notion that therapists can achieve some privileged access to some detached and disinterested observer status. These critiques of objective reality claims draw attention to the impossibility of persons standing outside of the phenomena that they are observing, and the impossibility of persons avoiding a generative role in the construction of the realities that they are describing. These critiques have emphasised that the distinction so often perceived between how things are in themselves, and how we take things to be, is non-existent.

Such critiques question many a cherished notion of the culture of psychotherapy. For example, they make it impossible for therapists to sustain the illusion that they can participate in therapeutic processes under conditions of neutrality. In fact, therapists are confronted by the fact that the assumption of neutrality is not neutral in its effects, and that it is the very conditions established by this illusion of neutrality that permits them to reproduce the structures of privilege and relations of power of mainstream culture. These are structures of privilege and relations of domination that marginalise persons who seek help, maintain hierarchies of knowledge, disqualify alternative modes of life and thought, preserve the therapist's monopoly on power, and render invisible the therapist's location in the worlds of gender, culture, ethnicity, sexual preference, class, etc. In deconstructing notions of expert knowledge and of neutral observation, therapists are freed to acknowledge and to embrace the ethical responsibility that they bear for the real effects of their work - for the real effects of their work in the constitution of the lives of the persons who consult them.

I am also sure that readers will have some familiarity with the exposés of the technologies and of the instruments of truth of the professional discourses that are referred to in the above discussion - technologies and instruments that incite persons in the reproduction of the 'truths' of human nature, in the reproduction of those ways of living that are championed by these 'truths'. These exposés implicate therapists as agents of the professional discourses because of their complicity in engaging the persons who consult them in acts in the regulation and optimisation of their own lives.

It is not my intention to discuss further the real effects of these professional discourses in the constitution of the lives of the people who consult therapists. There has already been considerable attention given to this subject in various places in the literature. Instead, in the next section, I will discuss the implications of these professional discourses in the life of the therapist. This discussion with be shaped by the questions: What are the real effects of these discourses in the constitution of the life of the therapist? Are there options for therapists to avoid becoming accomplices in the calculated management of their own lives? What possibilities are available to therapists to break from the modern technologies of the self in the constitution of their own lives?

Professional discourses and the life of the therapist

I have reviewed some of the real effects of the professional discourses in the shaping of the relationship between therapists and persons who consult them, and in the constitution of the lives of persons who consult therapists. But there are yet further considerations.

In regard to the lives of therapists more generally, could it be that these are exempt from the real effects of these professional discourses? Could it be that therapists are somehow immune to the constitution of their own lives through these professional discourses? Could it be possible for therapists to traffic in the technologies of modern systems of power, and somehow avoid the powerful incitements to join in the self-government of the self that leads to the sort of individualisation that is so highly venerated in this culture? Is it likely that therapists could journey into what is the heartland of this culture's technologies for the administration and management of life, and yet resist the powerful incitements to engage in the policing of their own lives?

Although it stands to reason that the professional discourses that are constitutive of the lives of persons who consult therapists are also constitutive of the life of these therapists, this has been a relatively neglected consideration. This consideration has been obscured by a primary focus on the generative role that the therapist plays in the construction of therapeutic realities. This focus has diverted attention from the extent to which this activity occurs in discursive fields that are also constitutive of the life, and the world, of the therapist. It has diverted attention from the fact that these discourses have real effects not just in structuring the therapist's participation in the therapeutic context and in the production of therapeutic 'truth', but also in how the therapist relates to their own life - in the shaping of the therapist's relations with the world, in the construction of the therapist's accounts of personal identity, and so on.

Take those classes of knowledge of the professional discourses that feature truth claims about the human condition. These are constitutive not just of the lives of the persons who consult therapists, but also of therapists' lives. For example, therapists often understand the difficulties that they experience in their work in terms of the professional 'truths' about problem formation, and in so doing identify the source of these difficulties to be a 'problem' that is located at a 'site' within their identity. In response to this, therapists intensify their engagement with the truth-seeking technologies - self-observation, self-measurement and self-evaluation - and as an outcome of this they are more wholly constituted as objects of the knowledges of the professional discourses. They routinely place their lives on the deficit end of the continuums of adequacy/inadequacy, and derive classifications of their problem. Thus, therapists become more tied to the established 'truths' of problem resolution - and in general to the formation of their selves through the knowledges of the professional discourses.

In joining with the assumption that constructs therapists as knowing observers who have, in regard to knowledge, achieved an autonomous and detached status, the therapist is centred in this work, but at the same time profoundly isolated from the persons who consult them. The fact that this occurs under circumstances in which the therapist is required, upon entering the culture of the professional disciplines, to forsake those knowledges and skills that are generated in the local contexts of their histories, means that this centring is experienced under conditions in which the therapist has available to him/her fewer interpretive resources than s/he would otherwise have. The centring of the therapist in the context of isolation and under circumstances that are forsaking of these knowledges and skills of personal history contributes very significantly to a sense of burden and fatigue that can become overwhelming.

This assumption that constructs therapists as knowing observers who have, in regard to knowledge, achieved an autonomous and detached status, also renders it impossible for them to acknowledge value dilemmas, and to engage in explorations of the expression of their values in ways that open space for possibilities in persons' lives, rather than closing this down. Options to explore non-normative value systems are also foreclosed. For therapists, the possibility of mistrusting what they are for when it comes to the lives of others, and of exploring different expressions of different values and the real effects of these expressions in the shaping of life, is lost.

The expert knowledge claims of the professional discourses can also have the effect of constructing a 'timeless' experience for therapists. The specificity and authority of expert knowledges, which are distributed from the top down, not only make it difficult for therapists to ever experience the attainment of an adequate grasp of knowledge, but also discourage them in the plotting of their experiences of therapeutic conversations into an unfolding account of their work. This deprives therapists of a sense of forward-going developments in their work that could orient them in yet further steps, and contributes to an experience of being 'frozen' in time as they go about doing what they can to 'get it right' in the performance of expert knowledge. The acquisition of requisite professional knowledge is a priority that is ever over the horizon and out of reach. The spectre of failure looms ever large, and spurs renewed efforts in the regulation and optimisation of their work and lives.

In the chapters that follow in part two of this book, I will review some of the ideas and practices that are associated with narrative therapy, and that differently constitute the work and the life of the therapist. These ideas and practices provide therapists with options to break generally from the formation of the self of the therapist through the knowledges of the professional disciplines, and from acts in the calculated management of their own lives.

Note

1. Michel Foucault's (1973b, 1979, 1980, 1984) work has been very influential in my understandings of these technologies. This influence is evident in much of what I have written in this section on professional discourses. Foucault is best known for his spirited deconstruction of the truth discourses of contemporary western culture, and of the practices of power and the technologies of self associated with these discourses.

6

The Therapeutic
Relationship

The one-way account of therapy

A one-way account of the therapeutic interaction is the account that is taken for granted in the culture of psychotherapy. The activities of the various organs of the different institutions of the psychotherapy world, including those of the professional journals and societies, are so clearly informed by the idea that the recipients of therapy are solely the persons who consult therapists, and that, if the therapy is successful, if all goes well, these persons will undergo some transformational process.

The extent to which this is the taken-for-granted account is reflected by the fact that it underscores most of the representations of the therapeutic practices of the different schools of therapy. Regardless of how a therapist's specific contribution to such transformational therapeutic practices might be conceived of by these different schools - whether it be in terms of the introduction of certain interventions, in terms of providing a new perspective on certain situations, in terms of engaging in certain processes of education, in terms of the introduction of hypotheses that perturb systems, or whatever - therapeutic interaction is virtually always represented as a one-way process.

According to this one-way account of therapy, it is understood that the therapist possesses a therapeutic knowledge that is applied to the life of the person who consults them, and this person is defined as the 'other' whose life is changed as an outcome to these therapeutic procedures.

Exceptions to this one-way presentation of the ideal therapeutic process are invariably problematised. In various places, including in the literature, considerable attention is regularly given to the extent to which this ideal is not achieved by many of the practitioners in the field. In training and supervision contexts, discussion is often focussed on those developments in therapists' work that contradict the rule of the one-way process. These contradictions are represented in negative terms - they are deemed to be undesirable. These are those contradictions that arise when the therapeutic interaction draws in the lived-experience of the therapist in ways that affect his/her actions, and this is considered to interfere with the therapeutic process. They are glitches that require close scrutiny, and that need to be resolved. Such contradictions might be constructed as 'counter-transference', as the expression of 'one's neurotic needs' (perhaps even of 'co-dependency'), as 'unresolved family-of-origin issues', as a 'vulnerability to the suction of systems', as 'blurred boundaries' and 'emotional over-involvement', and so on. The examples that I give here of what might be called the 'interpretations of contamination' are by no means the most exotic of those that are freely available in the culture of psychotherapy.

What are the effects of this one-way account of therapeutic process on the lives of the persons who consult therapists? This significantly reproduces the subject/object dualism that is so pervasive in the structuring of relations of power in contemporary western culture. In this relation, persons' lives are the object of the therapist's knowledges and practices - these knowledges are the 'expert' knowledges, and these practices are the 'expert' practices of the translation and treatment of the expressions of the lives of others: the evaluation, the documentation, and the techniques of remediation and correction. In this objectification, the person who consults a therapist is constructed as the 'other'. And, in that the ideal is for this person's life to change as an outcome of the therapeutic conversation while the life of the therapist remains as it was, this person is subject to a marginalisation of their identity.

More specifically, what are the effects of this one-way account of therapy on the stories of identity of persons who consult therapists? A very significant number of persons who seek therapy have arrived at thin conclusions about their lives and their identities. They 'understand' that they are bereft of the requisite knowledges or skills to address what it is that they find problematic in their lives. They 'appreciate' the fact that they lack the personal wisdom to know what might be good for their lives. They have 'realised' that they lack the personal qualities necessary to get themselves out of their predicaments. They have 'figured' that they are a personal failure and a burden to the lives of others. And so on. According to the one-way account of therapy, these deficits are to be attended to and made good by expressions of the expert knowledges and the expert skills of the therapist. In this one-way account of therapy, persons are constructed as recipients. For many of these persons, this status contributes significantly to the reinforcement of the thin identity conclusions that they bring with them to the therapeutic context.

The one-way account of therapy and the therapist's life

I have reviewed the extent to which this one-way account of therapy structures relatively inflexible power relations in the therapeutic context. I have also addressed the potential of this one-way account of therapy to contribute to and to significantly reinforce many of the thin identity conclusions that persons bring with them into this context. But, this account of the therapeutic process also has a significant influence on the shape of our relationship with our work, on the stories we have about our lives as therapists, and on the accounts that we have of our identity more generally. This account of the therapeutic process suspends our active participation in 'acts of meaning' in regard to our lives as therapists.

It is through personal narrative that we take in and give meaning to our experiences of the events of our lives. It is through personal narrative that we link together the events of our lives in sequences that unfold through time according to specific themes. It is through this meaning-making process that we experience being in the flow of time, and that we experience our lives moving forward[1]. And, in that action is significantly prefigured on the successful interpretation of the events of our lives, it is through this meaning-making process that new options become available for action in therapeutic practice.

This one-way account of therapy, in rendering invisible the way that this work touches our lives, excludes us from these acts of meaning in relation to the significant events of our work. These events float across the screen of our consciousness, never more than a blip, and disappear over the edge into a vacuum. They are not taken into the story-lines of our lives. What it is about the therapeutic endeavour that is potentially changing of our lives as therapists is lost. There is no unfolding of preferred developments in our work to be experienced. There is no sense of positive direction. The therapeutic context is not one that contributes to our stories of identity being more richly described. The events of our work do not relate to the significant themes of our 'other life', the one that takes place outside of therapeutic contexts. Our work does not re-acquaint us with the viability of our purposes. Therapeutic practice becomes an atemporal experience. Life for us is something that occurs elsewhere, in the other contexts of our lives, at those times that we are free of therapeutic responsibilities.

In that the one-way account of therapy structures a relationship to therapeutic practice that disengages us from acts of meaning in relation to those experiences of our work that are potentially shaping of this work, and of our lives, it contributes to thin descriptions of our therapeutic identities, and to thin conclusions about the nature of our practice. In stepping into this account of therapy, we deny ourselves the opportunity to plot the significant events of our work into the story-lines of our lives. And we deny ourselves that which would otherwise be sustaining of us in the therapeutic endeavour. We become prone to frustration, to fatigue, and to a sense of being burdened by the work. And this ultimately contributes significantly to our vulnerability to experiences of 'burn-out'.

A two-way account of therapy

A two-way account of therapy is one that emphasises the life-shaping nature of this work in respect to the therapist's life. In constructing a two-way account of therapy, the therapist takes the responsibility to identify, to acknowledge, and to articulate, within the therapeutic context, the real and the potential contribution that this work makes to his/her life. This is a contribution that can be identified in the development of our therapeutic practices, in our experiences of, and in developments in, our relationship to our work, in the stories what we have about our life as a therapist, and in the accounts that we have of our identity more generally.

There are many implications of this acknowledgement of the extent to which therapeutic interaction is constitutive of the lives of all parties to this interaction; of the acknowledgement that what is shaping of the lives of persons who seek our help is also shaping of what we commonly refer to as our work, and that what is shaping of our work is also shaping of our lives in general. These implications include those that are derived from a recognition of the fact that therapeutic interaction is informed by cultural discourses and the practices associated with these discourses, and that these will have real effects in the shaping of the lives and the relationships of all parties to this interaction - that these interactions will be specifically and mutually, but differently, constitutive of our worlds.

A two-way account of the therapeutic process serves to undermine the rigidity of the power relation of the therapeutic context, and the potential for this power relation to approach states of domination. In challenging the hierarchy of knowledge, a two-way account of therapy establishes a context in which the potential for persons to experience their lives as the objects of professional knowledge is diminished. In that this two-way construction of the therapeutic process introduces alternative relationship practices, it assists therapists to avoid the reproduction of the 'gaze' (Foucault 1973, 1979) in our work - the practices of evaluation, the documentation of persons' lives, the techniques of remediation and correction. A two-way account of the therapeutic process contributes to the structuring of relations that challenge the marginalisation of the identities of persons who consult therapists, that challenge the construction of 'otherness'.

Further, rather than confirming the thin conclusions of life and of identity that persons bring to therapy, a two-way account of the therapeutic process challenges this. A two-way account of the therapeutic process is acknowledging and honouring of the contribution of persons' knowledges and skills to the work and to the life of the therapist. A two-way account of the therapeutic process contributes to the generation of thick descriptions of persons' lives, and assists them to break from thin and deficit-centred descriptions of their qualities and purposes. A two-way account of therapy contradicts the notion that persons have gaps in their knowledges, skills and personal qualities that can only be addressed through recourse to the skills, knowledges and qualities of the therapist. Rather than constructing persons as recipients of whatever it is that therapists have to give, reciprocity is invoked.

Third, a two-way account of the therapeutic process engages us, as therapists, in acts of meaning that contribute to the generation of rich descriptions of our own work and of our therapist identities. As we orient ourselves to the potentially significant events of the therapeutic context, and as we plot these into the story-lines of our lives, we experience being in the flow of time. We gain a sense of the unfolding of preferred developments in our lives, and of our work going forward. This makes possible further explorations of these directions, and presents us with options for action that would not otherwise be visible. This plotting of the potentially significant events of our work into the story-lines of our lives not only has the effect of re-acquainting us with our chosen purposes, but also contributes to our sense of the viability of these purposes. In so doing, we transgress the oft-made work/life boundary distinction.[2]

Taking-it-back practices

In the following discussion I will present just some of the options that can be taken up in the acknowledgement of the two-way nature of the therapeutic conversation. These options can be expressed in what I refer to as 'taking-it-back' practices.[3]

(i) Inclusion

Rarely do persons who consult therapists make the decision to do so lightly. The call to set up the first appointment is a significant step in itself, one that is often quite daunting. For many it is the first of a number of steps into the unknown. It is a step that will take them into an unfamiliar territory, one that this the home ground of the therapist. It is a step into a vulnerable place in the power relation of therapy. It is a step that sets them on a course which requires that they open their lives to strangers. It is a step towards a possible journey that can only be entered through an act of trust.

The significance of these steps that are taken by persons in the hope that things might be different in their lives can be easily missed by therapists who are focussed on the many tasks of their frequently busy working lives. When these steps are taken for granted, the potential for therapists to appreciate the significance of them to the persons seeking consultation is lost. Also lost is the potential significance of these steps to the work and to the lives of therapists. Lost are the options for therapists to recognise the significance of the trust that is being invested in them. Lost are the possibilities that are available for therapists to acknowledge the privilege that is being granted to them by the persons who open their lives in the way that they do, a privilege that is rarely available to others in the usual day-to-day flow of life. Lost is the opportunity for therapists to take into their own lives the experiences of being so powerfully included in the lives of others. Lost are possibilities for the realisation of all of this in the shaping of the work and the life of the therapist.

However, when the steps that persons take in seeking consultation and in opening their lives to therapists are not taken for granted, and when these steps are acknowledged, it becomes possible for therapists to embrace the significance of these steps to their own lives as well. In these circumstances, therapists become more conscious of the effects, on their lives and on their work, of the trust that is being extended them, and of the acts of inclusion that they are the recipients of.

(ii) new associations

Many of the practices of narrative therapy assist therapists to join with the persons who consult them in the attribution of alternative meanings to the actions and to the events that constitute the plots of the stories of their lives, and in the attribution of new meanings to many of those events of their lives that have gone unstoried. The meanings that are attributed to these events and actions often contradict the dominant problem-saturated plots of persons' lives - these events and actions come to speak to the alternative plots or counter-plots of persons' lives. These alternative plots and counter-plots can be named and more richly described in narrative conversations.

It is in this way that the actions and events that are re-interpreted or newly read in these conversations come to be highly valued - they are interpreted as expressions of persistence, determination, struggle and protest, connection, and so on, and often come to represent the turning-points of persons' lives. It is through this re-making of meaning that many of these actions and events become the 'sparkling' actions and events of persons' lives, and a cause for celebration.

These sparkling events and actions occur in the different contexts of persons' lives, are set in particular scenes, and are often associated with particular objects of the world that come to take on powerful symbolic meanings. Joining with persons in an appreciation of these events and actions, and, in some instances, being privy to the reproduction of the actions and events themselves, contributes to the therapist's own world being more richly described through new associations - the symbolic meanings flow into the therapist's world, and many of the familiar objects of this world are newly appreciated. Also, it is through this phenomenon of association that particular scenes and contexts of the therapist's world are more richly experienced - scenes and contexts that to a degree mirror those scenes and contexts that frame the sparkling events and actions of the lives of the persons who consult therapists.

(iii) Re-engagement

In re-authoring conversations, the little events and acts that contradict the dominant plots of persons' lives take on a special significance, and, in so doing, provide options for the identification and thick description of the alternative stories of persons' lives. In these conversations, these little events and acts provide a gateway to the alternative territories of persons' lives. These events and acts speak to sub-plots, to different hopes and purposes, to other accounts of identity, and to many knowledges and skills of life that have gone unacknowledged.

The joining with persons in the identification of these sparkling events and acts, and in the exploration of these in re-authoring conversations, can have the effect of orienting therapists to much that has been overlooked in their own lives. As therapists begin to attribute significance to those little events and acts of their lives that have been neglected, they find opportunities to step into, and to map out, some of the alternative and neglected territories of their own lives - to name the sub-plots that are constituted of the neglected but lived-through experiences that are to be discovered in these territories, to fill the gaps in the story-lines associated with these sub-plots, and to engage in the revision of many of their identity descriptions. In this activity, therapists find themselves re-engaging with the histories of their own lives, and in the re-making of their lives and their work.

(iv) Re-membered lives

In joining in re-membering conversations with persons who consult them, therapists often find themselves reflecting on the relational contexts that have contributed to their own knowledges of life, and to their skills of living - the images of certain figures from their own histories are evoked, and experiences of these connections are relived. This provides therapists with a basis for the initiation of steps in the further re-membering of their own lives. For example, they may engage in conversations with figures from their own histories, conversations that they would not have otherwise had. These are conversations that will be identifying of and acknowledging of the contributions of these figures to the knowledges and skills of the therapist's work and life.

Thus, the re-membering conversations of narrative therapy are constitutive of the work of the therapist, and of their life more generally. They also contribute to a greater therapist consciousness of the knowledges and skills of their work and life that might otherwise be taken for granted, and to these knowledges and skills being more richly described. These re-membering conversations present therapists with possibilities for engaging in revisions of the membership of their own lives, revisions that support their expressions of the knowledges and skills of their work in difficult contexts in which they might otherwise be dispossessed of these.

(v) Re-voicing therapy

Therapeutic conversations provide therapists with the opportunity to join with persons over matters of life that are of very considerable importance - to be with these persons in explorations that are informed by their hopes that things might be different, and by their resolve to step into ways of living that are more in tune with the preferred purposes of their lives. Such is the significance of these conversations that the experience of being with persons in these explorations often ripples on in therapists' lives well beyond the boundaries of the therapeutic conversation itself. As an outcome of this, therapists often find that they carry with them the images of the persons who consult them into their work with others, and often into other contexts of their daily lives in ways that they might not have predicted. This contributes sustenance to the lives and the work of therapists, and can assist them to more fully acknowledge the voices of others.

Not only are the images of these persons evoked by events in various contexts of the therapists' life, but therapists can consciously call these forth on those occasions upon which they wish to experience the support of others - for example, in difficult and trying circumstances where there is some risk that their knowledges might be disqualified, in contexts that are eroding of their skills in acknowledging others, at times when their voice against injustice is being overwhelmed, and in environments that are dispossessing them of hope. In this way, these images contribute to therapists' lives and work being multiply joined and multiply voiced.

(vi) Solution knowledges

In narrative practice, it is in the interaction of therapists and the persons who consult them that solution knowledges are generated. Therapy is conceived of as a form of co-research that constitutes what therapy is - the solution knowledges that are derived in this context are taken up in the further expressions of this work. In a general way, these solution knowledges shape what therapists bring to subsequent consultations - they inform the conversations that are had, and contribute to the stock of available options for action that are identified in the course of these conversations.

More specifically, therapists also take a familiarity with the solution knowledges generated in certain therapeutic contexts into other contexts of their work. This familiarity serves to alert them to different traces of solution knowledge that are emergent in these other contexts, traces that might otherwise be missed. However, this is not to propose that the knowledges generated in one context are directly transferable to other contexts - that the solution knowledges appropriate to one person's life might be reproduced in the life of another person. And it is not to propose that those solution knowledges generated in one context be imposed on another context.

It is possible for therapists to share the solution knowledges derived in particular therapeutic contexts with other persons in other contexts without contributing to this sort of imposition, and without allocating some normative status to these knowledges. For example, in therapeutic conversations that are identifying of specific traces of a person's solution knowledges, these knowledges can often be more richly described by comparing them to similar solution knowledges that have been generated in other therapeutic contexts. This sharing of solution knowledges across contexts is facilitated by the documentation of these knowledges, which is common practice in narrative work - in the course of this work, though this documentation, the therapist builds archives of solution knowledges that can be made available to the persons who consult them (Epston & White 1992a).

In the sharing of solution knowledges across contexts, persons can be invited to reflect on them to determine the relevance of these to their own circumstances of life, and to identify possible connections between these and the traces of their own solution knowledges that have been distinguished in the course of the therapeutic conversation. If relevance and connection is established, the basis of this can be explored through appropriate questions: 'What is it about these solution knowledges that seems relevant to your circumstances?' 'What aspects of these solution knowledges do you find yourself relating to?' 'What do you perceive to be the links between these solution knowledges and your own preferred ways of being in life?' 'Does this contribute to you being on more familiar terms with the history of these ways of being in your own life?' 'What does an acquaintance with these other solution knowledges bring to an appreciation of your own solution knowledges?' 'Is there anything about these solution knowledges that is particularly capturing of your attention, or stirring of your imagination?' 'If so, are you aware of aspects of your own experiences of life that resonate with the images triggered by these solution knowledges?' The therapeutic conversations that are informed by these and other similar questions contribute very significantly to the rich description of the person's solution knowledges - rich descriptions of solution knowledges that are not simple reproductions of the solution knowledges drawn from other contexts. These conversations are constitutive, and provide new options for action.

At times, in the sharing of solution knowledges across contexts, relevance and connection is not established. On these occasions, therapeutic conversations can contribute to drawing out more fully some of the distinctions around those solution knowledges derived in other contexts, and those that are relevant and appropriate to the person's life. These conversations are invariably generative of rich descriptions of what otherwise would remain thin traces of the person's solution knowledges. In these circumstances, it is the distinctions that provide a structure for knowing - a structure that contributes to persons achieving a sense of being knowledged.

(vii) Skills of therapeutic practice

In narrative practice, the persons who consult therapists make a very significant contribution to the identification, development, and reinforcement of the appropriate knowledges and skills of therapeutic practice. This contribution is made in the co-generation of therapeutic conversations. It is also present in the general feedback given by persons in their responses to these conversations. This feedback can be read in the person's non-verbal responses, and is also given in their verbal responses. As well, it is available in their reflections on these conversations and on the relational practices engaged in by the therapist.

Apart from the feedback that is generally available to therapists in the course of this work, it is common in narrative practice for therapists to consult persons about their experience of therapeutic conversations. Many of these consultations are 'mid-stream' - that is, they are solicited in the course of the work itself. This is achieved by inviting these persons to reflect on the conversation and on the conduct of the therapist: 'Would you catch me up on how this conversation is going for you?' 'Is it taking a direction that seems appropriate to you?' 'Is it your sense that we are talking about what is important for us to be talking about?' 'Is this conversation addressing your agenda for this meeting?' 'If we are going in a direction that seems appropriate, would you share your sense of what it is about this conversation that is working for you?' 'Do you have any thoughts about other directions for our conversation that might be relevant?' 'Have any of my responses in this conversation put limits on what you feel you can talk about here?' 'Would you be prepared to reflect on the conversation that we have been having, and put me in touch with what seems more helpful and what seems less helpful about it?'

These examples of questions that solicit mid-stream feedback are but a few of the possibilities available to therapists. Because the therapeutic relation is also a relation of power that can be limiting, inhibiting, and shaping of persons' responses to these questions, before soliciting mid-stream feedback, it is important for therapists to contribute to an exposé of this power relation, and its potential to affect what might be expressed in this feedback. At this time, the therapist can also initiate a review of some of the other relational politics that might have a presence in the therapeutic conversation, and that might also be limiting of what might be expressed, or that might be shaping of expressions in ways that are diverting of them - these relational politics might include those of gender, culture, race, class, heterosexism, age, and so on. Such reviews are based on an exposé of the power relations in question. Illustrations of these exposés are given in *Re-authoring Lives: Interviews and Essays* (White 1995a). For example, in regard to the relational politics of gender, I discuss the imperative for male therapists have to:

> *... share, with the women who consult* [them], *what* [they] *see as the possible dangers of this, including the extent to which women's knowledges are so often disqualified in these contexts, and the possible limitations that might be associated with the fact of* [the therapist's] *gender. These limitations can be exposed in part by the therapist giving notice that, in the context of therapy, he will take responsibility for any misunderstanding or particular difficulties with achieving understanding, and will assume that these will relate considerably to the privilege that is associated with his location in the social world of gender ... in practical terms, it involves* [male therapists] *sharing with the woman some of* [their] *concerns, and asking some questions about any thoughts that she might have that could help to make* [his] *participation in the therapeutic interaction more accountable to other women ...* (1995a, pp.165-166)

It is also a common narrative practice for therapists to consult persons about their experience of these conversations after the event - persons are encouraged to reflect on their experiences of particular meetings and on series of meetings, and on the outcome of these meetings, by reviewing the subsequent developments in their lives. In this way, persons contribute to distinguishing the more helpful conversations and relational practices from the less helpful, and to a determination of those that were of a hindrance. It is in these consultations about therapeutic conversations and practices that therapists' expressions of this work are formed and reformed. It is in these consultations that therapists' knowledges and skills become more thickly described.

In that the therapeutic conversations of narrative therapy are co-generated, and in that the feedback about these conversations and about the relational practices of this work are so powerfully shaping of it, the persons who consult therapists contribute significantly to the therapists' further expressions of this work, and thus to the lives of those who follow in the footsteps of these persons. This contributes to options for therapists to be with others in ways that make a difference.

(viii) Remembering not to forget

The survival of many of the inequalities and injustices that persons and groups of persons are subject to in our own communities, as well as those inequalities and injustices experienced in more distant communities, is to a considerable extent dependent on a lack of consciousness on behalf of persons who live with privilege. In part, this lack of consciousness relates to the fact that persons who live with privilege do not experience the circumstances of life endured by those who are disadvantaged - persons who live with privilege either haven't stood in these places, or they vacated these places a long time ago.

But this lack of consciousness is also significantly an outcome of the forgetting practices of contemporary culture. Although this forgetting is often theorised in psychological practice, here I wish to emphasise the history of this tradition - of 'remembering to forget'[4]. These forgetting practices have a cultural dimension, and the inverse relationship between privilege and memory when it comes to these matters is, in part, an outcome of these practices.

It is these forgetting practices that support the denial of privilege, and prevent an acknowledgement of the foundations of this privilege - that is, the dispossession and/or the disadvantage of others. Living with privilege makes us more vulnerable to entering the thrall of these forgetting practices. Under this thrall it becomes possible for us to step into ways of being and thinking in the world that are exterior to a consciousness of the power relations of the micro-

and macro-worlds of life; to occupy locations in life that do not necessitate any acknowledgement of disadvantage, and of the abuses of power that are disqualifying, marginalising and silencing of persons and groups of persons.

As therapists, we are uniquely placed to break from the injunction to remember to forget. In joining with persons in the deconstruction of the problems that they experience, many of the forces that provide the context for these problems are named. And in this naming, the relations of power that support and maintain disadvantage and inequality are rendered more visible. It is in the exploration of these power relations that persons invite us to stand with them, however briefly and partially, and this provides us with the opportunity to look back on our taken-for-granted ways of thinking and being in the world. In breaking from the thrall of forgetting practices in this way, it becomes possible for us to think outside of the limits of what we would otherwise think, to challenge aspects of our own participation in the reproduction of dominance, and to identify options for action in addressing disadvantage and inequality that would not otherwise be available to us. Our lives are invigorated for this.

(ix) Purposes and intentions, values and commitments

Then there are the narrative practices that open space for persons to take a position on the problems of their lives, on events and acts that contradict the stories of incompetence and inadequacy that are associated with these problems, and on the solution knowledges that are identified through the exploration of these contradictions. These are practices that make it possible for persons to: (a) negotiate or renegotiate the meanings attributed to these problems and to these contradictions, (b) map out the effects of these problems through the different domains of life, and explore the consequences (both real and potential) of the solution knowledges that are associated with these contradictions, (c) engage in an evaluation of the effects of the problem and the consequences of the contradictions and the solution knowledges that are identified in this way, and (d) determine relevant justifications for these evaluations.

In justifying these evaluations, persons find themselves articulating accounts of their preferred intentions and purposes, and of what they stand for in regard to values and commitments. In response to this, therapists often find themselves entering a renegotiation of the meaning of various events of their own lives, and renewing their acquaintance with their own purposes and intentions, and with their own chosen values and commitments. This turns out to be sustaining of therapists in their work.

(x) Resistance

This renewal is also available to therapists as an outcome of the conversations that they have with persons that assist them to identify and to significantly acknowledge the extent to which they have kept alive the hope that things could be different in their lives, despite everything that has been discouraging of this - conversations that contribute to an acknowledgement of their persistence in acts of resistance despite formidable odds. Joining with persons in this acknowledgement provides therapists with options for a greater recognition of their own acts of resistance, and with ideas about how and in which contexts of adversity these might be further expressed.

(xi) Joy

There are other ripples of this work that touch therapists' lives. Narrative practices not only provide options for therapists to join in the identification and the exploration of the little events and acts that contradict the problem-saturated stories of persons' lives, but also provide the opportunity for therapists to join with these persons in celebrating the significance of these events and acts. The joy that is had by therapists in doing so contributes directly to their experience of their work, and invariably flows into other domains of their lives.

Taking it back

I have here reviewed some of the real and the potential effects of therapeutic conversations in the constitution of the lives of therapists and in the shaping of their work - these are all contributions that can be acknowledged within the therapeutic context itself. I hope that, in this review, I have been successful in emphasising the two-way nature of therapeutic practice. This review is not by any means exhaustive. There are many other ways that these therapeutic conversations are influential in the therapist's life and work - take for example the part that this work plays in us becoming better listeners, or the extent to which this work opens possibilities for us to develop more compassionate relationships with our own lives.

As the one-way account of therapy is marginalising of persons who consult therapists, and because it informs a power relation that is relatively inflexible, bringing forth the two-way nature of therapeutic interaction has a priority in narrative practice. This priority is one that is, in the first place, determined by the ethics of practice - it is an ethical commitment. Second, apart from these ethical considerations, bringing forth the two-way nature of therapy is accorded a priority as this contributes significantly to the rich description of the lives of persons who consult us. Third, this is accorded a priority because taking the responsibility to identify and to acknowledge the ways in which this work is actually or potentially shaping of therapists' lives and work, engages therapists in the re-authoring of their own lives and their own work.

This brings us to considerations of how these contributions to the life and to the work of the therapist might be acknowledged - considerations of how the therapist, having identified the shaping or potentially shaping nature of these interactions, might proceed in acknowledging this within the very therapeutic context from which these contributions emerge. It is one thing for therapists to identify how this work is changing or potentially changing of their lives and work. It is another thing for them to engage in some acknowledge-ment of this. It is yet another thing to perform this acknowledgement within the very therapeutic context that gives rise to these ripples - to take back, to these persons, some acknowledgement of extent to which the therapeutic encounter is actually constituting of therapists' lives.

Taking-it-back practices have already been illustrated at different places in this book: for example, in the course of my conversation with Sophia, and in the transcripts of the outsider-witness group responses to the stories of Sally and Paul. But there is much more that can be taken back.

I am able to take back to Sophia what it has meant to me to have Rupert in my life, to have him joining me in my work in ways that are an expression of her spirit, and what this has meant to so many children over the past fifteen or so years. I am also able to take back to Sophia what it has been like for her to evoke Bill's presence at Dulwich Centre in the way that she has, and for me to consciously re-evoke this in my work with men who are referred to me for perpetrating abuse - to have him standing with me in what he stood for, and to find support in this for my own knowing that there are other ways that men can be in their relationships with women, children and other men.

I can take back something similar to James - about how our explorations of better judgement have been significantly reinforcing of my work with men who perpetrate abuse, about how his inclusion of me and his trust touched my life, and about how this has been renewing of my commitment to find ways of working with men who abuse that are not totalising of them. I can also take back the fact that our shared explorations were also renewing of my own efforts to seek out and to challenge acts of dominance that I inadvertently reproduce in my own life as a man.

I can take back to Louise how her inclusion of me in the revision of the membership of her life has contributed to me being more attuned to the acts of inclusion that I am subject to by the significant persons in my own life, and to my ability to more directly acknowledge the significance of these inclusions.

I can take back to Pat how the image of her perseverance in her relationship with hope, of her refusal to be separated from this despite so much that was discouraging of this, has contributed to my conversations with others whose lives have been close to being overwhelmed by the effects of the abuses that they have been subject to - conversations about what these persons' survival is a testimony to. My interview with Pat has also encouraged me in further explorations of options in joining with these persons to mend what might be mended, particularly their relationship with the non-offending parent (usually the mother), which is so often a casualty of the abuses that they have been subject to.

I can take back to Ian the extent to which our conversation has contributed to my work with some of the persons who seek my consultation in regard to fear. I find that I am more able to join with these persons in the identification of some of the figures of their histories who may have been veterans of fear, and to engage these figures in the identification of the contexts of fear, and in the identification and the rich description of the sort of knowledges and skills that limit the effects of fear in one's life.

I can take back to Greg the new appreciation that I have for the little creatures that I now search out with my eyes as I pedal my bike to work and home each day, taking in the camaraderie of the galahs, the dignity of the cockatoos, and the raucous partying of the parrots - arriving at places refreshed by this, and more ready to take in the contributions that little creatures make to the lives of the persons who consult me.

I can also thank all of these folks for introducing me to the figures of their histories that, in the course of our conversations, they re-membered into their lives and their work. I know that the world would be in so much more of a sorry state if it wasn't for its Bills, Marys, Bobs, Helens, Paulines ... and its Sam Fangs.

These are but a few examples of the taking-it-back practices that are of the sort proposed in the above discussion. In engaging in these practices, I am not expressing a graciousness. And these expressions are not grand - 'you have turned my life around' - and they are not ingratiating. These taking-it-back practices are, first and foremost, expressions of an ethical commitment. Taking-it-back practices are about the performance of an acknowledgement of what this work brings to the life of the therapist. This is a performance that contributes to the rich description of the lives of all parties to the therapeutic conversation. This is a performance that is constitutive of the lives of these parties.

Further discussion of what I refer to here as 'taking-it-back' practices is warranted. The proposal for the performance of this acknowledgement, for this taking-it-back to the persons who are at the centre of these consultations, often raises questions for therapists: 'Won't taking it back contribute to the blurring of professional boundaries?' 'Won't this set up a context in which persons experience an expectation to please therapists?' 'And, won't this make it more difficult for persons to talk to therapists about what it is difficult to talk about?' 'Isn't there a significant risk that this will close options for persons to express distress or despair?' 'Isn't there a hazard that these taking-it-back practices will structure therapy as a context that is for therapists, not for the persons who consult them?' 'And won't this be disrespectful to the agenda of the persons who consult therapists?' These and other questions can contribute to a guide in the development of the sort of taking-it-back practices that do not reproduce the hazards that they refer to. These questions can also shape other questions that can be raised by therapists as they seek consultation from persons about the real effects of these therapeutic conversations and practices in general, and of taking-it-back practices in particular - including the consequences of these taking-it-back practices in regard to the therapeutic conversation itself.

However, although questions of this sort can provide a guide in the development of taking-it-back practices, and although these questions can play a significant part in orienting us to the consulting of persons about their experience of therapy, it is not likely that the negative outcomes referred to by these questions will eventuate if these taking-it-back practices are informed by the tradition of decentred practice that is referred to in various parts of this text. Taking-it-back practices are not a formula for the production of a form of therapist self-centredness, but are an antidote to this. When informed by the tradition of decentred practice, these taking-it-back practices present options for new avenues in the exploration of the territories of persons' lives. In the performance of these taking-it-back practices, the expressions and the agenda of the persons seeking consultation remain at the centre of the work.

Set backs

When presenting ideas about taking-it-practices to others, from time to time I am asked questions about the phenomenon that is often referred to as a set-back: 'What if things haven't worked out quite as well as the therapist and the persons who are consulting him/her might have hoped?' 'What if, between interviews, there have been untoward developments or set-backs that were not predicted?' 'And what if this has a negative effect on the therapist?' 'For example, what if this contributes to despair for the therapist, despair that affects the therapeutic conversation and that ripples into other domains of the therapist's life?' 'Does the therapist take this back to the persons who are seeking consultation?' 'In engaging in these taking-it-back practices, is the therapist to acknowledge to others what they experience as the negative contribution of these untoward developments to their work and lives?' As this inquiry touches on a theme that is central to the discussion in the next chapter which reviews some of the ethics of this work, I will only briefly address it here.

Needless to say, therapist despair is not generally experienced as a good outcome by persons who are seeking consultation. If these persons are first required to address the discouragement of the therapist before receiving assistance to break from their own discouragement, it is likely that they will only experience their difficulties as more insurmountable. So, how is the therapist to engage in taking-it-back practices when persons have gone away from narrative-oriented conversations, having identified proposals for action in relation to what it is that is troubling to them, and returned to report not only on the frustration of these proposed actions, but also on developments that they regard to be of the nature of a set-back?

Under these circumstances, options for taking-it-back practices become more available as the contexts of these set-backs are more fully appreciated. For example, the events surrounding whatever it is that is experienced as a set-back can be reviewed in a way that puts the therapist more in touch with the forces that were frustrating of the person's proposals for action, and that contributed to 'regress'. In contributing to the development of a greater consciousness of these forces, this review throws many previous actions and events of the person's life into sharp relief - all of those actions and events that have contradicted these forces, including those that led to the person's decision to seek consultation, and to follow through on this, take on an increased significance. In this review of the context of set-backs, the therapist becomes yet more respectful of the person's contributions to these actions and events, and is presented with a number of taking-it-back options that will contribute to the stories of the lives of all parties to the therapeutic conversations being more richly described.

Notes

1. For further discussion of narrative analysis, see Jerome Bruner's *Actual Minds: Possible Worlds* (1986) and *Acts of Meaning* (1990), and Paul Ricoeur's *Time and Narrative* (1984).

2. In breaking their work from this distinction, therapists are freed to explore and give expression to the limits that are defined by ethical considerations of the sort discussed in this and parts three and four of this book, and by the personal resources that are available to them.

3. When I have shared with other therapists my explorations of taking-it-back practices, some have proposed 'giving back' as a more appropriate description. However, because these practices have to do with an acknowledgement that is honouring of the history of those ripples of the therapeutic conversation that significantly touch our lives, I continue to prefer the description 'taking it back'.

4. I first came across this phrase in David Epston's work many years ago. In relation to working with young people who would respond to questions with 'I don't know' or 'I forget', he would sometimes ask, 'How did you remember to forget?'

7

Supervision as
Re-authoring Conversation

The power relation of supervision

Although 'supervision' is the title of this section, this is a term that provides an account of the relationship between the person seeking consultation about their work (here referred to as the therapist) and the person providing this consultation (here referred to as the consultant) that does not fit at all well with the practices that are described here. The term supervision is one that evokes a hierarchical relationship in which one party's knowledges are assigned a 'super' vision status, and in which the other party is subject to this super-vision in matters of work and therapist identity.

The term co-vision has at times been proposed as an alternative to supervision. This term is proposed in the expectation that it will contribute to the structuring of practices that provide an antidote to the hierarchy of knowledge and the inflexible power relations that are associated with the concept of supervision. Co-vision does provide an egalitarian account of the relationship between therapists seeking consultation about their work and consultants who provide this consultation, one that challenges the hierarchy of knowledge that is associated with the notion of supervision. Nonetheless, there are problems with the term co-vision when it is used to describe a relationship in which one person seeks consultation from another who has responsibility to provide this. This responsibility is one that is often formally sanctioned by an agency, by a professional association, or by an educational/training institution, or it is a responsibility that is observed more informally in professional networks. The status of the person who is sanctioned to provide this consultation may have been achieved by seniority, by credentials, by reputation, by organisational rank, by experience, and so on. As well, the person engaged to provide this consultation is usually financially rewarded for this. These and other factors speak to the privileged location of the person providing consultation. Thus, the term co-vision is problematic in that it obscures the power relation that is established by this privilege, a power relation that significantly influences the outcome of the consultation.

I believe the obscuring of such power relations to be perilous. Because of the fact of this power relation, the person providing the consultation has ethical responsibilities to the person seeking consultation that that person does not have to the person providing consultation - these are ethical responsibilities that are not reciprocated. If this power relation is obscured, it is less likely that the person providing the consultation will be able to observe these ethical responsibilities. It is less likely that the person providing consultation will engage in the monitoring of the real effects of the power relation on the work and the life of the person seeking consultation. If the power relation is rendered invisible, the options that are available for the person providing consultation to take responsibility to diminish the possible negative effects of this relation will be reduced. The consultant will find it more difficult to contribute to an exposé of the negative outcomes of this power relation, and to establish limits to its influence. The consultant will find it more difficult to initiate acts that are subverting of this power relation, acts that might render the context of supervision more egalitarian than it would otherwise be.

Not only does the visibility of this power relation open options for action for consultants, it also provides options for therapists. It makes it more possible for these persons to monitor their experience of the consultation, and to reference these experiences to the shared expectations and to the purposes that have been negotiated for the consultation. The visibility of this power relation also makes it possible for the persons seeking consultation to attend to, and initiate conversations about, the real effects of this power relation in regard to matters of their work and their lives more generally. It is in this context that questions can be raised about these consultations that would not otherwise be addressed.

In discussing the options that the visibility of this power relation brings to the person seeking consultation - to monitor the real effects of this on their life and their work, and to raise questions in regard to this - I am not describing a context in which the consultant may be held directly and uniquely responsible for the outcome of the therapist's actions in their work with the persons who consult them. As the therapist is responsible for the shaping of whatever it is that comes from the consultation, and for the unique expression of this in their life and work, the consultant's responsibility is one that is more general and indirect. In regard to the therapist's responsibility for the real effects of the power relation that is structured by their therapeutic practice, there are many options available to them to build into their work processes that make this work accountable to the persons who consult them. However, these practices of accountability are not the subject of this present discussion - they have been explored in other sections of this book.

I would like to emphasise that, in talking here about the fact of these power relations, I am not celebrating the exercise of power, but emphasising the special ethical responsibilities that are implicated in the exercise of power. And I am speaking to the priority that can be given to drawing out some of the available options for the deconstruction of this power relation and the taken-for-granted privilege that is associated with it.

A re-authoring conversation

Therapists seek consultation on their work for many reasons. Perhaps this is a requirement of their employment, or of registration and accreditation. Perhaps this is an expression of a commitment to the ongoing development of their work. Perhaps this is to do with a general dissatisfaction with their work, or over particular difficulties experienced in their work. Or, perhaps this is provoked by new challenges that are being faced. Whatever the initial impetus for the seeking of consultation, much of what therapists bring into these contexts for discussion relates to concerns of one sort or another: things in their work not turning out as they might have hoped, feelings of being stuck, personal doubts they are experiencing, difficult dilemmas they are facing around values and practice issues, and so on.

In relation to these and other concerns, therapists are not less vulnerable to engaging in internalising conversations than are the persons who consult them. In these internalising conversations, therapists frequently locate the source of difficulties in different sites of their own identity, and/or in sites of the identity of the persons who are consulting them. In my experience, with therapists who seek supervision from me, the first is more often the case - that is, it is more usual for the therapist to locate the difficulty in a site of their own identity, and to enter their lives into continuums of normality and abnormality - competence/incompetence, dependence/independence, and so on. Thin conclusions about personal failure or inadequacy are the outcome. This outcome is associated with an intensification of the modern practices of self-regulation, acts that lead to what I have elsewhere in this book referred to as the calculated management of the life of the therapist. All of this closes down space on options for action in the therapeutic arena, and undermines therapists' experiences of being knowledged.

In mirroring the practices of narrative therapy, the narrative approach to consultation assists therapists to break from these internalising conversations, and from the practices of the self that are associated with these conversations. Through the introduction of externalising conversations (White 1988/89), it is the experience of the therapist seeking consultation that comes to occupy the centre of the conversation. It is in this space that therapists have the opportunity to express their experience of various events of their work, to speak of the meanings that have been attributed to these events, and to explore the real effects of these experiences and meanings in the shaping of their work and, more generally, on the shape of their lives. In the course of these conversations, the thin conclusions that therapists have about their work and their identity are deconstructed. In this way these thin conclusions become less specifying and capturing of therapists' identities.

The deconstruction of these negative truths of identity provides possibilities for a renegotiation of meaning in regard to many of the events of therapy, a renegotiation that provides for alternative readings of these events. The deconstruction of these thin conclusions also frees therapists to engage in the explorations of the 'other' events of therapy - events that have been neglected, events that contradict the thin conclusions that are the outcome of the negative truths of identity. These contradictions provide a point of entry to the alternative territories of the therapist's work and life, and it is in these territories that traces of the therapist's preferred knowledges and skills can be identified - traces that can be explored through lateral and longitudinal dimensions of life, knowledges and skills that can be more richly described through re-authoring conversations. This rich description presents options and proposals for therapist action in the therapeutic context and in life more generally, options that were not previously available to the them. And this can include options for the expression of these knowledges and skills in contexts that are otherwise discouraging of them.

It is not my plan to here describe the maps that guide these re-authoring conversations. I have provided details of these maps in various publications (White 1991, 1995; Epston & White 1992b), and elsewhere in this book. All of these maps, including those that relate to re-membering conversations and to definitional ceremonies, are as relevant to this context as they are to the contexts in which persons seek help from therapists. And those practices, like 'taking it back', that are informed by ethical considerations are also as relevant. In observing these considerations, consultants can take steps to acknowledge the two-way nature of these consultations by identifying how these conversations contribute to the shaping of their own work and life.

There are many options available to the consultant for engaging in 'taking-it-back' practices. For example, in joining with the therapist in the generation of rich descriptions of the knowledges and skills that they have to bring to this work, the consultant may become more aware of echoes of these knowledges and skills in their own work. These become more richly described for the consultant in the course of these consultations. Or, in joining the therapist in the explorations of the options for action that are informed by the therapist's knowledges and skills, and in the shaping of these options into specific proposals, the consultant may become aware of options for action in his/her own work that would not otherwise have occurred to him/her. These experiences that provide opportunities for the knowledges and skills of the therapist to be more richly described, and that provide options for the consultant to think outside of what s/he might have thought, represent just a couple of the many possible contributions that can be identified by the consultant and that might be a focus for 'taking-it-back practices'. And these acts of taking it back further contribute to possibilities for consultants to be other than who they were at the outset of the consultation.

Supervision illustrated

Due to considerations of space, it is only possible to provide one example of narrative supervision here. In providing this example, I have decided to rely predominantly on the transcript of a conversation with Maria about some general concerns that she had about her experience of herself in her work. Another example of narrative supervision might begin with a focus on particular difficulties that a therapist is experiencing in their work with specific persons, or on explorations that have to do with specific problems that the therapist is being consulted about.

Maria[1]

Maria is employed in a women's health and counselling centre. Here she works with women who have been, and who are being, subject to abuse. She meets with these women in groups, and in individual counselling as well. Maria had chosen to work in this area because of her consciousness of the injustices perpetrated in the context of the power relations of gender, because of her awareness of the effects of these injustices on the lives of women and children, and because of a longstanding personal commitment to play a part in addressing these injustices. Although she has had an appreciation of the fact that it would only be reasonable for her to at times find herself quite distressed in this work with women who are subject to violence that is predominantly perpetrated by men, Maria was concerned about the fact that, of late, she seemed more vulnerable to despair, and felt that she was losing touch with something that was precious to her. That she was having this experience in an agency that was very supportive of her work, one that is well-known for its commitment to the values that Maria prioritises in her own life, was a further cause for her concern. And although there was the reality of insufficient funding of these services for women in the community, Maria believed that there was more to be understood about her despair. It was this that she sought consultation over.

An outsider-witness group of women who work in health and counselling services for women, colleagues of Maria, were present for the duration of the conversation that the following transcript is drawn from.

Transcript

There are so many experiences that have ... touched off or evoked that sense of despair. An overwhelming sense of 'How can I help this woman, what can I do?' I must admit that this has been true in more recent times. I feel like I'm loosing touch with something, you know ...

Losing touch with ... ?

Losing touch with my ability to keep believing that I am helping this woman, that it is making a difference ... to keep believing that even the smallest achievements are important. This is the sort of thing I talk to women about, and yet I am beginning to lose that myself. I feel really distressed about this. It's not what I stand for. I don't like it. It's more than I don't like it. It really distresses me. And yes, it has an effect on other areas of my life. This distress actually seeps through the other work that I do. At times when I go home I have it on my mind. You know, a sense focussing too much on negativity, on lots of stuff that I can't do anything about. Things to do with a wider system that doesn't seem to be supporting women who are experiencing violence. So, I have an idea of where I'd like it to be, but I feel that the gap between this and how it is is too big. And, at the same time, I know that women who come to see me do talk about how our connection has been useful when I check with them. But then there are the times when women will come to see me about situations that are so complicated, so desperate, and there is actually nothing more that I can do in a practical sense. I've done everything that I can do. I feel very distressed at the fact that there isn't anything that I can do. I feel really bad, I feel like ...

But, what do you do?

What do I do?

Yes. You're feeling like there is nothing that you can do, and at this time what are you doing?

I would spend a considerable amount of time with a woman talking about, or hearing her experience. And being very respectful about her experience, of her efforts in trying to keep her family together, or to keep things going, or in keeping her life together. I know that I focus a lot on that. I listen, and at times that's all that I feel like I can do.

What is she experiencing from you in these conversations? What's your guess? If I could interview one of these women that you thought you could do nothing for, what would she experience from you in the conversation itself?

My guess would be that she ... or my hope would be, that she would say I was supportive of her. Listening, hearing what she was saying.

So, that you were a person who was able to listen, and a person who was able to be supportive?

And respectful.

Respectful of what? What would she say she had experienced you being respectful of?

Respectful of the fact that whatever choices she'd made ... not judgemental of her as a person, as being a good or a bad person. That I'd be respectful of her efforts ...

Being with her in respecting those efforts?

Yes. Not judging her for things that even she might identify as having done that were wrong. I don't judge this, or not having done ... what she believed she should have done.

If I was to ask her if that was an unusual experience for her, or a regular experience, to be with another person in another place in life and not to experience judgement, and to experience being respected in this way, what do you think she would say? That it was a usual thing, or an uncommon thing for her?

She would probably say it was uncommon. I think that this is what, in general, women would say.

Right. So ...

But I don't see that as being ... I see that only as a start, I don't see that as being enough for a session. I ...

Sure. I wasn't hinting at that, but I was wanting to get some sense of what women experience in their conversations with you and what they would conclude about that. You were going to say something else?

I just said that I don't see it as enough for a session, but I think that there were times when I used to see it as enough. At particular times, women would say, would identify to me, that this was what in fact what they wanted. They didn't want to hear anything that was about suggestions, or solutions, or advice, or anything like that. Anything that would hint at giving suggestion, or even checking, 'Have you tried such and such a thing?' or, 'Can I make a suggestion?' even just checking, that for some women is not okay.

It's a judgement for many, I guess, to hear that.

Yes. I'm just wondering that maybe that should be enough for a session. You know, that maybe that is enough ... at times. That's part of what I'm not valuing any more, even that which I do. Just losing touch with that. Losing an appreciation of the effect that these conversations have on the women I work with.

Can I just share with you some thoughts about possible conversations? Is that okay?

Yes.

You've just been catching me up on where things have been going for you in the last couple of years, and some of this doesn't really fit with where you want to be in this work. I thought about what you said at the beginning of the conversation about getting back a sense of connection, that this is what you really want in your work. I was thinking about maybe asking you some questions about connection, about what this means to you, and about how you actually go about those skills of connecting to people. I've also been thinking about what you said about keeping on believing that you're helping, and about what forces are at play that actually block this appreciation of what you are doing. And then we've just been talking about how you are with women who consult you, about how you can be that way with these women. In ways that don't have you giving them advice when you know that this could be experienced as something that they could just fail, and so on. I am just wondering which of those conversations you would be most interested in us following up?

The point you made just previous to that. The one before that.

The one before that ... the second one? I mentioned a possible conversation around what it is that gets in the way of your belief that you're helping, around what takes you away from that belief. That's the one that you'd like to talk about most?

Yes.

So, would you like to start talking about that?

When I think about it, the first thing that comes to mind is a sense of self-monitoring that I've been trying to challenge for probably as long as I can remember.

Self-monitoring?

Yeah. Self-monitoring. It's almost like a regular check as to whether what I'm doing is really worthwhile. In some ways I find with whatever is happening around me, in particular in my workplace, I tend to really focus on anything that could highlight my sense of perhaps not being quite capable enough, or not doing enough, or not doing it as efficiently as I could. Or that the term of counselling could be shortened, saving some of the workplace resources. I would really like to shut them off, but ... The whole thing about needing to be efficient - I would really like to shake that off, but ...

Is it like ... How would you describe it? Is it like a voice of efficiency, or is it ...? What would be a good name for this?

The voice of being effective?

The voice of effectiveness?

Yeah.

Okay. And this gives you a hard time?

Absolutely!

It has you monitoring yourself, checking on yourself, measuring yourself against some idea of how you should be? It has you asking questions about your capabilities and so on?

Yeah.

So, the voice of effectiveness. Is that a good name for it?

I think so. Yeah.

Okay. So, could you say more about how that voice speaks?

Well, it speaks in many different areas of my life. I was just thinking that it speaks on a personal level as well. Quite loudly actually. Yeah.

In terms of accusations or ... ?

Yeah. Even in terms of ... Actually, I have a child. He's grown up, nearly twenty. I know that I've had that voice kind of run or rule my life for as long as I can remember, because even now I can reflect back on some aspects of my parenting approach. I think I always used to try and come from a position of being a really effective parent, or an efficient parent - that I could fit in lots and do it in a way that could be honoured and appreciated by other people. That I could make their connection with me worth their while, to be their friend or my child's mother. It's like whenever I've taken on a task that's related to my work or in relation to my personal life, the voice of effectiveness speaks really loudly. It tells me that unless I'm 'effective', I'm not doing it right.

Not doing it right. Okay. And what else does it talk you into about yourself?

That others then can see it.

That 'others can see through me'?

Yeah. And can see it too.

What would they see?

They would see my ineffectiveness.

'My ineffectiveness'?

I think inadequacy comes into it as well. Like a sub-voice.

Okay. Inadequacy like a sub-voice: 'They will see that I'm inadequate'. Is that right? So, it's a pretty powerful voice.

It evokes a lot of fear ... fear of failing and not being good enough in what I'm doing. Sometimes there are two parts of me that fight about this. One part saying: 'You know, you are doing a good job. You know that you are a valuable person and you're doing really good work', 'And you know you've been a good parent'. Then there is this other part that insists on trying to come up with opposition, by saying things like: 'But what about the times when you know you've failed?' or, 'What about the time when you didn't do this thing according to how you'd want to do it?' 'What about the fact that you might not have as much skill or knowledge as someone else?' And then the comparison comes up in a big way.

In my work situation what can precipitate these accusations are those times when I find that not only I, but other workers around me, are under other pressures. External pressures are placed upon us to go along with the restructuring of the organisation and other things. I know that I work in a really special place and I know that the other women there really care about each other and about me. And yet, at times I feel like people might be treating me slightly differently because of my 'inadequacy'. And then I automatically identify in my own head, 'Well, it must be because I am inadequate' ... It's not as though people ever come to me and say that, or even suggest that. But, it's something that I find myself doing, and that's the self-monitoring I was talking about. This happens particularly when it comes to doing my one-to-one work ... My sessions tend to go longer than an hour ... Even that has for me a way of reinforcing that sense that I should be able to do it within an hour, and I then get stuck with that so that if somebody was to ask me in goodwill, 'Oh, that was long session' ... automatically I am thinking: 'Oh gosh! They noticed my inadequacy. They noticed that I wasn't able to have it ended that short' ...

So, it can be quite a persuasive voice, and it somehow - this voice - sets itself up as an authority on your identity and in so many places in your life?

Yeah.

I have a few questions I would like to ask. But before I do that, I would like to check with you to see how this conversation is going so far.

It's good. I'm finding it helpful.

Why is that? What's helpful about it?

Because I'm beginning to get clearer about just how powerful this voice is and how pervasive it is ... I am getting clearer that it is about the voice rather than the people. I've always known that but I felt really almost tricked by this whole thing. Although I feel like I know that, now I'm becoming clearer that it's to do with the other voice being awakened again, or re-evoked or ...

It really does talk you into some pretty negative things about yourself generally, and has you treating yourself harshly at times. It has you treating yourself in dismissive ways? Or, what would you say? How does it have you treating yourself? I don't want to impose a word here. Is dismissive ... ?

Yeah. Dismissively. That would fit.

This would fit? In terms of how this voice has you treating yourself?

What would be the opposite of appreciative?

Disqualifying?

Disqualifying. Yes.

It has you treating yourself in disqualifying ways?

Yeah.

Yes? Do you know what forces do stand with this voice, historically ... or when ... ?

Yes. Just as you were talking a minute ago, this particular incident kept coming to mind for me. I would have been probably not even ten years old, but I remember one particular day - this is back in Italy in the country town where I grew up - I remember that my class went on a small excursion. We were walking down the main street of the town and I remember my brother, who was then in high school ... he and a couple of other young friends of his used to just stand around in front of us, especially girls that were going past. So, they saw us just going past, and on that day - I used to have a close friend, but she was away on that day - I was actually walking right at the end of the group and I was on my own. And I remember that it really hurt. [tearful] *I remember my brother and his two friends were both just saying, 'Oh, who would want to go with you anyway?' I don't even remember the exact words, all I remember is that pain. That 'No wonder you don't have any friends', and they were just laughing about it. My brother was leading it and he was having the time of his life. My sense is that he didn't really know how much it hurt me ... I know that when I feel really dismissive of myself or whatever, that has somehow come back. Not so much the picture, but that feeling that, 'Well, there you go, you know, a group of people said that'.*

So in a sense ...

It had its birth back when I was very young and people have been able to see that about me. Therefore there must be something there. I thought: 'I am not good enough. Not worthy of having friends'. I ... it's so powerful. I don't even know why.

It is powerful though, isn't it? It was probably at a time in your own life when you were quite vulnerable to ...

Yes, actually I was! I grew up just in a really small farmhouse away from town and that was actually the first year that I had gone to join the village school. I was feeling really intimidated and afraid. And I was actually feeling quite vulnerable. Yes. So ...

So, you grew up in a small farmhouse and this was the first time in the wider community for you?

For the first three years I had been going to just a local, very small school ... a home that had been turned into a small school, and it was really quite non-intimidating. I had to take the bus on my own and go to this other school and a whole new group of people to face. There was also this belief, or an attitude within that town, about country people, who were treated with lots of discrimination. It was very common for country people to be treated very differently ... with disrespect, or as a sub-human ... I certainly felt that. That there were sometimes comments that were made about country people being dumb, or being all kinds of things: uneducated, stupid, and all of that. So, yes, I was feeling quite vulnerable at the time.

You had come from a school where you had connections with others, and they were good connections?

Yes. They were good. I had a really close friend who then didn't come to that village school, but went to a different one, because they moved.

What was her name?

Maria (2).

Maria?

Yes. So, it was only my first year at the village school ... I had only managed to make a connection with the one girl who was away that day, and I remember feeling really alone. Very conscious of others not being interested in making friends with me. And then, of course, with my brother and his friends saying this, it had an incredibly painful impact on me ...

What would you call that? What would be a good word for what you experienced from your brother at that time when you were so vulnerable and feeling excluded and ... ?

I can't be clear about a word, but I think it was really traumatic for me.

Really traumatic?

Yes. Really traumatic. It was an attack on me as a person, and I actually remember bringing that up when I went back home. I talked briefly to my mother about it. She is usually good at picking up things that are wrong that are happening in my life. At this particular time she did say, 'Well, that was really wrong of them', which was good to hear. But she also then said: 'Well, that's your brother, you know what he's like. Just dismiss it'. And then of course I knew that would be the end of it. I couldn't do anything about my brother, because he would just humiliate me even more. It was a humiliating attack.

So, that's the word. 'Humiliation'. What's it like just to name that as humiliation? Is that important?

Yes. It is actually.

Why is that?

Because, it feels like it is something that he imposed on me rather than something that was really inside me that I took with me. The fact that I was feeling vulnerable, I can identify with that, and then he ... imposed this humiliating action. It's had a really lasting effect ...

We are getting to hear a little more about the history of that voice and who was represented in that voice. And we had been talking about the voice of effectiveness that has you treating yourself in those dismissive ways.

What's really a bit puzzling, though, at the moment, is that I am trying to think of my brother as he then developed as an adult. There have been changes ... Although we are not close, we do have a certain level of respect for each other, and we are acknowledging that we are respectful of each other.

Does that make it harder for you to speak to this in a way, because he has changed?

Yes. In a way. I guess I am also staying rather reserved about it. I am choosing not to have as much contact with him because of not wanting to be vulnerable. I am trying to avoid being in situations of feeling vulnerable again. So, I am guarding myself I think. I think that's giving me a little bit of a sense of having got back some sense of power in his eyes, because I think he does respect who I am now. He has shown that in different ways in conversations with other people, but he's never said it to me.

What if your friend Maria (2) told him that she had heard about this humiliation of you? What would she have said?

She would have been really shocked.

She would have been shocked and ... ?

[speaking for Maria (2)] *'You don't know the first thing about how she is as a friend ... Or, how ...'*

'You wouldn't know the first thing about ... ?

'You wouldn't know the first thing about who this girl is.'

About who this girl is? 'I have chosen her as my friend because ... '

'Because she is caring and generous'. [tearful]

Chosen you as her friend because you are caring and generous and ... ?

'Respectful.'

'Caring, generous and respectful.'

'Worthwhile.' And that she was missing me.

'I am missing her'?

Yes. She was missing me, I know. Maybe a few other things I can't think of right now.

'I would miss her if we couldn't spend time together, because my life is different from having known Maria (1) in some ways.' In what way would you say your life is a bit different for knowing Maria (2)? In what way would she say that her life was a bit different for knowing you?

I was someone she could talk to. She also had two brothers who were younger than she was, and parents who were always just not available to her. She used to be able to talk with me ...

So, 'There are some things about myself that I can appreciate, that I wouldn't otherwise be able to, that my connection with Maria (1) has put me in touch with'? What sort of things?

I think she felt like a valued human being, someone who had feelings. She used to say that to me. Whenever she tried to talk to her brothers, they would joke. So we shared that frustration. But also her parents were very dismissive of her needs and her requests and what have you. She didn't have anyone to talk to. She would come and talk to me. We shared a lot of similarities. She told me once that ... she never did find another friend that she could quite talk to.

Wow! She never found another friend like you?

Yeah.

Friends like you were pretty rare?

I guess she felt that. Yes.

Could you speak a little to those tears that you are experiencing?

A part of me feels like I don't know where they are coming from, and another part feels, of course I do. I think they are about realising that I have been dismissing so many good things, you know.

Yes. Yes.

They are about sadness. A sadness that ... Whatever the force is of those voices that are always measuring me up against someone else, against a standard or ... I feel really cheated, you know.

You've talked about a standard, the judgement, and how cheated you've been feeling about that?

Yeah.

So, Maria (2) could have set your brother straight. Even if he didn't listen, she could have set him straight in some ways on this.

She would have something to say all right. I haven't caught up with her since I was twelve. She stayed in Italy when I came here. She would be a really assertive woman. She used to be really assertive. With my brothers, she used to tell them in no uncertain terms where to go. To behave themselves ...

From the way that you are speaking it sounds to me that both you and Maria (2) had a consciousness about injustice. Would that be true? A consciousness that you both had back then?

Yeah. I think so. We certainly were aware of the injustices perpetrated at least by our brothers.

Even when your mother said to you, 'You know what he's like', you didn't buy that?

No, I didn't. I know that I wished that something else could have been done, but at the same time, I felt hopeless about that. I knew that if I told my father he may have talked to my brother, but there was already a big clash between them

... I didn't want to create even more problems by then him retaliating. It wasn't so much about protecting him, but about keeping myself safe.

Keeping yourself safe?

Yeah.

And, when your mum said, 'You know what he's like', that was somehow accepted by others too. But you didn't allow that to dispossess you of this consciousness of the injustice, is that right? You kept true to that consciousness?

Yeah.

What's happening for you right now?

I think that it's a sense of injustice which ... Yes. I had other stuff happen as well. Just in my childhood. I know I have always tried somehow to incorporate into my life some ways in which I could address ... to try and do something about injustice when it was happening.

Is that part of the history of your involvement in the work that you're doing?

Yeah.

So there is a long history of consciousness of injustice. I am wondering what it is that you'd actually be more free to appreciate about your work, what you bring to it, if you didn't hear this voice that says what you're doing doesn't count, or it's not enough?

'Who would want to be involved with me anyway?'

What difference would it make to what you could appreciate about what you are doing if you didn't hear that? What would you be more free to acknowledge?

I think I might be more focused or more aware of my efforts and the things that I do. Things like, for example in my work ... I wouldn't be comparing.

Okay, so you would break from that.

Yeah. I would break from comparing. I would break from that self-monitoring. I would break from measuring the amount of what I do ...

So, you would break from that whole orientation of measuring by amounts. You'd be free of that? I guess that this wasn't the measure of your relationship with Maria (2). It was something else.

No. It never was measured in amounts. It was something else. I think that one of the other things I might break from is that automatic assumption that when someone says, 'That was a long session' or, 'Is so-and-so still coming to see you?' they are coming from a place of judgement. And perhaps I might be in another workplace, and if somebody was to say really inappropriate things to me, I can see that if that voice wasn't affecting me I would be thinking, 'Well nothing is bothering me', and I would be able to be clear about people being inappropriate or being disrespectful. I wouldn't just walk away feeling uncomfortable ... I would say, 'Well, why do you think so?' Whereas now things have a way of stopping me from doing this. The voice actually silences me ... I react, but I don't make it heard.

So, you would be more likely to be saying 'I am not sure whether you are measuring me against something, or whether your response is something else, perhaps to do with you acknowledging my skills'?

Yes. I would say something. I would ask what they actually meant by that.

How would it be to find yourself doing that?

I think that would feel ... it wouldn't necessarily feel powerful, but somehow that word comes to mind. I feel like I would get a good balance of power back in me. Yeah.

There is so much to talk about in these conversations. I want to touch base with you about how this conversation is going for you.

It's good. Very good.

Why do you say it's good? Could you put me in touch with what you meant by that?

Yes, sure. When we started talking I felt like there was this incredible confusion. As I mentioned at the beginning of our session, I tried to prepare, I tried to think about it, but the more I thought about it, the more confused I was getting. But ... I now feel a lot clearer. I feel a lot clearer and I feel it's a relief. I'm talking about an influence from a belief, rather than it's something in me that ... I've read about it before, but this is different because I've actually experienced it. Yeah.

It's a good experience?

Absolutely. Yes. It is a very strong feeling of relief and a release as well. There is a totally different sort of feeling in here. I can breathe differently now. I have got a different perspective on how I could be doing things quite differently and challenging that voice, challenging those voices. And I might even, next time I see my brother, I'll think about how I might prepare to talk to him ... I want the next time I meet with him to be different, to reflect some of this process ...

I have some idea of what it would be like to have Maria's (2) voice in your life more in this matter. Even to write a letter to your brother, a letter from Maria (2) that you write. Perhaps: 'It has come to my attention that you've really humiliated my best friend who's really very important to me and this is really unacceptable. It is one of those injustices of the world that Maria (1) and I stand against', and 'I want to put you straight on Maria (1) and the things that you need to understand about her'. Not necessarily to send this to your brother, but to ...

I was just going to ask you about that ...

But maybe to keep it in your shirt-pocket over your heart. What would it be like to consult this on those occasions when this voice of effectiveness is starting to give you a hard time? What effect do you think it would have to privilege Maria's (2) voice more, to elevate her voice in that way?

I think it would have a strong effect. It would be a reminder of this very special process of today. It would be a reminder of who I want to stand for, of who I believe I do stand for. And, the fact that I am someone who is valuable to be with and who has contributed and is worthwhile. I could keep that with me.

I was just thinking about somebody asking you about having such a long session and you saying, 'I've got some things to say to you, but I've got to read a letter first'.

[Laughter] *Absolutely!*

When I asked you what things would be like if the voice of judgement or the voice of effectiveness wasn't there, if you were free of that, what you would then be free to do, you seemed to know instantaneously. You didn't say, 'Well, I don't know'. You knew exactly what you would say. You were very clear about those sorts of skills. How would you name those skills that had to do with addressing difficult things? What's a good name for those sorts of skills?

What would I choose to call that? Umm ...

Like if you were free just to act in a way that fits with everything that Maria (2) knew about you.

Well ... it would be for me the ability to be able to be genuine about who and what I stand for ... true to what I stand for, but true isn't necessarily ... about skills.

There is a know-how attached to that ... so, I would like to ask you more about this. But not now. Right now I want to know whether or not these are the sorts of things people go away from you experiencing. Like a stronger sense of what they stand for, or some options for taking action in their life that have to do with what they see as really genuine to them. And, not so much dictated to by other people's expectations. Is that what people would go away, from their consultations with you, taking with them?

Yes. The interesting thing is that I never had any doubt about that. I've always known that people do go away with that, and yet that voice has always been so powerful, has always tried to convince me that ... But, no. That's a lot clearer now. It means that what works for me also works for ... I can't be another way. My belief is in justice and in treating people with respect, and that's what I do. And I do that in all areas of my life and my work.

So, what we are talking about has to do with you including yourself, your own life, in expressions of those knowledges and skills? Of being free to do that?

Yes. And I can see myself liberating more of my creative ability or my artistic ability which I think has been dormant for a while. I think I can reawaken this. This conversation might open up more space for this as well. It's just come to mind.

How did that come to mind?

Just looking at the colours. [pointing to a Mexican papier-mâché tray] *Just thinking about how much I enjoy art-forms. I used to do some of that as a child. I used to paint. I've gone away from that over time. I feel that by becoming more free of that voice, and recognising it as something that is coming externally, I can have more space to bring that ability back into my life.*

That's great!

I used to draw fruit quite a lot. We never had much fruit, but I used to draw it a lot. [laughter] *I hadn't really thought of that for a long time. I can include some of that creativity in my work. Not necessarily painting, but being creative.*

Postscript (authored by Maria Fiorito)

   I remember that initially I felt somewhat apprehensive about being interviewed in the presence of my work colleagues. However, I soon became aware of shifting into another space, where it felt safe to journey back through my life, sharing self-doubts, self-criticisms and exposing 'vulnerabilities'. This decision to share my life with others in this way was quickly reinforced. One of the first things that I became aware of in hearing my colleagues' re-tellings was the ripple effects of this sharing - my colleagues had experienced aspects of themselves and their own work being affirmed.

   I was also personally touched by my colleagues' re-tellings. One of these colleagues, Monica, spoke of her deceased grandmother - about how important this grandmother's voice was for Monica, about how in times of special need, this grandmother's presence gave her strength and a sense of renewed commitment. Monica said that she thought her grandmother would think highly of me, and would be supportive of who I am and of my work. I felt extremely privileged to not only have received a special gift, but to have also fulfilled a wish. Because some time ago, when Monica first spoke to me about her beloved grandmother, I recall thinking how special she was and how I wished I could have known her. Through Monica's re-telling, I've been given the opportunity to get to know her and experience her wisdom and love.

Lately I've been thinking about other 'Marias' (including those who are no longer alive) who play an important role in my life in valuing and affirming who I am, as well as bringing life-enriching qualities to my life. I've been taking their presence with me into my work as well as into my personal life. I've become aware of a chain of acts of resistance in my life that have been present from a young age. The links in this chain have been kept strong by these people's influence. In order to privilege their voices in my life I have recently designed, on their behalf, a statement of values, skills, and qualities. In my work, I've been bringing to women opportunities for them to re-member people in their past who either directly or indirectly influenced their lives in favourable ways, and to find ways in which they might privilege these people's voices over the voices of people who devalued and dismissed them.

I've been reflecting on one of the possibilities that Michael suggested for a conversation, one that could have been shaped by the question about what connecting to people means to me, and about the skills involved in doing this. In the course of this reflection, it's become clearer to me that what's important about connecting to the women who consult me is that it renders my values and intentions visible. It is then possible for me to join with them, not only in affirming their experiences of struggle and resistance, but also in supporting them to achieve preferred changes in their lives. I believe that my experiences of discrimination and isolation have provided me with the ability to understand and empathise with others who are experiencing hardships in their lives.

I've been more appreciative of my 'country values' and of my ethnic and cultural background - realising that this is not only shaping but also enriching of my life. I am more likely to share this with others, including, when appropriate, the women who consult me. I've found that this often assists women to re-discover important values they had lost connection with, and to take these back into their lives. I'm more able to value the contribution I make to women who consult me, and I've been incorporating more creative tools in my work, which is an outcome of feeling re-connected with my childhood love of story-telling, drawing, painting, and being surrounded by colourful things.

Note

1. Maria Fiorito, c/- Dulwich Centre, Hutt St PO Box 7192, Adelaide 5000, South Australia.

8

Training as
Co-Research

In addressing the notion of training as co-research, I will not here provide an overview of the many dimensions of training in narrative therapy. I will restrict the focus of this discussion to some of the practices of training in narrative therapy that take the form of co-research. In taking this focus, many other aspects of training will be neglected - for example, the priority that is given to explorations of the tradition of thought that narrative ideas are situated in, the location of narrative practices in the broad fields of discursive practices, the emphasis that is placed on ethical, philosophical and political considerations, the review of micro-maps that orient therapists in re-authoring conversations, and the exploration and further development of the more specific practices and skills of this work. Some of these considerations I have discussed elsewhere (White 1989/90).

A significant part of training in narrative therapy occurs in contexts that are structured as definitional ceremonies. In these contexts, the training team works together with a faculty member in providing consultation to persons who seek consultation. At times these persons choose to attend these consultations unaccompanied, and at times with others who form their relationship networks - partners, members of families of origin and/or families of choice, friends, acquaintances, and so on. There are usually four stages to these consultations, and these I have outlined in 'Reflecting team as definitional ceremony' (White 1995b), and elsewhere in this book. In that each stage constitutes a re-telling of a telling, this provides opportunities for persons to experience a multiple contextualisation of the events of their lives, for engagement in the generation of rich descriptions of their personal narratives, and of the knowledges and skills of living that are associated with these.

In the first stage of this four-part process, two members of the training-group team up as co-therapists and engage the persons who are seeking consultation in a therapeutic conversation. The faculty member and the rest of the training group provide an audience to this consultation. In the second stage, this audience constitutes an outsider-witness group whose members engage each other in conversation about their responses to the first conversation. At this time, these members of the outsider-witness group have the opportunity to interview each other about these responses. During the second stage, it is the persons seeking consultation and the co-therapists who constitute the audience.

In the third stage, the co-therapists interview the persons seeking consultation about their responses to the conversation that took place between members of the outsider-witness group, with the faculty member and the rest of the training group again taking up the audience position. In the fourth stage of this definitional ceremony, the whole group (the co-therapists, the persons seeking consultation, the faculty member and the rest of the training group) meets to reflect on this series of conversations and to participate in the deconstruction of the specific contributions of the co-therapists and of the outsider-witness group, and, more generally, in the deconstruction of the therapeutic process.

The fourth stage of this ceremony also provides a forum for the exploration of ideas about other possibilities for this work This exploration often contributes to the generation of proposals for other conversations that might be had with the persons whose lives are at the centre of the consultation, conversations that might contribute significantly to the re-authoring of the stories of their lives and relationships. As this ceremony draws to a close, the persons whose lives are at the centre of these consultations are invited to respond to these proposals. Which of the proposals do these persons consider to have promise? Which of these do not seem that relevant to the issues of concern and the tasks at hand?

From this point, the co-therapy team takes the initiative in leading a critique of the work. This is a critique that is facilitated by the 'wisdom' that invariably becomes available through hindsight. Together, and at times in the presence of the persons whose lives are at the centre of this work, the co-therapists undertake the task of reviewing the videotape of the consultation. After so doing, they select a five-to-fifteen minute segment of the interview for the purposes of a microanalysis of the therapeutic conversation. Through this microanalysis, the co-therapists develop a critique of their contribution to the conversation, and of their expressions of therapeutic practice. As part of this critique, they develop ideas for the elaboration of the lines of conversation that contributed to rich descriptions of the stories of the lives of the persons who are at the centre of the consultation, and speculate about the points of entry for, and options for the generation of, other re-authoring conversations that might have been had. These are points of entry and options for conversations that went unnoticed by the co-therapists as they were participating in the flow of the conversation.

This critique also usually includes some reflection on what constructions and what power relations of the dominant culture may have been unwittingly reproduced in therapeutic conversation. For example, some co-therapists might determine that some of their responses reflect constructions that are informed by the taken-for-granted privilege that they enjoy as members of the dominant culture (if they are of this dominant culture), and that these responses are of the same order as those that have provided the very context for the generation of the problems of the persons seeking consultation. Or they might determine that in some of their responses they have unwittingly reproduced some of the power relations that are pervasive in contemporary society; for example those that relate to the politics of gender, sexual identity, class, culture, race, and so on. Before this critique is brought back to the training group, it is shared with the persons whose lives are at the centre of this work. Their responses are solicited and recorded.

The videotape segment chosen by the co-therapists, along with their critique and the responses of the persons seeking consultation to this, is then presented to the training group. This invariably provides the basis for a discussion that is generative of specific ideas for the furthering of the therapeutic conversation, and the basis for a further exploration of the practices and ethics of narrative therapy. In this way, the narrative work of the training group becomes more richly described.

This discussion is recorded in one form or another, and then taken back to the persons whose lives are at the centre of the consultation. The co-therapists then solicit further feedback, from these persons, on the various ideas and proposals from the group discussion: on how they might have responded to these options had they been incorporated in the consultation, on how these options might be taken up in further conversations, and on any critique of the reproduction of particular relational politics. At this time, the co-therapists also interview these persons about what they believe to be the real effects, on their lives and relationships, of their participation in the co-research itself - about how this has influenced their relationship to the problem for which they sought the consultation, and about their responses to the acknowledgement of the part that they have played in contributing to the ideas and practices of narrative therapy being more richly described.

It is important that all parties to this consultation understand that this critique is not a reproduction of what is usually referred to as criticism. In engaging in, and in leading this critique, the co-therapists are not stepping into the subject position of the familiar power relations of modern culture. They are not making themselves available to others to be judged against some norm of appropriate conduct. They are not submitting themselves or their work to the evaluations of others according to some criterion of correctness, against some measure of the 'right'. They are not taking a one-down position in relation to the rest of the training group, faculty members, or the persons who are seeking consultation. There is nothing about these practices of critique that constitutes an opportunity for others to participate in acts of assessment and regulation of the lives of the co-therapists. And these practices are not about exercises in 'self-government' either. There is nothing about these critiques that has the co-therapists engaging in the sort of self-surveillance and self-evaluation that would have them policing their own lives and work. These critiques are not reinforcing of the sort of calculated management of the self that reproduces contemporary forms of self-subjugation.

Take those aspects of the critique that have to do with the detection of options for re-authoring conversations that were not visible to the co-therapists in the flow of the conversation at the time of the consultation. This critique does not constitute a criticism. It does not provide the basis for some evaluation of the co-therapists against some image of how they might otherwise be in their work. It is understood that whatever it is that is detected in hindsight is, invariably, less available for detection in foresight - that, regardless of the apparent wisdom of the critique, this is a wisdom that is not usually available to foresight, and therefore it cannot speak to what the co-therapists should have done at the time of the consultation. And, although this critique is often further developed by the other members of training group and the faculty member, this is framed by an acknowledgement that, after the event of the consultation itself, it is not possible for anyone to determine how the persons at the centre of the consultation might have responded to any alternative proposals for re-authoring conversations.

Further, there is, in the training context, a general recognition that the relevance of any proposal that emerges from this discussion can only be determined by the insider group - that is, the co-therapists and the persons seeking consultation - and that the translation and expression of any proposal is the business of this insider group. This recognition is in keeping with the understanding that no other member of the group can translate such proposals into appropriate expressions on anyone else's behalf. Such translations and expressions will be determined by the meanings that the members of the insider group uniquely negotiate in relation to the proposals, and by the particularities of their lived experience.

And what of those aspects of the critique that are derived through attention to the power relations of culture, class, sexual preference, age, gender, and so on? These are aspects of the critique that are oriented by an acknowledgement that therapeutic practices can never be exempt from considerations about how these might be reproducing of these power relations. These are aspects of the critique that are oriented by an acknowledgement that therapeutic context is not a space that is free of the local politics of culture. This is an acknowledgement that stands, regardless of the extent to which, in the training course proper, explicit attention is given to the development of an exposé of these politics. Within the context of this acknowledgement, the reproduction, in therapeutic practice, of the power relations of culture is a phenomenon that can be expected. The identification of this phenomenon does not then provide a source of criticism or a foundation for shaming practices. Instead, it is understood that any critique that renders visible the reproduction of these power relations provides, for participants and faculty, a space for the exploration of alternative relational practices, and a window through which can be perceived the limits of their thought - one that in turn provides options, through inquiry, for the transgression of these limits. This transgression is the outcome of participants and faculty taking up options to step past the boundaries of the previously known.

The following account of co-research in the training context does not reflect all of the possibilities of co-research in this context - no single example could ever do so. But it will provide readers with a practical step-by-step illustration of this practice, and may act as a guide to preliminary explorations of training as co-research. In this example, Michelle Murphy and Mark O'Donahue make up the co-therapy team.

Kathy[1] (authored by Michelle Murphy)

I (Michelle Murphy) first met Kathy in February 1995 when she attended an eight-week 'Discoveries' group for survivors of childhood sexual abuse, a group based on narrative ideas. Kathy had only recently remembered the sexual abuse perpetrated on her by her father when she was a child. As Kathy spoke of this, she became increasingly conscious of the effects of the abuse on her life. This included: addiction to alcohol for twelve years, 'people-pleasing', feelings of worthlessness, uselessness and self-hate, suicidal thoughts, a sense of failure as a wife and as a parent to her two teenage sons, difficulty making friends, inability to continue her employment as a child-care worker, and overwhelming depression and despair that she thought to be abnormal. Kathy also worried that she was drifting apart from her family as, in wanting to protect others from the pain that she keenly felt, she had kept to herself the details of the memories of the abuse that she had been subject to.

At the end of the 'Discoveries' group meetings, Kathy felt she had made important changes. However, she also thought that she would benefit from some individual therapy sessions. After five of these sessions, I asked Kathy if she would be interested in attending Dulwich Centre with me as I was part of a training group there that I believed would provide an audience that would powerfully bear witness to her new story. After I explained how the proposed visit to the Centre would be structured, Kathy thought the idea to be a good one. She said that she believed that for her to overcome the anxiety of speaking in front of such a group would be a momentous achievement in itself.

Following the visit to the Centre, along with my co-therapist (Mark O'Donahue), I reviewed the videotape of our session. I then again reviewed this videotape alone, endeavouring to select five minutes of interview that I felt most uncomfortable with. This was difficult, as there seemed so many options to choose from! Then I attempted to deconstruct the chosen piece so that I might understand why it was that I felt uncomfortable. For example, I pondered over what particular ideas or beliefs were guiding my questions or restraining me from asking alternative questions at that point in time. I then brainstormed possible alternative questions that may have been more useful to ask Kathy. I documented the outcome of these explorations, so that I could take them to Kathy, and then back to the training group.

Not fully exploring potential unique outcomes

(a) Excerpt from interview

Kathy: *I started thinking 'Oh, am I never going to get better?' I was on the phone to Ian* [Kathy's husband], *crying, 'I don't think I'm ever going to get better, you know'. And then after that I just thought, 'Yes, I am'. It was like I just thought, 'I'm not going to believe that'. And so I've chosen not to believe that. Because, like, if I don't ever get better, there's not much point in doing all this, is there?*

(b) Critique

In critiquing the videotape I noticed that when Kathy made a positive comment or described a unique outcome, like the one above, this was often immediately followed up by a negative or qualifying comment that took the shine off the sparkling event just discussed. I have recently had a sense that such follow-up negative comments are often offered by the person in order to provide a 'more balanced picture' or so as not to be seen as 'blowing their own trumpet' - 'I am not as together as this sparkling event would reflect'. However, I have felt that this practice has often worked to disqualify or cancel out the power of the unique outcome to the person.

In watching the training tape of my work with Kathy I realised that, at some level, I was also influenced by the idea that a disqualifying statement cancels out a unique outcome. In the past I have responded to this situation by trying to find a different unique outcome, because I mistook this disqualifying statement as an indicator that the person did not believe this sparkling event to be unique or important. Consequently, I was implicitly reinforcing the idea that the sparkling event was not worthy, even though I had not taken the time to explore with the person the potential for this to be constituted as a unique outcome.

This realisation has provided me with two concrete ways in which I can improve my future work. The first is for me to be more vigorous in asking questions immediately following the expression of a sparkling event. Not waiting for the follow-up qualifier would be helpful in this, and would involve me in challenging the belief that it is always rude to interrupt. The second way would involve returning to a thorough exploration of the sparkling event regardless of the strength of the disqualifying statement. This would require me to challenge the idea that one negative event cancels out a positive event, and that once you have gone past these events in the flow of the conversation, you cannot go back.

When Kathy had spoken about her phone conversation with Ian in which she told herself she was going to get better, I could have asked questions that would have engaged both of us in an explorations as to whether this might be a unique outcome, rather than ignoring this information when it was followed by a qualifying comment. I have developed a list of possible alternative questions that I could have asked, and they are reproduced shortly.

Experiencing confusion

(a) Excerpt from interview

Kathy: *Recently I've got in touch with this anger and I haven't known what to do with it. It just sort of simmers there sometimes. I have realised that one thing I get angry about is when my rights are violated.*

I think I've got the right for the boys to listen to me. But if they don't, when that right is violated, I get really angry. But I'm angry at myself. I get really angry at myself and I think, 'Oh, gosh you're so useless - you can't do this'.

That's one thing that I've been thinking about quite a bit the last few days. I get really angry when I can't control the boys. I've also noticed that I control Ian quite a lot. I didn't realise how much I do this. I know that's quite a thing with people who have had abuse. I've been doing a lot of reading and it said that you can become quite controlling. I didn't realise I was quite controlling. But when I can't control something, then I think I'm useless, you know ... and so that anger comes up.

(b) Critique

At this point in the interview, I had felt very uncomfortable with Kathy labelling herself as controlling. I also believed that her feelings of anger were more connected with her rights being violated rather than her control being challenged. However, I didn't really have a clear idea on how best to address this discomfort. Additionally, I was confused about the connection between anger and uselessness. I was also confused about the sequence of Kathy's rights being violated, then feeling angry about this, then feeling angry at herself, then believing herself to be useless, then telling herself, 'You can't do this'.

In being confused in this way, I did not respond. I hoped things would become clearer as the conversation progressed. At this point, I was also concerned that I might be wasting everyone's time by not having clear intentions guiding my questions. Unfortunately, the conversation then progressed in an entirely different direction, and an opportunity was lost to explore this anger, which I know, from previous conversations with Kathy, was a very important issue for her at this time.

Upon reviewing the tape I realise that it might have been acceptable for me to express my confusion as genuine curiosity, and to invite Kathy to clarify these questions for me. Again, I have developed a list of alternative questions that I could have asked, and these are reproduced shortly.

Phone contact

Kathy called me the day after the interview at the Centre. I remember feeling a slight sinking feeling as she began to speak, as it has been my experience that non-scheduled phone-calls usually signified a crisis or set-back. To my delight, I was wrong. Kathy had called to tell me about a unique outcome that she was extremely excited about. Her boys had been fighting again. In the past she had felt responsible for their 'terrible behaviour' and had tried to stop them - her efforts had been reinforced by a neighbour who had threatened to move because of this fighting.

On this occasion, however, instead of yelling at the boys, and then feeling angry and useless because they ignored her, Kathy told them that they were allowed to continue their fight so long as they did this in the street, because they were violating her right to a non-violent home. Additionally, they were to explain to the neighbour their decision to fight with each other. One of her sons then retaliated by calling her 'useless', and said that she couldn't solve any problem. He then went to his room. Kathy followed up by telling him that she was not useless and was not going to take this on.

Kathy said that in the past she would have believed she was useless and would have cried the rest of the night. She then told me that her son later apologised for his behaviour. Kathy was ecstatic about this change in her thinking and actions, and had asked Ian whether he thought she should call me to share this news. Ian thought that I wouldn't have time to listen to such news because I was a very busy person. Fortunately, Kathy trusted her own judgement. She believed that I would appreciate the significance of this outcome.

After speaking with Kathy, I reflected on the meaning of the event of the phone-call. Kathy had not only thought about the importance of gaining an audience to these preferred developments, but she had actively engaged the people she knew would participate with her in this way. She had trusted her own judgement, and not privileged her husband's judgement as she would have done in the past when she was more caught up with 'people-pleasing'. This event also marked a turning-point in my practice. I felt I had been able to engage in conversations with Kathy that were transformative of her life without imposing knowledge. And the fact that she sought an audience to these developments suggested to me that she was now aware of steps that were available to her in the shaping of her own life. I chose to share this news with my colleagues, as the importance of sharing unique outcomes had been demonstrated so well to me by Kathy.

Interview with Kathy

My next meeting with Kathy was scheduled four days after the visit to the Centre to allow us to reflect upon the session and to give me time to complete my critique. We reviewed the videotape together, and I asked Kathy for her impressions of our conversations and of the reflecting team response.

Kathy said that she had realised during the session that 'I won't ever be hopeless again'. She had also become very clear about the fact that 'I'm not a controlling person', and that 'over-responsibility' was pushing her around in her relationship with her boys, making her feel angry and useless. Following a review of the videotape, Kathy said she could see that when her sons misbehaved this re-connected her to the self-blame she had experienced in relation to the abuse she had endured.

In regard to the responses of the reflecting team, Kathy appreciated the comment that she had experienced a double dose of training in being a 'people-pleaser' - from the abuse, and from her socialisation as a woman. Kathy had also really appreciated the fact that many members of the team had noticed that she had a good sense of humour. This was important to her, as she had believed other people perceived her to be a 'depressive'. This reflection had made her feel lighter and happier.

We then discussed my critique of the previous interview and pondered the alternative questions that I had developed. Kathy thought these questions could provide useful avenues to pursue in future sessions. In this review, Kathy planned some future directions:

(i) Viewing the videotape with her husband, mother and two best friends who had asked to see it.

(ii) Exploring anger and its connection to over-responsibility and to the violation of her rights.

(iii) Interviewing her mother on changes she has noticed in Kathy.

(iv) Collaborating with her husband in writing down a list of positive qualities expressed by her boys, and naming her contribution to the development of these.

(v) Working on 'taking the credit' for her achievements.

(vi) Telling her church group about these achievements.

(vii) Exploring the connections between her present anger and her past experiences.

(viii) Using the experience and knowledge she had gained through the process of therapy to help other women in similar situations.

Kathy found this shared reviewing of the videotape, and this planning of her future directions, very useful. At the end of this meeting, I gave her a copy of the videotape and a copy of the critique of this. This critique included a list of alternative questions that I had developed. I also distributed copies of the critique and questions to the training group, and together we reviewed these with reference to the segments of videotape that I had selected.

Kathy's responses to the alternative questions

Two weeks later I saw Kathy again and she provided me with typed answers to the alternative questions that I had proposed in the critique. At this time I also shared with her the training group's responses to the critique. Kathy had found this exercise very useful as she was able to answer the questions at her own pace, and felt that in responding to these she was taking an active part in her own therapy outside of our appointment times. She believed that this would lead to a faster recovery. One complication was that she was not able to clarify the meaning of some of the questions, but this did not bother her as she chose to leave these questions unanswered. I have included a sample of these questions here, along with Kathy's responses.

(a) Questions exploring the 'voice of hope'

Q. What would you call this voice that said 'Yes, I am going to get better'?

A: *I would call this voice the voice of hope.*

Q. How do you account for the strong appearance of this positive voice at this particular point?

A: *I'm sick of being negative and giving myself negative self-talk. I want to get better.*

Q. What enabled you to hear the clarity of this positive voice at this time?

A: *My depression doesn't last as long or isn't as deep. Therefore it has become easier to hear the positive voice more.*

Q. What does this positive voice reflect about your intentions for your life?

A: *I want to get better. I don't want this negativity to control me. I want more for me. I deserve better.*

Q. You sound quite clear that you have *chosen* to believe this positive voice ... What might that reflect about what role you think you play in your getting better?

A: *I realise I play a big part in getting better. No-one else can do the work for me or change my negatives to positives. They can help me see things clearer and offer me a different perspective, but I've got to be willing and open to it.*

Q. Has there been other times that this positive voice has been so strong?

A: *Yes. The day with Bradley when I chose not to accept him telling me that I was useless and couldn't solve anything.*

Q. What is the history of this positive voice?

A: *It has been very silent. As up till now I hadn't been aware of how much I have hated myself and the large part this has played in my thinking. I also wasn't aware there was another way of thinking. There has been a voice inside me that quite a few times during my growing up would cry out silently inside but never out loud. It was always an angry upset voice which couldn't understand why things had to be so. But I never voiced these feelings out loud. I guess I never fully acknowledged them and I pushed them back down.*

Q. Who out of all the people you know would be least surprised that you are listening to this positive voice?

A: *Probably my friends Judy and Cathy, as they have been the two people who I have not put on a front with, and have been totally honest with about my struggle over the last three years.*

Q. Was there a time in your past when you can recall hearing this positive voice?

A: *I remember very clearly once Mum said to me, 'you understand'. It was something to do with Alice needing more attention, and I stood there, with my hands clenched and in my mind I was going, 'I don't understand, I don't understand!' I was angry and mixed up but I didn't say this. This could have been my positive voice telling me I had rights to state my feelings.*

Q. Who in your past would be aware that you had this positive voice?

A: *I can't think of anyone who would have been aware of it because I never said anything and obviously my body language was not noticed or read correctly.*

Q. What qualities do you think they would say a person needs to be able to listen to this positive voice?

A: *I'll answer this from what I think a person needs. Qualities ... to be able to recognise the truth over a lie, to be willing to hear and try to accept the truth. Persistence to keep trying to overcome the negative thinking. Tenacity. Bravery ... to be able to face trying to overcome a lifelong way of thinking and acting. Strength to reach out for help when things aren't going so well.*

Q. If you were to turn the volume up on this positive voice, how might that affect your relationship with Ian and your boys?

A: *It would be good for our relationships. I would be more confident. I'd be able to relax with the boys more. I'd believe in myself and my abilities more (especially as a mother).*

Q. How might this increased volume of the positive voice affect your relationship with the negative voice/the voice that lies?

A: *The negative, lying voice would lose its power over me. Its ability to knock me low would be much less.*

Q. What difference might your boys notice in you when you are 'tuned in' to this positive voice?

A: *A more confident, happy, relaxed mother, who isn't on their backs about making noise etc. all the time.*

Q. How have you kept this positive voice alive throughout your life?

A: *Remember the truth and how far I've come. Fall back on all my strategies if I need them.*

Q. What will help you keep 'tuned in' and help you 'turn the volume up' on this voice during the coming week?

A: *I didn't know it was alive until recently, but I intend to try to keep it alive.*

Q. Who might you like to tell about your current project of keeping 'tuned into' this positive voice?

A: *Ian, Cathy, Judi, the boys and maybe Mum.*

Q. What might they gain from this consultation?

A: *Be more aware of my struggles. Perhaps help me recognise the positive and give me encouragement.*

Q. What might you gain from this collaboration?

A: *Understanding from them. Freedom to ask for help. Comfort knowing they love me and will help me.*

(b) Questions exploring my confusion about Kathy's understanding of her anger

Q. So when did you become aware of this voice saying your rights are being violated?

A: *Only after a counselling session we had where you asked me had I considered the connection (if there was one) between my rights and the anger. Until then I hadn't thought about my rights at all.*

Q. Is this the point that you realised you do have rights?

A: *Yes.*

Q. What difference did this make to you?

A: *I felt a bit surprised because I had never consciously considered the fact that I do have rights. It also made me more aware of what rights I do have. For example, to express my feelings, to be listened to etc.*

Q. How was this realisation connected with your anger?

A: *I realised I felt angry when these rights were violated. Even back as a child I was angry, but I couldn't express what was really inside, what I was really feeling. I've only recently realised, though, that this anger was connected with not being able to speak out about what I was feeling, and not being aware of my right to do so.*

Q. How were you able to unmask this second voice that was trying to trick you into believing you had no rights anyway?

A: *I guess you helped unmask it. Because I don't think I was consciously aware of it.*

Q. What is the relationship between feelings of anger and feelings of uselessness?

A: *I believe my feelings of uselessness come from viewing myself as weak for not standing up for my rights. I took on the false guilt for the abuse, then became a people-pleaser after being fostered. Maybe on a deep level I realised I had rights to say how I feel, to say what I want. But for fear of rejection I didn't do this, and therefore over a period of time I viewed myself as weak and pretty useless for not standing up for my rights, and felt angry at myself because of it.*

Q. What does your anger tell you?

A: *That I am not happy with having my rights violated and not happy with viewing myself in this way.*

Q. How have you felt about anger in the past?

A: *In the past I have not expressed it out loud. As a teenager I felt suicidal and as an adult I drank.*

Q. What might have been the purpose of this second voice that said you had no rights and therefore had no right to express anger?

A: *To keep false guilt alive. Keep my bad feelings about myself alive. To give me an excuse to turn the anger on myself because I saw myself as weak.*

Q. Kathy, I remember you saying that you have spent a lot of time when you were young trying to please people. What type of relationship would a person have to develop with anger to be a people-pleaser?

A: *Anger is always inside, because you do things for the wrong reasons. You aren't honest with yourself or others about your true feelings. You become angry, resentful and rebellious.*

Q. What sort of values and beliefs does someone have who gets angry when their rights are being violated?

A: *They must believe they have rights and that these rights are important.*

Q. How will this new understanding of the history of your anger and its connections make a difference to your view of your anger now?

A: *It will help me try and place the anger where it should be placed, instead of directing it at myself all the time.*

Q. How may this new view of anger affect your relationship with Ian and your boys?

A: *I hope it will help our relationship because I'll direct the anger where it should be directed or at least realise its origins and therefore hopefully not see myself as useless and weak.*

Q. What may people be seeing in you that is different from now on?

A: *Not sure about now, but as I try and externalise this anger away from me, I'll start feeling better about myself and then hopefully appear more confident and happy and relaxed.*

Q. How will you keep these positive changes to the forefront of your mind in the next few days?

A: *Talk to Ian and the boys about my anger, our neighbour, false guilt, etc. Try to get their understanding and support. Try to remember to put blame where it is due in a given situation and not on me. Try to remember to externalise it.*

I saw Kathy for three more sessions in which we discussed issues that had been highlighted by the viewing of the videotape, and her answers to the alternative questions that I had provided. I also consulted her about what she understood to be the consequences, to her life, of joining me and the team in this co-research. Kathy judged these consequences to be positive. She decided to enrol in a social work course, and saw this decision as a milestone - previously she had not thought herself intelligent enough for this. When I called Kathy recently to discuss this contribution to this book, she informed me that she had just earned another distinction, this time for a sociology essay on the social construction of gender roles in western culture.

Postscript (authored by Michelle Murphy)

The principles of narrative work need to inform the relationships between therapists generally, and between therapists in training, just as they do between therapists and the persons who seek consultation. This is a challenging goal, and when it is achieved there can be a shared acknowledgement that none of us are exempt from the reproduction of the ideas that provide the very context for the generation of the problems of persons seeking consultation. I have found this shared acknowledgement to be of immense relief, and it marked a turning-point in the progress of my work.

Previously, where I had been able to feel compassion for the persons I worked with, I had not been able to afford myself the same luxury. This shared acknowledgement also assisted me to develop the practice of critiquing my work, and contributed to a feeling of excitement at sharing my new understandings with colleagues, without being concerned that I would be subject to shaming practices. Critiquing my own work and brainstorming possible alternative questions with others in the context of training provides for safety in the exploration of new ideas and practices.

Critiquing my practice has also enabled me to unmask problematic 'taken-for-granted ideas and beliefs' about this work. For example, in reviewing the videotape I realised that I was influenced by the idea that 'the therapist should always know what direction their line of questioning was leading and have clear intentions in that respect'. The critiquing process allowed me to more strongly connect with narrative principles that emphasise instead transparency and the knowledges of the persons who are consulting us. This decreased my anxiety and has allowed me the freedom to be more exploratory and curious.

I used to think that to be a capable narrative therapist you had to have special abilities in deconstructing language and in rapidly articulating eloquent and pertinent questions, while keeping an outward appearance of comfort and composure. However, the collaborative nature of this training, and of this work more generally, has emphasised to me that some of the most valuable therapeutic experiences usually involve less spectacular qualities - qualities like thoroughness, persistence, patience, reflection and an appreciation of the importance of collaboration in the co-authoring of the stories of person's lives.

Note

1. This is an edited version of Michelle and Kathy's account of their co-research. Michelle and Kathy can be contacted c/- Northern Metropolitan Community Health Service, Tea Tree Gully and Ingle Farm Branch, Kylie Crescent, Ingle Farm 5098, South Australia.

PART III

The Ethic of Collaboration and Decentred Practice

Introduction

In the first two parts of this book I discussed and illustrated some of the options in the conception and the practice of therapeutic lives that can provide therapists with an antidote to burnout and to fatigue - engaging in re-membering conversations, the convening of definitional ceremonies, identifying the two-way nature of the therapeutic interaction and expressing this in taking-it-back practices, constructing supervision as a re-authoring conversation, and envisioning training as collaborative research. The experience of despair in this work can be taken as a signal for therapists to review these conceptions, to take steps to renew their engagement in these practices, and to enter into explorations that question the known limits of these practices in a quest to exceed the boundaries of them.

In part three of this book I take up a more general discussion of the ethic that informs the conceptions and practices proposed thus far. This is begun through further explorations of what it is that therapist despair 'speaks' to, and through a review of the notions of effective action that are associated with this despair. The discussion will then take us into the practice considerations of the 'ethic of collaboration' - practice considerations that assist therapists to break from despair, and that are reinvigorating of their work and their lives.

This review of the ethic that informs this work then turns to the hazards of the privileging of the micro-world of therapy over the macro-contexts of persons' lives. This privileging of the micro-world of therapy is the outcome of therapist-centredness, and it contributes significantly to experiences of burden, fatigue, and exhaustion. Therapist-centredness also establishes the conditions for a vulnerability to burn-out. Some of the decentred practices of narrative therapy are then discussed. These are practices that not only assist therapists to avoid the negative outcomes that are associated with therapist-centredness, but are also powerfully sustaining and provide opportunities for therapists to think outside of what they would otherwise have thought.

9

The Ethic
of Collaboration

I am here going to discuss further responses that are available to therapists in addressing the experience of despair, responses that take them into a more general exploration of the ethic that informs the conceptions and practices proposed thus far in this book. But before doing so, I again want to emphasise that the considerations addressed in this book are not the only ones relevant when it comes to matters that relate to therapists' experiences of despair. The emphasis on these considerations here does not constitute a denial of the extent to which therapists' experiences of despair can also significantly be an outcome of the politics and the economics of service delivery; of the unsatisfactory level at which service delivery is resourced, and of the extent to which this reproduces disadvantage in the lives of persons and groups of persons who are already struggling with inequalities in the distribution of resources in our communities; of the extent to which this places extraordinary demands on therapists because of their consciousness of the fact that the persons who are seeking services have few, if any, other options to turn to; of the extent to which agency structures, requirements, and priorities, often render them relatively unsupportive to therapists in their work.

The question of to what else it is that despair speaks to is a complex one.

There are many despairs. There is the despair that is experienced on the way to despondency, one that is an outcome of a longstanding consciousness of injustice, disadvantage and inequality - a consciousness that is not matched with a wider acknowledgement of this. There is a despair that is experienced on the way to resignation, one that is the outcome of a critique of injustice, disadvantage and inequality, and a non-acceptance of these circumstances - a critique that is not matched and joined by others in solidarity. There is a despair that is experienced on the way to capitulation, one that is the outcome of a history of acts of resistance to injustice, disadvantage, and inequality - action that is not supported by others. There is a despair that is experienced on the way to hopelessness, one that speaks to a history of a longing for and a desiring of a different world - a longing and a desiring that have gone unacknowledged and unsustained. There is a despair that is experienced on the way to depression, one that speaks to the preciousness of long-held dreams and visions - dreams and visions that are becoming lost to dishonour and to disqualification.

It is through active re-engagements with history that what it is that these despairs speak to can be identified. And it is through re-membering conversations and definitional ceremonies that what it is that these despairs speak to can be honoured. In regard to the realms of injustice, disadvantage, and inequality, it is through this re-engagement with history, and through these re-membering conversations and definitional ceremonies that therapists can be confirmed in their consciousness, joined in their critique, and acknowledged in their actions. And it is through these re-membering conversations and definitional ceremonies that therapists' longings, desires, dreams and visions can be powerfully authenticated. These practices that are identifying of what it is that the despairs speak to, and that establish forums that are acknowledging of this, provide an antidote to these despairs. This not only checks the drift into despondency, resignation, capitulation, hopelessness and depression, but rejuvenates so much that is on the other side of these despairs. This is as true for therapists as it is for the persons who consult them.

And yet there is a further consideration of the context of despair[1], one that overlaps and is interlaced with those referred to above. There is a despair that is an outcome of a deep frustration and a sense of personal failure that is experienced by many workers in their efforts to bring about changes in persons' lives. This is a despair that is significantly a product of living with taken-for-granted privilege and with its promise - of having access to the resources, to the opportunities, and to positions in structures of power that make it possible, in at least some domains of life, for therapists to achieve sought-after ends in a specified and usually brief period of time through singular and independent action. This is the notion of effective action that is associated with the ethic of control. Although many of the ideas and practices that shape therapeutic interactions are informed by this notion of effective action - workers are encouraged to speak of themselves as 'case managers', to construct their efforts to assist others in terms of 'engaging in interventions', to think of the shaping of 'service delivery' as 'targeting groups' and 'implementing strategies', and so on - rarely are the contexts of therapy ones that are at all favourable or amenable to accounts of effective action that are informed by this ethic of control.

For example, the excesses of power that are required to achieve sought-after ends through singular and independent action are generally not available to therapists - their work settings are generally under-resourced, they are subject to various organisational constraints to action, and, as front-line workers, they are not generally well placed in regard to positions of influence. As well, therapists often find themselves being consulted by persons whose circumstances of disadvantage render it impossible for them to relate to therapists' conceptions of action when these are informed by the ethic of control - their disadvantage denies them access to solutions of the sort that are informed by this ethic. Further, it is very often the case that it is these very circumstances of disadvantage that are significantly generative of, or complicating of, the problems for which persons seek therapy. Thus, therapist action that is informed by this ethic of control renders invisible the nature and the significance of the task that persons are undertaking in pursuing their determination for things to be different in their lives. This makes it more difficult, not less, for all parties to the therapeutic conversation to acknowledge all of the sparkling events of persons' lives, and of the therapeutic conversation itself, that might not directly speak to the known and sought-after ends, or that might not fit the criteria of what counts when measured against a specified time-frame for the achievement of these sought-after ends. As well, therapist action that is informed by this ethic of control is action that is accountable to 'global' norms and 'universal' principles, and not to the feedback of the persons who are seeking consultation. In regard to these considerations, for therapists to propose action based on the presupposition of privilege is to render all parties to the therapeutic conversation vulnerable to a sense of personal failure, and to the experience of despair.

An experience of despair that relates to a deep frustration in their efforts to bring about changes in the lives of the persons who consult them, and a sense of personal failure over the outcome of these efforts, can serve to alert therapists to their participation in the reproduction of the ethic of control. This experience of despair can provoke therapists to review, to question and to break from those notions of effective action that are informed by this ethic, and to engage in explorations of options for action that are informed by an alternative ethic - one that I will here refer to as the ethic of collaboration[2]. This ethic brings with it a different account of effective action. Effective action is recast. Rather than singular and independent action that is delivered into persons' lives, the ethic of collaboration recasts effective action as that which is determined and taken in partnership with others. And, rather than action that is measured by its success in the achievement of sought-after ends in a time-frame that is specified ahead of the initiation of this action, the ethic of collaboration recasts effective action as those actions that consist of the steps that contribute to the establishment of a foundation of possibility in persons' lives in the time that is required to take these steps.

This reading of despair and recasting of effective action provides for a reinvigoration of therapists' work. It contributes to possibilities for therapists to refuse the incitement that they experience to think about what they do in terms that are informed by the ethic of control, in terms that are expressions of the taken-for-granted privilege that is associated with this ethic. In joining collaboratively with persons in multiple actions that contribute to the foundations of possibility in persons' lives, therapists become relatively decentred in this work, and less likely to experience burden. In this recasting of effective action, many events of persons' lives that would otherwise be irrelevant, that would not otherwise 'measure up', are attributed a special significance. In this attribution, these events contribute to the foundations of possibility in persons' lives. In breaking from global principles and universal norms, it becomes possible for therapists to become more accountable to the persons seeking consultation in developing an understanding of the task at hand, in developing a consciousness of the contexts of persons' lives, and in developing an appreciation of what it is that constitutes the preferred real effects of the therapeutic conversation. All of this is an antidote to the despair experienced by therapists that is the outcome of action that is informed by the ethic of control.

Notes

1. This discussion of despair in the context of taken-for-granted privilege is substantially influenced by Sharon Welch's *A Feminist Ethic of Risk* (1990).

2. Sharon Welch (1990), deconstructs the notion of responsible action that is informed by the ethic of control, and proposes an alternative notion of responsible action that is informed by an 'ethic of risk'. I found her discussion of these accounts of responsible action to be very helpful; this discussion was informative, and provided me with a 'double description'.

10

Decentred Practice

In therapeutic practice, there is always the potential for the therapeutic context to become a micro-world that is split off from the contexts of persons' everyday lives. When this is the case, there is the risk that the particularities of what it is that is taking place in persons' day-to-day lives, in the macro-contexts of their everyday existence, will cease to have relevance to the therapeutic conversation, and in regard to feedback about the consequences of these conversations. This condition restricts the opportunities available for therapists to exercise any commitment they might have to identify and take responsibility for the real effects of their work on the lives and the relationships of the persons who consult them. Rather, their work becomes increasingly accountable to theories and principles that are considered to have universal relevance.

When the therapeutic context becomes a micro-world that is privileged over the macro-contexts of persons' lives, there is also a very considerable risk that the power relations that are significantly shaping of persons' lives - those that are structured around knowledge, gender, class, culture, race, age, and so on - will be rendered invisible in these therapeutic conversations. This contributes to a general diminishment of consciousness of these power relations, and to a reduction in the options for addressing them. This is so not only for the power relations of everyday life, but also for those that are reproduced in the therapeutic context. The privileging of the micro-world of therapy is invariably associated with an assumption that the therapist is somehow exempt from participating in the reproduction of these power relations in the therapeutic context.

Apart from these implications, the privileging of the micro-world of therapy has the effect of centring the therapist in this work - because of the power relation of therapy itself, when the micro-world of therapy is privileged over the macro-contexts of persons' lives, there is a significantly increased likelihood that the knowledges and the consciousness of the therapist will occupy the focal point of therapeutic conversations. In these circumstances, the knowledges and the consciousness of the therapist become exclusive, and the knowledges and the consciousness of power relations that are generated in the history and in the everyday contexts of persons' lives become marginal to the therapeutic endeavour.

Needless to say, developments of this sort are hazardous to persons seeking consultation. But they are also hazardous to therapists. For example, as therapy becomes less accountable to the everyday developments in persons' lives, and as it increasingly becomes a context for the reproduction of what is 'known' by therapists, it fails to provide opportunities for therapists to think outside of what they might otherwise have thought. This, over time, contributes to the therapist's knowledges and skills being more thinly described, and to a growing experience of monotony. As well, when this work becomes therapist-centred, the therapist is more at risk of finding it burdensome, and more likely to experience fatigue, exhaustion and burnout. Apart from these consequences, the privileging of the micro-world of therapy is isolating of therapists.

How are these negative consequences of the therapeutic endeavour to be avoided? Much of the forgoing discussion in this book has been devoted to the exploration of decentred practice, and it is these practices that diminish the potential for the therapeutic context to become a micro-world that is split off from the contexts of everyday life. This decentring provides opportunities for therapists to:

1. Exercise a commitment to identify and take responsibility for the real effects of their work on the lives and the relationships of the persons who consult them.
2. Contribute to an acknowledgement of the power relations of everyday life

that provide the context for the problems that persons bring to therapy.

3. Contribute to an acknowledgement of the power relations of therapy itself, and to steps that will provide opportunities for the monitoring of this power relation.

4. Establish therapy as a context in which the consciousness and the knowledges of the persons seeking consultation are at its centre.

Practices

I will now briefly review the practices that I have already discussed in this book that are decentring of the therapist. Following this, I will focus again on the practices of 'accountability' that are expressed in narrative work. I do this because, of all decentring practices, these are the ones around which there is the greatest potential for misinterpretation.

The practices of narrative work that are decentring of therapists and that have been discussed in this book, include:

(a) Re-membering conversations, which bring to the centre of this work the knowledges and skills that have been generated in the significant memberships of persons' lives through their histories, and that identify options for new memberships that are potentially generative of yet other knowledges and skills of living.

(b) The telling and re-telling of the stories of persons' lives that contributes to the multiple contextualisation of the actions and the events of life, that links the stories of persons' lives to shared purposes, values and themes, and that is generative of thick description.

(c) The structuring of forums of acknowledgement which engage outsider-witness groups in these tellings and re-tellings, and in the authentication of the preferred claims of persons' lives.

(d) Taking-it-back practices in which therapists embrace an ethical responsibility to identify the ways in which these therapeutic conversations are shaping of their work and lives, and in which they acknowledge the contributions of the persons who consult them to this.

(e) Practices of acknowledgement that do not reproduce the tradition of the applause, and that do not centre the therapist through acts of judgement in matters that relate to persons' lives.

(f) Practices of 'transparency' that engage therapists in situating their expressions by rendering visible, to persons seeking consultation, the different contexts of these expressions, including those of culture, race, gender, and class, and that encourage therapists to embody their speech acts by acknowledging the purposes and the lived-experience that shape these acts.

This list of decentring practices is by no means exhaustive, and many of the regular practices that inform the re-authoring conversations of narrative therapy also contribute significantly to the decentring of the therapist. These include: (1) the focus on the unique outcomes of persons' lives, (2) the acts of meaning-making that persons are invited to enter into in relation to these, including those that contribute to the naming of the counter-plots of their lives, and to the determination of new identity descriptions, and (3) those conversations that contribute to the rich description of the knowledges and skills of living that are associated with these counter-plots, and that these identity descriptions are emblems for.

Accountability

In decentred practice, the knowledges and consciousness of the therapist - and, for that matter, the knowledges and the consciousness of groups and associations of therapists - is not primary in providing a basis for a review of the real effects of the therapeutic conversation on the lives and the relationships of persons seeking consultation. Instead, it is the knowledges and consciousness of the persons consulting therapists that is primary to, and privileged in, these considerations.

This provides for a version of accountability that is bottom-up rather than top-down. Considerable attention has been given to the development of structures and processes that establish contexts for this version of accountability, much of which has been inspired by the folks of The Family Centre, in Lower Hutt, New Zealand. For example, structures and processes of accountability have been derived for therapists working in partnership with others across various interfaces, including those of race and culture (Tamasese & Waldegrave 1994) and gender (Hall 1994). Perhaps accountability is an unsuitable word for describing the initiatives that have been taken in the development of these structures and processes, for it often conjures images of top-down hierarchical processes that are evaluative and judging of persons. Rob Hall and Dallas Colley have referred to 'partnership accountability' (Hall 1994), and perhaps the bringing together of these terms goes some way in addressing this concern about this term.

This approach to accountability is not one that is associated with submission. It is not one that is accompanied by structures of top-down regulation. It is not one that is associated with practices of evaluation and judgement of the therapist. It is not one that has any connection to any form of institutional requirement. It is not one that has to do with the notion of the therapist 'not getting it right'. And it is not an added burden to the work of the therapist - it is not a hardship. Rather, it is an approach that emphasises a bottom-up accountability that is formed in collaboration with persons who consult therapists.

There are many possibilities for therapists to build in these sort of accountability processes in their work with persons who consult them. For example, I have discussed the emphasis that can be given to processes of accountability in work with men who have perpetrated abuse (White 1995a)[1]. In this work, attention is given to the exploration of knowledges about alternative ways of being for men, and to the development of specific proposals for action that are informed by these knowledges. Once established, feedback on these proposals is solicited from women and from children. This provides some check on the unwitting reproduction of those men's ways of being in the world that are oppressive to others. I have also discussed the development of processes of accountability in my work with women who have been subject to abuse by men (White 1995a). This accountability is often facilitated by engaging other women as consultants to the therapeutic conversations. Special attention can be given to the review of any developments in therapy that might be reproducing of the power relations of gender. These processes of accountability are decentring of the knowledges and of the consciousness of the therapist in regard to the many considerations of the real effects of this work.

As I have already stated, this approach to accountability is not burdensome, but one that is sustaining of therapists. In decentring the consciousness of the therapist, this version of accountability provides options for rendering visible, to them, the limits of their thought. It also provides options for therapists to think past these limits, thereby extending them. For example, this approach to accountability privileges the voices of persons, who are seeking consultation, on therapists' expressions that reflect taken-for-granted privilege, and that reproduce the marginalisation of others. These circumstances provide opportunities for therapists to link these expressions to their location in the social worlds of gender, race, culture, class, sexual identity, and age. In so doing, therapists come into a fuller knowing of the limits of who they are, and find before them opportunities to go beyond these limits.

In contributing to possibilities to think outside of what they would have otherwise thought, this version of accountability brings to therapists options to be other than who they were at the outset of their conversations with the persons who consult them. And, to reiterate, this is not a hardship. These experiences are a powerful antidote to monotony - under these circumstances therapists will not find therapeutic conversations to be the 'same old thing over and over again'.

Decentred practice and injustice

In narrative therapy, the therapist invariably explores options that structure their work in ways that are decentring of them and that contribute to the tellings and the re-tellings of the stories of persons' lives. These are not just any tellings and re-tellings, but ones that contribute to these stories being more richly described. These re-tellings contribute to powerful acknowledgements, and are authenticating of persons' preferred identity claims. When an outsider-witness group is engaged in these tellings and re-tellings, its members become conscious of their contribution to what I have referred to as, following Barbara Myerhoff, 'ceremonies of redefinition'.

Although all conversations with persons seeking consultation provide options for therapists to decentre themselves through the engagement of outsider-witnesses in these tellings and re-tellings, none require a greater privileging of this practice than do those conversations that address injustice. This is as true for therapists who are expressing the injustices of their own lives as it is true for the persons who consult therapists over injustices that they have experienced. Let me tell you a story.

Aileen[2] and Beatrice

Aileen attended a workshop at Dulwich Centre, and volunteered to be interviewed about her life and her work. At the outset of the interview, I inquired about the history of her presence in this workshop - asking questions about what it was about the ideas, values, and practices of narrative work that struck a chord for her, and about the history of these preferences in her own life. One of the most important resonances for Aileen was that narrative ideas offered the possibility for her to remember her mother's life, as well as her relationship with her mother, in a radically different way. Her first explorations of this possibility had been through her own writing as a student in the University of Waikato's narrative-based counselling program. Two years later, Aileen found reading the story of the Power To Our Journeys[3] group (Brigitte, Mem, Sue & Veronika 1996) to be profoundly moving and enabling for her.

Aileen proceeded to explain. Her mother, Beatrice, had been diagnosed with schizophrenia in the 1950s, and had been treated for this until her death in 1988. Beatrice's struggle with schizophrenia had not been easy for Aileen. Beatrice's life was centred around recurring episodes, frequent admissions to hospital, coping with the effects of different treatments, and struggles to reclaim her life and her family in-between all of this. Through this time, Aileen's relationship with Beatrice was dominated by confusion, bewilderment and a great deal of pain. At the time of Beatrice's death there was an uncomfortable distance between them. Aileen's memories of her mother were of someone inseparable from and dominated by schizophrenia. It was this that narrative ideas and the story of the Power To Our Journeys group had assisted her to challenge.

Upon reading the story of the Power To Our Journeys group, Aileen had several powerful realisations. She just knew that Beatrice could have contributed to the knowledges of this group. Beatrice would have had these insider knowledges. She also would have been able to join with the spirit of the group's work, and would have experienced joy in doing so. And Aileen also knew that this would have made a very great difference to her mother's life, and to her relationship with her mother.

Reading the story of the Power To Our Journeys group also contributed to an increased awareness of what her mother had gone through - disqualification, stigma and marginalisation. Looking back, Aileen could not recall one occasion upon which Beatrice had been acknowledged for her efforts, for her struggles, and for her desire to have a different life. And she could not recall one occasion upon which Beatrice had been seriously listened to.

Although these realisations had the effect of changing the terms of Aileen's relationship with Beatrice - and this was welcome, for it had opened possibilities for Aileen to experience the presence of Beatrice's voice in ways that contributed to her work and to her life - there was also distress associated with them. Aileen was left with a sense of some significant injustices that Beatrice had been subject to and that had never been acknowledged, let alone addressed.

In response, I said that I thought that it was never too late to acknowledge and to address injustices of the past. I located one of the documents of knowledge of the Power To Our Journeys group, and Aileen read this with the idea of determining in which parts of this Beatrice could have made a contribution - where might she hear her mother's voice expressed in the knowledges of this document? In this reading, Aileen found her mother's voice to be very present. With the approval of the Power To Our Journeys group, I have included this document here.

I then had a proposal to share with Aileen. Would it be acceptable to her for me to ask the Power To Our Journeys group to consider her mother for honorary life membership. Before receiving Aileen's response to this proposal, I was quick to inform her that I was not a member of the group - in fact I am not eligible - and that I couldn't speak to this proposal in a way that would influence the outcome. Aileen was delighted - no, joy-filled - over this proposal. The bestowing of an honorary life membership of the Power To Our Journeys Group to Beatrice would certainly be a wonderful outcome, but the fact that this was even being proposed was, of itself, an honouring of Beatrice. The proposal itself would provide Aileen with a sense that there had at last been some action that provided redress to some of the injustices that her mother had been subject to.

Naming the Backlash for What It Is

1. *In many ways the voices are quite predictable in their actions. Whenever we take a new step in life, or subject ourselves to pressures, or whenever we are having a really great time, like playing a beautiful piece of music and feeling proud of ourselves, the voices get unsettled. In fact engaging in anything that makes us a little bigger in the world disturbs them profoundly. We upset their applecart, and they then endeavour to exercise power over our lives to turn us back.*

2. *Whenever the voices get into a slinging match, and get on to our cases, they are engaging in what best could be described as a BACKLASH. They engage in this backlash in their attempts to silence us, to make us less visible in the world, and to recruit us into hurting our own lives and into destroying our connections with others. In these efforts the voices have to talk rubbish, but they can be very convincing nonetheless.*

3. *It is very important for us to recognise a backlash for what it is. These experiences of a backlash are not experiences of failure. They speak more to how our successes shake the voices up. Backlashes are proof of our success in the steps that we are taking in life. And naming the backlash for what it is, is to steal its thunder.*

4. *We are now all developing an increasing ability to predict these backlashes, and these predictions turn out to be particularly important. If we can predict a backlash ahead of its arrival, we can prepare ourselves for it. We can organise support from friends, plan nurturing rituals, stock pleasurable things to eat and drink, and do other things that have to do with pampering ourselves some. We can also get ready by going over with others the various tactics that we predict the voices may engage in to punish us.*

5. *In fact, the prediction of the backlash is quite vital, because if we are not prepared, then the backlash is more likely to have the effect that the voices desire. And this is not good. How would you like to be subject to five blaring radios, ten television sets tuned simultaneously to four TV stations, two video recorders running continuously and half a dozen symphony orchestras powering away and not being able to tune any of these in quite well?*

6. *Although these steps that we take in life do make us vulnerable to these backlashes, we do know that they challenge and eventually shrink the voices' power, even if we don't realise this at the time. We know that 'from little things big things come' and to take the steps that we decide to take (not ones that have to do with outside expectations that a person should determine their worth by doing things like going to work or showering) is all that is important.*

7. *We've been very creative in the work that we have done together and separately to diminish the power of these backlashes. For example, one of our group has tried understanding, and developing an appreciation of the fact that these voices are like people who have hassles and take it out on others. Another member of our group used realisations that the voices really couldn't get her because they have no arms and legs. Yet another group member decided to go on the initiative, and went out looking for them, and even cooked meals for them. But they never rocked up. We all have engaged in humour as an antidote, and this has at times been very effective. Other tactics that we have developed have been included in previous documents.*

8. *We hereby declare that we have the knowledges that are necessary in handling backlashes, and we will remain committed to predicting these and naming them for what they are in our on-going work to reclaim our lives.*

At the very next Power To Our Journeys group meeting, I shared Aileen's story with the group. I first talked with the group members about Aileen's connection to their story, and the link between this and her presence in the intensive training workshop at Dulwich Centre, providing as best I could an account of how their story rippled into Aileen's relationship with her mother, and into her life and her work. I also said that Aileen wanted this proposal to be considered entirely on its merits, and that she understood that I had no voting rights on this or anything else that came before the group. I also informed them that Aileen would not have wanted it any other way, that she did not have any expectations about the group's deliberations, and that the proposal, of itself, was healing of some of the injustices that Beatrice was subject to, and was strengthening of their connection with each other - Beatrice's voice was already more available to Aileen.

The members of the Power To Our Journeys group responded in turn to Aileen's story, which had moved them all. The decision to offer Beatrice a life membership was unanimous. I asked the group members if they would be prepared to catch me up on what it was that had contributed to this decision. Their responses, as ever, were very personal. For example, one group member said that to offer Aileen's mother an honorary life membership was doing something to address the terms of her relationship with her own mother, who had died several years ago, going to the grave still believing that she had somehow caused her daughter's condition. During this conversation about the proposal to offer Beatrice an honorary membership, this group member felt that she was achieving something that had seemed just so impossible to her in the latter years of her mother's life - she was putting to rest all of the self-accusations that had so plagued her mother's life, and breaking from her own anguish over this.

Aileen's story was substantially also a re-telling of the story of the Power To Our Journeys group, a re-telling that provided the basis for yet further tellings that more richly described the work of the group, its identity, and the lives of the members. This was partly facilitated through the introduction of questions like: 'What is it like for you to experience the ripples of your work going out into the world and touching the lives of others in the way that it does?' 'How does knowing that you have contributed to changing the terms of Aileen's relationship with her mother in the way that you have affect the image that you have of your work?' 'How does this affect your sense of who you are as people?' 'In playing this part in addressing the injustices experienced by Beatrice in this way, what does it say about the spirit of your work?' In response to these and other questions, group members derived yet new descriptions of their work and their lives.

I will include here a copy of the letter that went out from the group members to Aileen, notifying her of the unanimous decision to offer Beatrice an honorary life membership of the Power To Our Journeys group. A copy of the certificate of membership that was to be given to Aileen to hold on her mother's behalf was sent along with the letter, and I am also including a copy of this here. Aileen accepted the offer on Beatrice's behalf, and wrote to the group informing them of the significance of this:

Dear Aileen,

Michael told us about your mother, Beatrice Devline, and about some of her struggles in life. We understand that for most of her life she kept trying against all odds - against disqualification, stigma, prejudice, ignorance and rejection, and against the injustices that were perpetrated in the name of treatment.

The fact of Beatrice's struggle is not lost to us. In hearing her story, we have become more able to speak about what it is that would otherwise be silencing of us. We draw sustenance from what we know of the story of her life.

We have unanimously decided to offer your mother honorary membership in the Power To Our Journeys group. Please let us know how you think Beatrice might have responded to this invitation, and what you think she might have wanted to be said about her life.

We look forward to hearing from you.

Yours sincerely,
Power To Our Journeys group.

CERTIFICATE
of
Honourary Membership
of the
"Power To Our Journeys" group

This is to acknowledge the spirit of Beatrice Devline's struggle to navigate life's journey in a world that didn't affirm her. It is also to honour the special knowledges that she developed and put to this task. The Power To Our Journeys group are at one in solidarity with Beatrice in this struggle and in the development of these knowledges.

Beatrice Devline
is hereby granted honorary membership
in the
"Power To Our Journeys" group
We welcome her and celebrate her journey

Signed; ....
Spokesperson: ....
Date: ....

Dear Power To Our Journeys group members,

I was very moved to receive the honorary membership certificate to the Power To Our Journeys group on behalf of my mother. The certificate is being framed and I will hang it beside a portrait of my mother, aged nineteen, painted by her father before she left Scotland as a war bride in 1946.

I think my mother, too, would have framed this membership invitation and hung it in pride of place. She would have been moved to tears by your invitation as for her it would have been recognition that she was not alone in her struggles and that other people had some understanding of what she had achieved through her struggles. That would have been a very special recognition for her. I imagine she would have felt a great deal of joy in being linked to your group and would have drawn further sustenance from the special knowledges that you all have. This invitation too would have been recognition of her creativity, her courage and her knowledge; special things about her which sustained her. I have an image of my mother waving this certificate under the noses of some of those who discounted her!

My mother, I believe, wanted her life remembered in several ways. Foremost would be her ability to connect with and support those around her who were also disqualified and rejected by others. Her warmth and practical care spoke of a different meaning of care to the care often spoken of by some professionals. She would have liked her resilience to be remembered; the steps she took in her life to stand for herself and what she knew, which drew on both her creativity and her courage. Many failed to recognise the significance of those steps or discounted them, but she would want those steps remembered as evidence of her resilience. Sometimes these were huge steps, like taking my brother and me as young children back to her family in England when the voices first asserted their power. Sometimes the steps might be seen by others as small, like cooking a meal, but such steps were all part of her achievements.

This invitation has huge significance for me as well. There have been many invitations to me in the past to see my childhood and relationship with my mother in terms of deprivation and damage. But I have come to stand very strongly against such descriptions. Reading your article last year, my conversation with Michael, and this certificate all add strength to that stand. It is with pride that I wear one of your T-shirts and explain to those who ask what it means, that my mother is now an honorary

member of the group. With each conversation it is my hope that I am
making her life and your group more visible.

With thanks and love,
Aileen.

Notes

1. For further discussion of therapeutic responses to men who perpetrate abuse, see Alan Jenkins' (1990) *Invitations to Responsibility.*

2. Aileen Cheshire, School Counsellor, Selwyn College, Kohimaramara Road, Kohimaramara, Auckland, New Zealand.

3. From the Power To Our Journeys group:

    This is a support group for people who struggle through their lives hearing voices. It is an empowering group enabling our stories and our 'insider' knowledges to be heard and recognised. We have developed close and respectful friendships that help us through the hard times. Each step we take together is about our survival, but these also have to do with justice - because there is so much injustice around issues in the mental health field that needs to be addressed. We also pick daisies, fly kites, eat chocolates, and sponsor dolphins.

PART IV

Casting
Narrative
Therapy

Introduction

There are interpretations of narrative therapy that read it as a proposal for a recycled structuralist/humanist psychological practice. This reading takes narrative therapy into the discourses of psychological emancipation, and casts it as a liberatory approach that assists persons to challenge and overturn the forces of repression so that they can become free to be 'who they really are' - so that they can identify their 'authenticity' and give true expression to this.

This casting of narrative therapy is in direct contradiction to the tradition of thought and practice that has informed its development - that is, the tradition of poststructuralist thought. It is a casting that is generally informed by structuralist concepts and practices, and more specifically by the repressive hypothesis and the psychologies of emancipation that are associated with this hypothesis. Because of this, and in order to distinguish the proposals of narrative therapy from what it is at times taken to be, I have included here a discussion of the repressive hypothesis and the notion of psychological emancipation.

Although the term 'repression' is not so much in vogue today, and doesn't have the common usage that it did in recent history, the idea itself permeates most of the mainstream psychological theories, and has also become a taken-for-granted idea not just in popular psychology, but in popular culture generally. It is my hope that this discussion will be of some assistance in untangling the ideas and practices that I have referred to here in this book, and in other places, in the name of narrative therapy, from those ideas and practices that are informed by these structuralist conceptions.

I have placed this section, which untangles structuralist and poststructuralist thought, last in this book. I have chosen to do so because this discussion doesn't necessarily make for easy reading. It is my hope that, because there are echoes of this discussion in much that I have already written in this book, readers will be sufficiently acquainted at this point with some of the distinctions around structuralism and poststructuralism to engage with this last section. Although narrative therapy is constituted of a body of skills - there is a 'know-how' that can be clearly identified - it is also constituted by poststructuralist thought. I believe that not to grasp the structuralist/ poststructuralist distinction, and to therefore interpret narrative therapy as proposal for a recycled structuralist/humanist psychological practice, has specific consequences - consequences that contribute to therapists' work and life being thinly described. Several of these consequences are reviewed in the discussion in this section.

Because poststructuralist thought and practice are directly challenging of many taken-for-granted and cherished notions about life and about identity, those who are interested in exploring this tradition can find it quite confronting. However, this is a worthwhile challenge. These explorations open possibilities for us to break from reproducing, in our work and in our lives, the grand narratives of human nature that are ever-present in contemporary culture, and open options for action in the therapeutic context and in the world that could not otherwise have been entertained. Some of these options are in the form of questions that take therapists into conversations, with the persons who consult them, that are significantly shaping of their own lives in ways that they could not have imagined. I believe that such questions are only available to therapists when they can break from the pursuit of 'uncovering' the 'truth' of life, and from the grand narratives of human nature of contemporary culture that incite this pursuit.

The last section of this chapter explores such options by locating narrative work in poststructuralist thought and practice, and by reviewing the implications of this in terms of how it orients therapists to their work and to the world more generally.

Much of the discussion in this section is informed by my reading of Michel Foucault, and it would be impossible for me to fully cite him here[1]. Foucault, a French intellectual who regarded himself to be a Historian of

Systems of Thought, made a very significant contribution to critical thought and poststructuralist studies, the subject of much of which was the professional disciplines.

Note

1. My understanding of Foucault's thought is principally informed by the reading of primary sources (1965, 1973a, 1973b, 1979, 1980, 1984, 1987). However, there are secondary sources that provide good introductions to, and overviews of, this thought. For example, I recently happened across Jon Simons' *Foucault and the Political* (1995), which provides an excellent review of Foucault's later work.

11

Narrative Therapy and Poststructuralism

The will to truth, the repressive hypothesis, and the emancipation narrative

Foucault (1988a, 1988c) traces the history of the central philosophical question of the contemporary era in western culture: 'What is the truth of who we are?' This question of the contemporary era he associates with the production of a 'will to truth', which displaced what could be described as the 'will to self-renunciation' of the era before it.[1] This will to truth informs a great incitement for us to know and to speak of the 'truth' of who we are - of the essence of our being, of our human nature. This has become a paramount concern of both professional and popular culture.

In recent history, this will to truth has been coupled to the repressive hypothesis. The great lament of contemporary culture is the outcome of this joining: 'How Comes It that we all start out Originals and end up Copies?'[2] This lament has a rising trajectory that can be traced through the past three hundred years, and is perhaps reaching its zenith in late 20th-century western culture. A multitude of contemporary versions of this lament pervade popular culture. In most everything that has to do with questions about modern life, inquiry is informed by this lament: 'What is it that stands in the way of us becoming truly who we really are?' 'What is it that frustrates and blocks the expression of our true human nature?' 'What are these forces of socialisation that obscure who we uniquely are?'

The terms of these and many other similar questions that are prompted by this lament foreshadow those responses that might be entertained. It is repression, in various of its guises, that is found to be guilty (Foucault 1984). It is repression that obscures our deepest wishes and desires, those that speak to the truth of our human natures. It is repression that hides from us the truths about who we are. Repression is not once guilty, but doubly so. Not only does it obscure the truth of our human natures, it is also the force that frustrates the expression of this truth. It is repression that keeps us from personal fulfilment, that complicates our efforts to return to the original. It is repression that is the force that stands in the way of us achieving a life that is true to our human natures. And, more than this: in that the frustration of our authentic needs and deepest desires leads to all manner of maladies, repression is thrice guilty.

This 'guilty' verdict provides the basis for responding to the urgent questions of the will to truth, those questions that speak to priorities that override all others: 'How do we become what we are?' 'How could I live a life that is an expression of my authenticity?' 'How can I actualise my real self?' The answer goes: 'Through liberating the self from the forces of repression'. It is by challenging repression that we are freed to become who we truly are. Here, the narrative of the emancipation of human nature is joined to the couple formed by the will to truth and the theory of repression[3]. It is said that it is through challenging repression in the name of personal emancipation that the truth of who we are will be revealed to us. It is through this challenge that we can escape what has been imposed on our identities, and arrive at the foundation of the self - that is, 'true personal knowledge'.

This joining of the will to truth, the repressive hypothesis, and the emancipation narrative has spawned the production of many modern knowledges and practices of the self and of life, knowledges and practices that are all in the service of living a life that is free of repression. These include the knowledges of human 'needs' and practices for the fulfilment of these needs. But nothing is settled. There is an ever-rising clamour of claims and counter-claims about the nature of the true self, and of proposals and counter-proposals for how this might be set free. It is everywhere that these claims and proposals are echoed - in the popular magazines, in the burgeoning self-help literature, in the selling of consumer products, in media advertising, in the promotions of the self-improvement industry, and so on. Today, these claims and proposals know no bounds - even the processes of aging are understood to be repressive of the real self, one that is expressed in youthfulness, and even this can be recovered through certain processes.

The workings of this will to truth are visible in their particularities in the ongoing development of technologies for the measurement of persons' lives against images of the 'ideal' and 'natural' states of being, and for the documentation of these lives - technologies that are becoming ever more sophisticated. These are the technologies that make possible the assessment and evaluation of individual lives, and that recruit persons into self-surveillance and self-judgement.[4]

But this great lament is not just a preoccupation of popular culture. Foucault (1973b) links the elevation of this will to truth with the success of the professional disciplines in the production of the great meta-narratives of human nature and of human development, those that inform the universal theories about life that are held to be true regardless of culture, class, gender, race, circumstance, place, era, etc. This will to truth has inspired the development of formal systems of analysis of human life that make possible the interpretation of it and its reduction to formal categories that speak to the truth of its core elements.

Poststructuralist inquiry and the constitution of lives

Our inquiries into matters of life do not have to be informed by the will to truth. We do not have to be mesmerised by the great lament of contemporary culture: 'How Comes it we all start out Originals and end up Copies?' Much of what has been proposed in this book offers a challenge to the inquiry into life that is informed by this will to truth, and resists this lament. In our questions about life, we do not have to observe what Foucault called the 'formal ontology of truth'. In breaking from this will to truth, we can engage with a different class of questions - questions about what we are today. This is a class of questions that is informed by a tradition of thought that is often referred to as poststructuralism.

> *This question is very different from what we call the traditional philosophical questions: What is the world? What is man? [sic] What is truth? What is knowledge? How can we know something? And so on. The question, I think, which arises at the end of the eighteenth century is: What are we in our actuality? You will find the formulation of this question in a text written by Kant. I don't pretend that the previous questions about truth, knowledge, and so on have to be put aside. On the contrary, they constitute a very strong and consistent field of analysis, what I would like to call the formal ontology of truth. But I think that a new pole has been constituted for the activity of philosophising, and this pole is characterised by the question, the permanent and ever changing question, 'What are we today?' And that is, I think, the field of historical reflection on ourselves.* (Foucault 1988b, p.145)

These poststructuralist questions about 'what we are today' inform an inquiry into how lives are constituted through the knowledges and practices of culture - into how it is that the knowledges and practices of culture inform our modes of life and thought. It is through poststructuralist inquiry that we can break from the mission to discover something about 'given' nature, and instead work to develop some understanding of how it is that we are produced as subjects. It is through poststructuralist inquiry that we can explore the ways in which identity, subjectivity, and relationship are all products of cultural knowledges and practices.

In breaking us from the will to truth, and from explorations into the veracity of the various truth claims that are informed by this will, poststructuralist inquiry makes it possible for us to explore the history of these claims about the truth of human nature, and the practices of life that are associated with such claims. This is an inquiry that renders visible the use to which these claims have been put. This is an inquiry that contributes to the identification of the real effects of these claims and practices in the constitution of life.

So, where does poststructuralist inquiry take us when it contributes to the deconstruction of contemporary assertions about human nature, about the repressive hypothesis, and about the narrative of psychological emancipation? It takes us into considerations of how it is that lives are actually constituted through this triumvirate - to how persons' lives are shaped by these notions and the practices of living that are associated with them, to how these notions and practices style acts of living. As well, poststructuralist inquiry provides for an exposé on the extent to which this is a particularly insidious achievement. The joining of claims about nature, repression and psychological emancipation powerfully ties persons to the reproduction of our cultures 'truths' of identity in their pursuit of liberation - persons are ever more tightly bound to their subjectivities through their efforts to liberate themselves. These are the subjectivities that are specified by these 'truths' (Foucault 1984). Because the reproduction of these 'truths' of human nature is in the name of freedom, the constitution of our lives through these 'truths' is naturalised, and this hinders the development of a consciousness of this constitutive process, and exempts persons from any engagement in the monitoring of the real effects of these 'truths' in the constitution of their lives.

Poststructuralist inquiry exposes the ruse - that, in the name of psychological liberation, persons are incited to reproduce the dominant forms of individuality of contemporary culture (Foucault 1984). It is through poststructuralist inquiry that what this triumvirate of claims disguises becomes visible. It is through poststructuralist inquiry that notions of 'growth', 'self-actualisation', and 'fulfilment' are recast as emblems for certain modes of life and thought that are most venerated in contemporary western culture. Under poststructuralist analysis, it turns out that it is not repression that obscures the truth, but that it is the repressive hypothesis that actually obscures the fact that persons are being incited to reproduce the subjectivities that are specified by the 'truth' (of human nature).

In summary, poststructuralist inquiry contributes to a deconstruction of the systems of interpretation and understanding that constitute the repressive hypothesis. Under poststructuralist inquiry, these systems do not reveal elements that are at the core of the self, and the associated technologies of documentation and measurement do not accurately classify these elements. Instead, the self, and what it is that is taken to be human nature, is the product of these systems of interpretation, and of these technologies of documentation and measurement. These systems of interpretation and these technologies make life up. They constitute the modern subject; they specify subjectivity. They also have certain effects on therapeutic practice, and it is these that I will now review.

The will to truth, the repressive hypothesis, and the emancipation narrative: effects on therapeutic practice

(i) The confirmation of the known

When our work is oriented by the will to truth, by the repressive hypothesis, and by the theory of psychological emancipation - by the goal of assisting persons to become who they really are once they are free to be so - it becomes virtually impossible for us to orient ourselves to all of those events and expression of persons' lives, including those expressed in the therapeutic context, that don't fit with the grand narratives of human nature, that don't reproduce culturally venerated ways of being and thinking. All of those expressions of life that contradict the theory of repression, that cannot be read into the narrative of psychological emancipation, and that do not qualify as authentic expressions of human nature - that don't fit with these normative proposals for life - are lost.

When this is the case, all of these events and expressions - the unique outcomes and the exceptions of life - that potentially provide for a point of entry to explorations of other ways of being and thinking in the world, to other knowledges of life and skills of living, pass like blips floating across the screen of consciousness before disappearing off the edge into a vacuum. All of these events and expressions that otherwise might be rendered significant in regard to what it is that is happening in persons' day-to-day lives don't rate a mention. And with this goes opportunities for us to join persons in acts in the formation of selves that contradict those that are venerated in dominant culture - acts in the formation of the sort of selves that are expressions of resistance to much of that which is specifying of the 'authentic' selves of the contemporary world.

Under these circumstances, rather than finding, in this work, occasions for stepping outside of the boundaries of what is familiar and known, occasions for the challenging of the limits of our thought, we are confined to a reproduction of, and a confirmation of, all that which we are already familiar with and already know. As an advocate of the known, we experience a special burden. We have placed ourselves at the end of history[5], and become frozen in time. The door is closed on opportunities for our work to become something that it wasn't, and for us to become other than who were. Our lives become thinly described, as does our work.

(ii) Obscuring acts of meaning

Not only do the will to truth, the repressive hypothesis and the theory of personal emancipation make it difficult for us to engage with events and expressions that don't fit with the grand narratives of human nature, it also renders invisible the extent to which persons are active in the shaping of their lives as they live their lives. Expressions of life are expressions of lived-experience that are shaped by the meanings ascribed to this experience, and by the practices of life and relationship that are associated with these meanings. These expressions in turn contribute to lived-experience - expressions of life are constitutive of what life is.[6]

Although the meanings that are shaping of expressions of lived-experience are inevitably historical and cultural, they are not strictly determined. There exist multiple and competing systems of understanding of life and of the world, and the fixing of meaning is an achievement that is arrived at through personal and community acts of negotiation - meaning is determined in the social domain of life, and contestation of meaning is a feature of this domain. On this account, persons are active participants in the shaping of their own lives, and of the lives of others.

In rendering us oblivious to the extent to which persons are active in shaping their lives as they live their lives, the repressive hypothesis and the theory of personal emancipation rule out possibilities for us to join persons in the development of some appreciation of the extent to which they are active in the negotiation of meaning, of the extent to which they are participants in the production of their accounts of their experiences of life, and of the extent to which this is an activity that is shaping of their own lives. This also rules out the possibility for us to join with persons in the exploration of alternative meanings that contradict those that are routinely reproduced in their lives - it shuts the door on a curiosity about alternative meanings, and the development of a fascination with these.

The will to truth, the repressive hypothesis and the theory of personal emancipation also rule out options for us to acknowledge our own participation in the negotiation of meaning, in the shaping of our own lives and work, and in the shaping of the lives of the persons who consult us. This forecloses on options for us to engage knowingly in acts of meaning in the re-making of our lives and our work - on options to experience a greater sense of personal agency.

(iii) Constrained lives

The bringing together of this question of truth, the repressive hypothesis, and the theory of personal emancipation, has the effect of creating a web that is powerfully constraining of therapeutic interaction. The therapeutic context becomes one for the challenging of repression, and for the reproduction of the 'truths' of human nature. And doing so in the name of personal liberation establishes a ruse that disguises what is actually taking place - the fact that therapy is a context for the reproduction of those 'truths' that are constitutive of the grand narratives of human nature and human development.

When this is the case, in our work, and in our personal lives, we become ever more tightly bound to those forms of life and thought that are informed by these truths. In pursuing this agenda to release nature from what has been constraining of it, we become unwitting accomplices in the reproduction of the dominant and culturally sanctioned versions of identity, of the popular and revered forms of personhood, of the most familiar and mainstream subjectivities.

For the persons who consult therapists, the outcome of this is a renewed commitment to those ways of being that are championed by the 'truths' of the grand narratives of human nature, a redoubled engagement with the practices of self and of relationship that are associated with these 'truths', and a significant narrowing of options for other ways of thinking and being in life. For us, as therapists, the outcome of this includes increased constraints on options to acknowledge the expressions of the persons who consult us, and on options for us to acknowledge the alternative expressions of our work. As well, a renewed commitment to this question of 'truth' is significantly limiting of the possibilities in regard to our ways of being with the persons who consult us.

(iv) The marginalisation of ethics

The ruse that represents therapy as a context for the emancipation of human nature discourages a review of the consequences of the therapeutic encounter itself, and a monitoring of the real effects of those ways of being and thinking that are privileged as an outcome of this encounter. Defining therapy as a process that is challenging of repression and liberating of nature renders unnecessary a review of the real effects of this on the lives of persons who consult therapists, and renders unnecessary any ongoing review of the real effects of this on the lives and the work of therapists. When therapy is established as a context for the identification and expression of the truths of human nature, success is determined by the extent to which therapy contributes to things being as they ideally should be in the lives of persons who consult therapists - by the extent to which persons have arrived at a point at which their lives reflect the states of being that are expressions of the norms, rules and laws of this nature.

Taking these norms, rules and laws of human nature as a foundation for our work, as therapists we exempt ourselves from considerations of personal ethics - from an acknowledgement of and a responsibility for the real effects of this work on the lives and relationships of persons who consult us. When therapy is about releasing human nature from what binds it, when it is about the recovery of authenticity, there is nothing to be monitored. In these circumstances, questions about therapeutic practice, about the structures of practice, and about the ways in which this practice and these structures are constitutive of the lives of all parties to the therapeutic interaction do not occur - these questions are irrelevant.

The outcome of this for persons who consult therapists is not trivial. This outcome includes the unquestioned performance of those ways of being that are championed by the grand narratives of human nature, the further erosion of narrative resources in the ascription of meaning to one's experiences of life, and a diminishment of a consciousness of one's participation in the production of one's own life. The outcome for therapists is the same. And, as well, this exemption from any requirement to address the ethical considerations in this work reduces the opportunities for us to be accountable to the persons who consult us, rather than to the 'truths' of human nature. This decreases our options to address the possible negative effects of the power relation of therapy, and dispossesses us of a source of renewal in our work - of what it is that might contribute to our work becoming other than it was.

(v) Concealing the power-knowledge relation

The bringing together of the 'truths' of human nature, the repressive hypothesis, and the narrative of emancipation obscures the fact of power. It is to propose that 'truth' is opposed to power. It is to propose the arrival at some state of being associated with ways of knowing that are free of the operations of power, free of techniques of the self that are forming of this self, and free of the practices of relationship of contemporary culture.

This proposal obscures the link between knowledge and power. This proposal obscures the fact that the production of 'truth', and its reproduction in persons' lives, is made possible through relations of power (Foucault 1979, 1980). When this link between knowledge and power is obscured, it becomes impossible for us, as therapists, to identify the ways in which the 'truths' of human nature are taken up in relations of power, and to establish therapy as a context for reviewing the real effects of these power relations.

(vi) The dissolution of history

The joining of the truths of human nature, the repressive hypothesis, and the narrative of emancipation inevitably casts history in problematic terms. Repression is the stuff of historical forces. In order that persons might become free to be who they truly are, history is something to be undone, to be resolved. And in that the outcome of resolving the forces of history is the achievement of some ideal state - a life that is an expression of the 'truths' of human nature - history becomes something not only to be resolved, but to be dissolved (Foucault 1984). In reclaiming the 'original' through the resolution of history, history ceases to have relevance. Having arrived at the original through the resolution of history, the goal is for a dissolution of history so that the future might be the same as the present - a present that is impervious to the ravages of time. This is a present that will be forever, one in which time would cease to have any bearing on how life is lived. Thus, the achievement of this ideal state of being is dependent on the end of history.

In practice this restricts us and the persons who consult us to deficit-centred or problem-saturated accounts of history - not just of the history of the persons who consult us, but also of our histories of our own work. As well, in a therapy that is premised on the idea of resolving the forces of history so that the effects of history might be erased, the option for us to join with persons, and with our own lives, in creative re-engagements with history are powerfully restricted. The sort of re-engagement with history that might contribute to persons' and therapists' lives being more richly described becomes unavailable.[7] In working towards the end of history, in the therapeutic context, history becomes unwelcome.

'Truth' and narrative therapy

In my written work, and in my teaching and consultation, when discussing narrative practices, I have drawn out some of the available options for deconstructing the dominant stories of identity that constitute persons' lives in ways that they judge to be dead-ended. I have also drawn out some of the options for the identification and the rich description of the alternative stories of persons' lives, options that open new possibilities for action in the world. These options that are identifying and richly describing of the alternative stories of persons' lives provide the basis of the re-authoring conversations of this work. In these re-authoring conversations, alternative descriptions of personal and relationship identity are derived. As these conversations evolve, these alternative descriptions begin to 'fill out' various identity categories - for example, the identity categories of desire, personal quality, want, need, whim, motive, purpose, intention, values, beliefs, goals, hopes, aspirations, and so on.

Many of the descriptions derived in these re-authoring conversations significantly contradict those descriptions that inhabit the identity categories of the problem-saturated stories of persons' lives. And many of the practices of self and relationship that are associated with these alternative identity descriptions contradict those practices of self and relationship that are associated with the identity descriptions of these problem-saturated stories.

I have not at any time proposed that these alternative identity descriptions and practices of self and of relationship speak of the 'truth' of persons' desires, needs, intentions, motives, or of any other category of identity. Nor have I proposed that these alternative descriptions refer to the real, natural or authentic expressions of the self, or of human nature. I have always referred to these descriptions as 'accounts' of desire, motive, intention, and so on, never as desires, motives or intentions *per se*. It is my understanding that we are as multi-desired, as multi-motived, and as multi-intentioned in life as our lives are multi-storied.

As well, I have not at any time proposed that narrative practices are exterior to culture as it is known. There is nothing revolutionary about these narrative practices - they do not stand outside of the discourses of culture. Take, for example, those re-authoring conversations that derive alternative descriptions that pack out the identity categories of desire, motive, purpose, and so on. Trafficking in identity descriptions like these is inevitably a cultural activity - in engaging with persons in this activity we are trafficking in those ways of understanding that are the hallmark of contemporary western culture. In these conversations, we are reproducing the conceptions of self of this culture, and the ways of life that are associated with these conceptions. But, in stating this, I do not believe that narrative practices are necessarily culture-bound. There are cultures that do not traffic in descriptions that relate to the categories of identity that reproduce a western sense of self, and, when engaging with persons of these cultures in narrative conversations, other culturally specific identity categories are privileged. For example, in joining in narrative conversations with Indigenous Australians, the categories of identity that are invariably privileged are those of kinship and spirituality.

Knowledge/power and narrative practice

In that narrative practice cannot claim a place that is exterior to cultural discourse, it also does not stand outside of fields of knowledge and power. The identity categories that are packed out in this work, and the alternative modes of life and thought that are associated with these, and that are more richly described in re-authoring conversations, are not exterior to fields of knowledge and power. This is as much the case for identity categories like 'membership' as it is for the more mainstream versions that are discussed above. These modes of life and thought have a trajectory that can be traced through the history of culture - they are constituted of knowledges and practices of life that are historical.

Although I have, at different places in this book, described work that assists persons to refuse those subjectivities that are informed by practices in the calculated management of the self, and work that gives rise to experiences of alternative subjectivities, I have not at any time been under the illusion that these alternative subjectivities represent a radical break from cultural modes of life and thought, or that they are exterior to fields of knowledge and power. Although we do not have to be unwitting accomplices in the reproduction of the subjectivities that have been imposed on our lives for the past several centuries (Foucault 1988c), the alternative modes of life and thought that give rise to alternative subjectivities are inevitably historical. These alternative modes of life and thought exist in discursive fields - they are constituted of knowledges, of techniques of the self, of practices of relationship, and of the power relations of culture.

This conclusion about the inescapability of relations of power does not constitute a celebration of this fact. Nor does the inevitability of relations of power provide an excuse to knowingly or unknowingly reproduce relations of power in our work. Rather, this consideration is one that contributes to a consciousness that there is nothing about narrative practices that exempts us from the reproduction of power relations, and one that encourages us to embrace a responsibility to structure into our work processes that might be identifying of these relations of power, and that might contribute to the monitoring of the real effects of these power relations on the lives of the persons who consult us - and, as well, on our own lives and work. The identification of these relations of power, and this monitoring of their real effects, provides therapists with the opportunity to engage in acts that are limiting of the excesses of these power relations, that challenge those aspects of them that are determined to be toxic in their effects, that contribute to the destabilising of them, and that render them vulnerable to reversals or inversions in ways that contribute a greater diversity of power relations.[8] These are the acts and practices that structure the therapeutic context as more egalitarian than it would otherwise be.

In narrative work, various practices that are informed by this consideration have been established. These include those that are formed by a principle of transparency (White 1991) that encourages the therapist to deconstruct his/her work, those that render this work accountable to the persons who consult therapists, those that are shaped by a commitment to the deconstruction of the modes of life and thought that are more richly described in this work, and those that I have referred to as taking-it-back practices. And, although these practices hopefully establish narrative therapy as a context for attenuating, and at times avoiding the reproduction of, many of the modern relations of power, this is not a question that can be left to hope. We are ever charged with the exploration of practices that might further contribute to the exposé of the relations of power in this work. It is this scrutiny of our work that makes it possible for us to assume an ethical responsibility for the real effects of this work in the constitution of life. It has been my understanding that to engage in narrative practices is to engage in activities that are actually constitutive of life.

Closing comments

In this last section of this book I have engaged in some critique of structuralist discourses on human nature. In this critique I have been interested in: (a) the proposals for living that are championed by these discourses, (b) how these proposals are taken up, (c) the use to which they have been put in the shaping of life and culture, (d) the modes of life and thought that they are constituted of, (e) what values they speak to, and (f) how they are inextricably linked to fields of power and knowledge. I have been particularly interested in the effects of these discourses in the constitution of the work and the life of the therapist.

In closing this section, I would like to emphasise that this critique is not a criticism of all that humanism stands for - it is not a disqualification of all of those ways of being and thinking in the world that humanism is an emblem for. And this critique does not constitute a disqualification of many of humanism's achievements on a personal and a social level - in the support that many persons have drawn from it in challenging the various acts of domination they are being subject to, and in the significant role that it has played through its employment by the various human rights movements that have challenged different forms of discrimination and oppression.

Notes

1. For summaries of Foucault's explorations of this subject, see 'Technologies of the self' (Foucault 1988a) and 'The ethic of care for the self as a practice of freedom' (Foucault 1988c).

2. Clifford Geertz (1986, p.280) quoting Lionel Trilling quoting an eighteenth-century aesthetician.

3. My appreciation of the joining of the emancipation narrative to this couple is principally derived from Michel Foucault's *The History of Sexuality* (1984). I recommend this book to those readers who are in search of a more extended account of this phenomenon.

4. For a discussion of these technologies, see *Discipline and Punish* (Foucault 1979).

5. For further discussion of this notion of the end of history, see Foucault (1984).

6. For further discussion of these processes, see Edward Bruner and Victor Turner's *Anthropology of Experience* (1986).

7. The re-engagement with history that is a feature of re-authoring conversations is not an 'academic' activity - it is not conceived of as some conversation about some of the events of a person's life that simply provides some different perspective on these events. The re-authoring conversations that provide the basis for this re-engagement with history are powerfully evocative of alternative images of persons' lives. These images trigger off reverberations that reach back through persons' lives, and these touch on experiences of particular events of personal history - experiences of particular events of personal history resonate, and 'light up'. In this way, these re-authoring conversations provide contexts in which persons engage in expressions of their experiences of particular events of history - contexts for the performance of these experiences. The therapist is engaged in this performance in different ways,

including as an outsider-witness who participates in acts of meaning, and who plays a significant role in the authentication of some of the alternative identity claims that are expressed in this performance.

8. For a discussion that distinguishes the pervasive power relations of culture from its states of domination, see 'The ethic of care of the self as a practice of freedom' (Foucault 1988c).

Conclusion

It is my hope that the ideas and practices that I have presented in this book will contribute to options for readers in the shaping of their work as a context that is both sustaining of them and a source of inspiration in their ongoing explorations. There are many different possibilities for taking up these ideas and practices in ways that can achieve this.

Although the examples of re-membering conversations and of the tellings and re-tellings informed by the definitional ceremony metaphor that are given in this book were drawn from conversations with therapists in workshop contexts, such conversations and ceremonies are not restricted to these contexts. I have joined with therapists in re-membering conversations with their peers in a variety of settings, including in workplaces where the aim has been to effect change in agency culture. And I have also joined with others in the convening of definitional ceremonies in a variety of settings, including those that are associated with wider community projects.[1] I trust that those readers who decide to pursue some engagement with the outsider-witness practices described in the book will enjoy this, and will at some stage have the opportunity to be at the centre of some re-tellings of the stories of their work and their lives.

I hope that readers will take the opportunity to engage in explorations of taking-it-back practices in their consultations with persons who seek their help, and have a first-hand experience of the contribution of these practices to their lives and work. I also hope that readers will have the opportunity to explore supervision as a re-authoring conversation, and training as collaborative research. And, as there is much more that is yet to be said about the ethic of collaboration and about decentred practice, I invite readers to fill in some of the gaps in the accounts of this ethic and this practice that I have sketched out in this book.

As I complete this book, I find myself thinking a lot about you, the reader. I am curious about the history of your interest in this book. I am wondering about which of the ideas and practices expressed in this text you relate to most strongly. I'm interested to know how these ideas and practices speak to your preferred values and ways of being in your work with the persons who consult you, and in your life generally. I have a desire to know about the experiences of life that have clarified for you what is important in regard to these values and ways of being in the world. I am even wondering about what I might be taking back to you if we were to have this conversation ... but that is another story.

Note

1. For example, the 'Reclaiming our stories: Reclaiming our lives' (Aboriginal Health Council of South Australia, 1995) and the 'Speaking out and being heard' (South Australian Council of Social Services, 1996) projects.

References

Aboriginal Health Council of South Australia, 1995: 'Reclaiming our stories, reclaiming our lives.' *Dulwich Centre Newsletter,* 1 (special issue).

Andersen, T. 1987: 'The reflecting team: Dialogue and meta-dialogue in clinical work.' *Family Process,* 26:415-428.

Anderson, H. & Goolishian, H.A. 1988: 'Human systems as linguistic systems: Preliminary and evolving ideas about the implications for clinical theory.' *Family Process,* 27:371-393.

Bachelard, G. 1969: *The Poetics of Space.* Boston: Beacon Press.

Brigitte, Mem, Sue & Veronika, 1996: 'Power to our journeys.' *American Family Therapy Academy Newsletter,* Summer, 64:11-16. Reprinted in 'Companions on a journey' (1997), *Dulwich Centre Newsletter,* 1 (special issue).

Bruner, E. 1986: 'Experience and its expressions.' In Bruner, E. & Turner, V. (eds), *The Anthropology of Experience.* Chicago: University of Illinois Press.

Bruner, E. & Turner, V. (eds) 1986: *The Anthropology of Experience.* Chicago: University of Illinois Press.

Bruner, J. 1986: *Actual Minds: Possible Worlds.* Cambridge, MA: Harvard University Press.

Bruner, J. 1990: *Acts of Meaning.* Cambridge, MA: Harvard University Press.

Epston, D. & White, M. 1992a: 'Consulting your consultants: The documentation of alternative knowledges.' In Epston, D. & White, M., *Experience, Contradiction, Narrative & Imagination.* Adelaide: Dulwich Centre Publications.

Epston, D. & White, M. 1992b: *Experience, Contradiction, Narrative & Imagination.* Adelaide: Dulwich Centre Publications.

Foucault, M. 1965: *Madness and Civilisation: A History of Insanity in the Age of Reason.* New York: Random House.

Foucault, M. 1973a: *The Order of Things: An Archaeology of the Human Sciences.* New York: Vintage Books.

Foucault, M. 1973b: *The Birth of The Clinic: An Archaeology of Medical Perception.* London: Tavistock.

Foucault, M. 1979: *Discipline and Punish: The Birth of The Prison.* Middlesex: Peregrine Books.

Foucault, M. 1980: *Power/Knowledge: Selected Interviews and Other Writings.* New York: Pantheon Books.

Foucault, M. 1984: *The History of Sexuality, Volume 1.* Great Brittain: Peregrine Books.

Foucault, M. 1987: *The Use of Pleasure.* London: Penguin Books.

Foucault, M. 1988a: 'Technologies of the self.' In Martin, L., Gutman, H. & Hutton, P. (eds), *Technologies of the Self.* Amherst: The University of Massachusetts Press.

Foucault, M. 1988b: 'The political technology of individuals.' In Martin, L., Gutman, H. & Hutton, P. (eds), *Technologies of the Self.* Amherst: The University of Massachusetts Press.

Foucault, M. 1988c: 'The ethic of care for the self as a practice of freedom.' In Bernauer, J. & Rasmussen, D. (eds), *The Final Foucault.* Cambridge, MA: The MIT Press.

Geertz, C. 1973: 'Thick description: Toward an interpretive theory of culture.' In Geertz, C., *The Interpretation of Cultures.* New York: Basic Books.

Geertz, C. 1983: *Local Knowledge: Further Essays in Interpretive Anthropology.* New York: Basic Books.

Geertz, C. 1986: 'Making experiences, authoring selves.' In Bruner, E. & Turner, V. (eds), *The Anthropology of Experience.* Chicago: University of Illinois Press.

Hall, R. 1994: 'Partnership accountability.' *Dulwich Centre Newsletter,* 2&3:6-29.

Jenkins, A. 1990: *Invitations to Responsibility: The Therapeutic Engagement of Men Who Are Violent and Abusive.* Adelaide: Dulwich Centre Publications.

Myerhoff, B. 1982: 'Life history among the elderly: Performance, visibility and remembering.' In Ruby, J. (ed), *A Crack in the Mirror: Reflexive Perspectives in Anthropology.* Philadelphia: University of Pennsylvania Press.

Myerhoff, B. 1986: 'Life not death in Venice: Its second life.' In Turner, V. & Bruner, E. (eds), *The Anthropology of Experience.* Chicago: University of Illinois Press.

Ricoeur, P. 1984: *Time and Narrative.* Chicago: University of Chicago Press.

Rorty, R. 1991: *Objectivity, Relativism, and Truth: Philosophical Papers, Volume 1.* New York: Cambridge University Press.

Rosaldo, R. 1992: *Culture and Truth: The Remaking of Social Analysis.* Boston: Beacon Press.

Simons, J. 1995: *Foucault and the Political.* London: Routledge.

South Australian Council of Social Services (SACOSS), 1995: 'Speaking out and being heard.' *Dulwich Centre Newsletter,* 4 (special issue).

Tamasese, K. & Waldegrave, C. 1994: 'Cultural & gender accountability in the "just therapy" approach.' *Dulwich Centre Newsletter,* 2&3:55-67.

Welch, S. 1990: *A Feminist Ethic of Risk.* Minneapolis, MN: Fortress Press.

White, C. & Hales, J. (eds) 1997: *The Personal is The Professional: Therapists Reflect on Their Families, Lives and Work.* Adelaide: Dulwich Centre Publications.

White, M. 1988: 'Saying hullo again: The incorporation of the lost relationship in the resolution of grief.' *Dulwich Centre Newsletter,* Spring. Reprinted in White, M. (1989), *Selected Papers.* Adelaide: Dulwich Centre Publications.

White, M. 1988/89: 'Externalizing the problem.' *Dulwich Centre Newsletter,* Summer. Reprinted in White, M. & Epston, D. (1990), *Narrative Means to Therapeutic Ends.* New York: W.W.Norton.

White, M. 1989/90: 'Family therapy training and supervision in a world of experience and narrative.' *Dulwich Centre Newsletter,* Summer. Reprinted in Epston, D. & White, M. (1992), *Experience, Contradiction, Narrative & Imagination.* Adelaide: Dulwich Centre Publications.

White, M. 1991: 'Deconstruction and therapy.' *Dulwich Centre Newsletter,* 3. Reprinted in Epston, D. & White, M. (1992), *Experience, Contradiction, Narrative & Imagination.* Adelaide: Dulwich Centre Publications.

White, M. 1995a: *Re-Authoring Lives: Interviews & Essays.* Adelaide: Dulwich Centre Publications.

White, M. 1995b: 'Reflecting team as definitional ceremony.' In White, M., *Re-Authoring Lives: Interviews & Essays.* Adelaide: Dulwich Centre Publications.

White, M. & Epston, D. 1990: *Narrative Means to Therapeutic Ends.* New York: W.W.Norton.